BLOOD
&
MONEY

Why Families Fight Over Inheritance
And What To Do About It

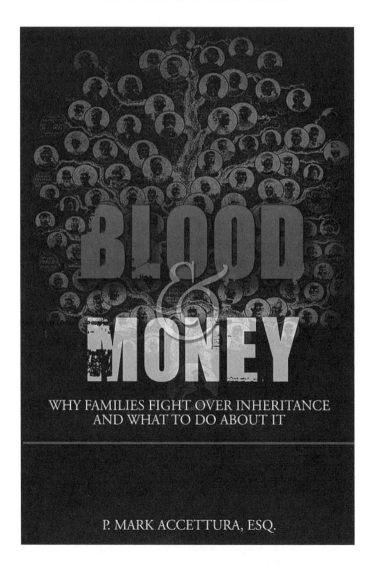

BLOOD

MONEY

WHY FAMILIES FIGHT OVER INHERITANCE
AND WHAT TO DO ABOUT IT

P. MARK ACCETTURA, ESQ.

BLOOD & MONEY

Why Families Fight Over Inheritance
And What To Do About It

BLOOD & MONEY

Why Families Fight Over Inheritance
And What To Do About It

P. Mark Accettura, Esq.

Collinwood Press
Farmington Hills, Michigan

BLOOD
&
MONEY

Why Families Fight Over Inheritance
And What To Do About It

P. Mark Accettura, Esq.

Collinwood Press, LLC

35055 W. 12 Mile Rd., Ste. 132

Farmington Hills, MI 48331

The information contained in this book is not intended to be comprehensive and should not be construed by readers as individual legal advice. The laws pertaining to inheritance disputes are inherently complex and constantly changing. Any planning strategy must be reviewed in light of current and future law changes. Therefore, readers should consult an experienced elder law attorney for specific legal advice regarding their individual needs.

Cover Design and Page Layout: Jessica Angerstein

Library of Congress Catalog Number: 2011910661

Printed in the United States

International Standard Book Number: 978-0-9669278-4-9

To my wife,
my sons,
my parents,
my sisters,
and the families
I have had the
privilege to serve

TABLE OF CONTENTS

Inheritance

When I was ten years old, my father died. And at that time, of course, I thought my father was the best and finest man there ever was. And some years later when I was eighteen and I began to mingle in the adult community, I introduced myself to strangers and they would ask me if John Estrada was my father. When I said yes, they would say, "Well, let me shake your hand. He was a fine man and a good friend of mine." And then they would tell me wonderful stories about him. Since that time, I have hoped that when I am gone, some people might meet my children and say to them that I was a good man and a good friend. To me that is a finer inheritance than any material possession.

~ Fred Estrada[1]

PREFACE

Blood & Money began as a personal inquiry into why people fight over inheritance. As an estate and elder law attorney for thirty years, I have witnessed people behaving at their worst. People who are normally thoughtful and connected with their emotions frequently revert to fighting children, figuratively scratching, punching, and pulling each other's hair. Even where there is no overt conflict, it seems that nearly every family has some amount of tension percolating just beneath the surface as they address family inheritance issues.

The combatants are almost always the same. They are typically siblings fighting amongst themselves or children fighting with stepparents. In private they tell me, "she's always been jealous of me," "I don't trust him," or "he's just plain nuts." It seems that the disputants always trace their problems back several years, if not all the way back to childhood. For some, the trouble starts with the involvement of non-family: "everything changed when dad remarried," or "we all got along until my brother-in-law started calling the shots." It is clear that inheritance conflict doesn't come out of the blue; it is a continuation of long-term relationship problems that resurface upon the illness or death of a loved one. And they aren't just about money or greed; they are about more, much more.

I used to believe, naively, that inheritance fights were instigated by greedy heirs. I had fallen into the trap of blaming the living and pardoning the dead. Over time I began to appreciate that in many if not most cases the decedent himself or herself was a central part of the problem; they just weren't physically present to fight over the mess that they had a hand in creating. This new orientation led me to examine how mental health and one's family dynamic are themselves part of the inheritance that passes from generation to generation.

When an unhappy family dynamic ripened into foul play it invariably began long before a loved one's death. Aggrieved family members, not waiting for nature to take its course, would take matters into their own hands, manipulating their loved ones as they began to fail. One of my early goals was to explain how the slow progression of dementia leads to an extended period of murky legal capacity and opens the door to what we now know as *elder abuse.*

My search for why families fight led me to the relatively new field of evolutionary psychology. I was enlightened to the fact that a financial inheritance is but one component of what we inherit from our parents; we also inherit our basic human nature and our earliest concept of self. While the law uses the term *inheritance* to denote a financial bequest, biologists, psychologists and other scientists use the term to describe the transfer of one's genome from one generation to the next. That the term *inheritance* is used to describe the passage of both goods and genetic traits is no mere linguistic coincidence. Instead, it is a coincidence in the sense of *synchronicity,* a term coined by Swiss psychologist Carl Gustav Jung to describe events that may seem on the surface to be unrelated but which in actuality are linked components of the human experience.

The term *inheritance* as used in the pages that follow reflects this multifaceted use of the term and thus, unless specified otherwise, includes legal, financial, and genetic inheritance. As we will see in Chapter Four, the psychology, aura, legacy, and memory of those that came before us are part of our own living identity, and serve as the psychological base from which we build.

Reliance on evolutionary psychology to explain human behavior is not without controversy. Darwin's evolutionary theory was not well received when originally introduced, and continues to be controversial. Today, some Christian fundamentalists reject evolutionary theory. They believe in a strict reading of the Bible, and attribute evolution to God's *intelligent design.* We may never know which view is right. For purposes of our discussion, I choose to adopt prevailing scientific thinking, leaving open the possibility that God's hand and *creationism* may play a larger role than we know.

Before undertaking the writing of *Blood & Money* I had to ask myself whether inheritance is still relevant in the twenty-first century. From an economic perspective, inheritance has arguably become less important than at any time in history. Family sustenance no longer depends on the family farm, and family businesses rarely survive to the next generation. With rapidly changing technology and increased mobility of the workforce, education, individual skills, and personal connections have become the most important ingredients of success. And the speed of change will only increase. Wealth will turn over more quickly with the young Turks of today becoming yesterday's news. With the half-life of ideas and enterprises becoming shorter and shorter, "old money" will become a term of antiquity, with new, newer and newest money taking its place.

Although we may be in the middle of the largest intergenerational transfer of wealth in history, the size of inheritances is likely to be negatively impacted by the greater economic demands being placed on the elderly. Increased life expectancy and the near extinction of the multi-generational household have greatly increased the need for expensive substitutes like senior housing, assisted living, and nursing homes. At the same time, the stress brought by an aging citizenry on the government programs of Social Security, Medicare, and Medicaid make it likely that individuals will shoulder an increasingly larger portion of the cost of their care. These factors all lead to the likelihood that financial inheritances will be smaller and less important to the overall financial success of succeeding generations.

Despite these assaults on financial inheritance, the genetic and psychological significance of what we inherit will never lose its relevance. Our very birth is a form of inheritance. We are shaped by our genome, prenatal and early parenting, birth order, and our relationship with our siblings. The imprint of these early relationships shapes us and is the starting point from which we begin our lifelong journey of self-awareness and personal development. Although the property we inherit may become less relevant from a purely economic perspective, it will never lose its symbolic importance as representations of our parents' love.

Chapter Three on terror management was actually the last chapter written. After "finishing" the book I had the gnawing feeling that something was missing. Indeed, I had overlooked perhaps the most essential element of inheritance conflict: the terror that the passing of a loved one conjures amongst the living. Although it now seems obvious that the death of a loved one would scare the hell out of those left behind, I did not fully appreciate the role of death in inheritance conflict until nearly four years into the project. Looking back, I understand my oversight. Like most humans, I myself had spent a lifetime avoiding conscious thoughts of death. The thought that we live in constant terror of death, as many social scientists now believe, hadn't crossed my mind.

The decision to make the Brooke Astor story one of the focal points of the book was a coincidence. I had decided to write *Blood & Money* a few months before Philip Marshall filed his 2006 bombshell petition to have his father removed as his grandmother's power of attorney. I was only casually following the case when Meryl Gordon published her excellent book, *Mrs. Astor Regrets: The Hidden Betrayals of a Family Beyond Reproach.* After reading Ms. Gordon's multigenerational tale of family dysfunction and the story of Brooke Astor's life, I decided that her case would be a perfect illustration of the essential elements of inheritance disputes, namely: dementia, testamentary capacity, undue influence, dysfunctional families, in-laws, chronic shortages of love, the operation of the legal system, and prevention.

My hope is that professional and lay readers alike will better understand the family dynamics that plague the inheritance process. I have included numerous anecdotes of the rich and famous to make the materials accessible to all readers and a generous bibliography and footnotes for the professionals. I have little doubt that you will recognize those with whom you conflict in the pages that follow. The challenge is whether you are able to see yourself, as each of us plays a role in our family dynamic, good or bad.

I was committed to write a book that does not merely restate the problem. For that reason, I have included sixty-one specific recommendations to limit or avoid family conflict. I also offer a recipe for family harmony, and challenge the reader to live more consciously as writing this book has forced me to do.

The Appendix, *How We Got Here – A History of Inheritance* chronicles how we arrived at our present legal and cultural view of inheritance. It was a daunting task, and to my knowledge not one undertaken by any other writer or legal historian, but I thought it was important to chronicle how the prevailing cultural, religious, and legal views of inheritance evolve to meet the needs of society and set individual expectations.

There are some housekeeping matters that require attention. First, I use the term "testator" throughout the book to describe anyone who arranges his or her affairs in contemplation of death. Although the term technically only refers to one who makes a will, I have chosen for simplicity to use *testator* to include those who employ revocable trusts and will substitutes like beneficiary designations, joint ownership, and pay-on-death ("POD") and transfer-on-death ("TOD") designations. Also, although I have endeavored to be as gender neutral as possible, the historical nature of the material naturally leads to terminology like "man," "man's," "he," "him," and "his." No slight to women is intended.

Where appropriate, I have attempted to add a little whimsy and humor to an otherwise serious subject. The mock Astor Playbill in Chapter Five, the one-liners, photographs and images that begin a number of the chapters, and the "recipe" in Chapter Eleven, are intended to entertain. Although the transition between the weighty and the whimsical may at times be somewhat abrupt, I hope that the mixture will make the reader's experience more enjoyable. Besides, when it comes to family there should always be room for a good laugh.

In addition to law, the inquiry herein required study and expertise in the fields of evolutionary psychology, gerontology, psychiatry, general psychology, and neuropsychology. I am grateful to the following friends, experts, and advisors who helped me bring these disparate fields of study together under one roof.

- Julia Belian, M. Div., JD
  (Associate Professor of Law, University of Detroit/Mercy Law School)
- Jeffrey S. Burg, JD (Law);

- Joseph Gluski, MD (Psychiatry);
- Gordon, Meryl (Author of *Mrs. Astor Regrets: The Hidden Betrayals of a Family Beyond Reproach*)
- Manfred F. Grieffenstein, PhD (Forensic Neuropsychology)
- Samuel A. Hurwitz, Esq. (Elder Law)
- Rev. Kenneth R. Kaucheck, J.C.D. (Roman Catholic Canon Law)
- Peter A. Lichtenberg, PhD, ABPP, Institute of Gerontology, Wayne State University (Gerontology, Psychology, and Medical Rehabilitation);
- Norbert L. Kerr, PhD Professor of Psychology, Michigan State University (Evolutionary Psychology and Sociometric Theory);
- Ira Lourie, Psy.D (Neuropsychology)
- Gina M. Torielli, Professor of Law, Thomas M. Cooley Law School;
- John Witte, Jr., Emory University School of Law, *Jonas Robitscher Professor of Law; Alonzo L. McDonald Family Foundation Distinguished Professor: Director, Center for the Study of Law and Religion.*

Also, special thanks to Brian Dickerson, Pietro Sarcina, James Knaus, Rebecca Coyle, Kimberly Rapp and Jessica Angerstein.

INTRODUCTION

"Inheritance disputes are not so much about money. People fight over the love they feel they did not receive."
Psychiatrist/Author Reuven Bar-Levav, M.D.

The old adage that "money makes people do funny things" doesn't do justice to the real problems and root causes of family conflict. To attribute inheritance disputes simply to greed ignores the underlying forces that lead families to fight. Money is not the core reason that families fight; money is how we keep score in the fight for the intangibles of love, approval, and primordial survival. Money and possessions also help allay the fears of those left behind. When families fight, greed is rarely the principal motive.

There are five basic reasons why families fight in matters of inheritance: First, humans are genetically predisposed to competition and conflict; second, our psychological sense of self is intertwined with the approval that an inheritance represents, especially when the decedent is a parent; third, we are genetically hardwired to be on the lookout for exclusion, sometimes finding it when it doesn't exist; fourth, families fight because the death of a loved one activates the death anxieties of those left behind; and finally, in some cases, one or more members of a family has a partial or full-blown personality disorder that causes them to distort and escalate natural family rivalries into personal and legal battles. These sources of family conflict are not mutually exclusive; in most cases, some combination of the five elements present themselves in a combustible cocktail of family rivalry and conflict. Chapter One, *Behaving Like Animals,* introduces the field of evolutionary psychology. Applying Darwin's theory of natural selection to human behavior, evolutionary psychology is the starting point in explaining family conflict and inheritance disputes. According to evolutionary psychologists, conflict between parents and children, sibling rivalry, the prejudice against stepchildren, and even elder abuse are natural and adaptive behaviors. In the wild, and occasionally among humans, such conflict results in siblicide, parricide, and infanticide.

Parents and siblings play a pivotal role in the development of our early concept of self. Parental love and acceptance help us survive infancy and are essential to normal psychological development. Birth order, sibling rivalry, assigned roles, early family environment, innate intelligence and character, and life experiences outside the family combine to make us the people that we become. Despite the myriad of influences that impact our concept of self throughout our life, the love and approval of our family never loses its primary importance. The strong emotional reaction that accompanies the disapproval of family or the slightest form of rejection underscores the ongoing importance of family.

The death of a loved one, especially a parent, rekindles past rivalries and perceived inequities. The decedent's last wishes, measured in money, prized objects, and assigned responsibilities, represent the decedent's final statement of each beneficiary's relative importance and position in the family. It is not the particular item, bequest, or assignment that is at issue; it is what the thing represents: love, validation, and importance.

Our relative worth is measured both by what we receive and what is bestowed on others. A professional athlete making ten million dollars a year feels cheated when someone on his team with the same statistics is making fifteen million dollars. He doesn't care that the average worker doesn't make ten million dollars in a lifetime; he still feels wronged. The same is true in the competition over who in the family is more important and more loved. In such a quest, the value of one's inheritance is relative to what one's relatives receive. It is for this reason that families fight over inheritance even when there is enough for everyone. Outsiders view their behavior as silly and petty, but to the contestants, there is nothing frivolous about inheritance fights; they are a matter of psychic life and death. With so much at stake and with victory defined by who gets more, it is no wonder that some heirs take a scorched earth approach. In their eyes, it is better that no one get anything than for a rival to get more.

The freedom to choose how one's property is to be disposed of at death – known as the *freedom of testation* – is a fundamental right under Anglo-American law. Current U.S. law allows perhaps the broadest testamentary freedom in the world; parents are free to disinherit children, even minors, in all states except Louisiana. Chapter Two, *Disinheritance* explores the dark side of this unparalleled freedom. With no presumptive heirs, toxic testators are free to poison their legacy and desperate family members can manipulate vulnerable elders to exclude their rivals.

Chapter Two also introduces *sociometric theory.* Early man learned to curb his natural lusts, greed and desires as *quid pro quo* for membership in the group. Scientists believe that the consequences of rejection or expulsion were so dire, that man evolved to feel a physical pain, called *social pain,* in response to even the slightest hint of actual or perceived rejection. It is for this reason that inheritance battles are experienced as a matter of psychic life and death. To be excluded from an inheritance is to be permanently exiled by one's family, to be left out in the cold.

In the civilized world, we regulate our animal urges in exchange for membership in society. However, if the individual feels he has been excluded without the possibility of re-entry, he is no longer compelled to self-regulate. Studies of Columbine and other school shootings show that the vast majority of the shooters had experienced acute social rejection. Many inheritance battles, especially ones that take the form of preemptive grabs, are the result of real or imagined fear of being permanently excluded.

The decedent's death itself is an important factor in family conflict as it activates the inner terror of those left behind. Survivors scramble to pacify their innate fear of death that they have spent a lifetime suppressing. They allay their anxieties by attaching themselves to the symbols of the decedent, like mom and dad's prized possessions; or they gird themselves against their generalized fears with the universal tools of power: money and wealth.

Social scientists believe that fear of death is the motivating factor behind most human behavior. Born with an instinct to survive and procreate, yet aware of our biological finitude, man is left with an existential dilemma: what is the meaning of life if we're just going to die? One branch of modern psychological theory suggests that man has resolved this seemingly irresolvable problem by repressing conscious thoughts of death. Ever-present but safely tucked away in our subconscious, *Terror Management Theory* (TMT), discussed in Chapter Three, posits that we reconcile our fear of death either by believing that we survive in the afterlife *(literal immortality)* or that the physical world, its structures, and institutions has meaning that survives our death *(symbolic immortality)*. When the monster fear of death escapes from the dungeon, as can occur on the death of a loved one, survivors engage in all kinds of behaviors that look crazy to outsiders, but in reality are geared to returning the monster of death to the cage of the subconscious.

Some families fight because one or more of their members, including the parent/testator, has significant mental health issues. The difficulties of such family members magnify and distort natural family rivalries into family battles that take on lives of their own. The pathology of one or more family members creates an unhealthy family dynamic that plagues the family during life and survives the decedent in the form of a *toxic inheritance.*

One author posits that as much as half of the legal cases that go to trial are instigated and perpetuated by people who suffer from Cluster B personality disorders. As listed in the Diagnostic and Statistical Manual of the American Psychiatric Association (DSM-IV-TR), Cluster B disorders include *borderline, narcissistic, antisocial,* and *histrionic* personalities. While less than ten percent of the U.S. population suffers from Cluster B personality disorders, experts believe that another ten percent manifest traits of one or more of the four illnesses. Chapter Four, *Toxic Inheritance,* analyzes the four Cluster B personality types and explores how each might contribute to inheritance conflict. The stories of Leona Helmsley and Sumner Redstone in Chapter Four and Brooke Astor in Chapter Five are examples of how such toxic legacies pass from generation to generation.

We tend to overlook the role of parents and testators in inheritance disputes, attributing such conflicts almost entirely to "greedy" children. We visualize heirs feeding off the fallen decedent like a pack of hyenas on a wildebeest. In reality, parents play a major role in inheritance disputes. Suffering from their own problems and personality disorders, toxic parents hurt their children during life through unhealthy ways of being and after their death either through a toxic inheritance scheme, or by completely failing to plan.

We start the discussion of how and when inheritance battles begin in Chapter Five with the well-publicized case of Brooke Astor. Her story illustrates many of the issues discussed in this book and serves as a backdrop to the chapters that follow. It is a story of great wealth gone astray, of elder abuse, and of the slow progression of dementia. It is also a story of a mother's neglect, a son's betrayal, a daughter-in-law's greed, and a grandson's hurt. It illuminates the murky waters of testamentary capacity and undue influence. It is a story of toxic inheritance and the vulnerability of an elder in the twilight of competence. Brooke's story offers a textbook example of the legal protections, legal remedies, and prevention techniques available to avoid or at least minimize family conflict.

Chapter Six, *Vulnerability in the Twilight of Competence,* explains how and why an elder's declining capacity makes them vulnerable to abuse. For many, inheritance disputes bring to mind images of movie scenes such as in *Rain Man,* where anxious family members meet in the lawyer's office to learn their fate. In reality, inheritance conflicts often begin long before the death of the testator. Long-held feelings are converted to action when testators begin to fail. Family members jockey for position, frequently engaging in some form of elder abuse in an attempt to alter history in their favor.

The media tends to focus on elder abuse perpetrated by outsiders. Scams foisted on seniors by home repair companies, bogus sweepstakes solicitations, and banking scams are widely reported. In reality, the greatest threat to the elderly is from within. According to the National Center on Elder Abuse (NCEA), adult children are the most frequent abusers of the elderly, with other family members and spouses being the next most likely to abuse. The true extent of the problem is difficult to gauge, however, since the vast majority of financial abuse is never reported. The factors that lead to financial elder abuse are the same as those that lead to inheritance conflict. It is thus fair to say that when perpetrated by family, financial elder abuse is an impatient inheritance dispute that begins while the testator is still living.

A basic understanding of dementia and neurodegenerative diseases such as Alzheimer's is essential to the discussion of elder abuse and inheritance conflict. The fact that sufferers retain some capacity even through the moderate stages of the disease helps explain why someone with dementia or Alzheimer's may nevertheless possess testamentary capacity. Early testing for age-related dementia allows for early diagnosis, treatment, and implementation of the preventive steps discussed in Chapter Eleven.

Testamentary capacity, the subject of Chapter Seven, is the guardian of testamentary freedom. To possess testamentary capacity a testator must have the capacity to know the nature of his assets, the natural objects of his bounty, and the effect of a will. Sometimes referred to as being of *sound mind* (or the Latin antithesis, *non compos mentis),* testamentary capacity is measured at the exact moment of the execution. A will executed when the testator lacked testamentary capacity is invalid and without legal effect.

Proper execution is intended to ensure testamentary capacity. Modern law requires that the testator be the age of majority, and that his testamentary act be witnessed by at least two witnesses (some states also require a notary public). The law relies on competent, credible, and disinterested witnesses to attest to the capacity of the testator and to the fact that the testator was not under the influence of another. The weight accorded to those *not* present at the signing, including friends, family, neighbors, and even mental health professionals is substantially less than that accorded to disinterested witnesses present at the signing, especially the drafting attorney.

Will contests based on the doctrine of *undue influence* discussed in Chapter Eight have a much higher success rate than pure testamentary capacity challenges. Undue influence occurs when someone in a position of trust uses that relationship to influence a susceptible victim to change their distribution plan to one that is unconscionable. Influencers wait for their victim to decline and become dependent. They then employ a cocktail of isolation, deceit, and brainwashing to foster dependency. Once they have gained the trust of their susceptible and dependent victim, they begin to change deeds, bank accounts, and estate planning documents.

Chapter Nine, *Legal Protections* explores the legal protections available to secure and protect vulnerable elders from physical and financial abuse. Once abuse has been discovered, early intervention is essential to prevent premature dissipation of the elder's assets. Generally speaking, the more time that elapses between the wrongdoer's bad acts and intervention, the more difficult it is to restore the elder to his or her rightful position. Without early intervention, misappropriated assets are quickly lost, witnesses die, and the ability to prove the elder's capacity at or near the time that wills, deeds, gifts, and other documents were executed becomes more difficult. It is for this reason that timely action is required.

Will and trust contests are covered in Chapter Ten, *Legal Remedies*. Such contests are brought by petition to the probate court as a remedy against the wrongful acts of others who would deprive an heir or beneficiary of their rightful share. The most common challenges to wills and trusts are petitions alleging that the testator lacked testamentary capacity or was the victim of undue influence.

Occasionally, the state has an interest in pressing criminal charges against wrongdoers who have committed especially heinous acts. Such was the case when Tony Marshall, son of Brooke Astor was indicted on eighteen criminal counts. While law enforcement is generally not interested in becoming involved in family disputes, it may choose to prosecute cases involving physical abuse or high profile financial abuse involving larceny, extortion, fraud, forgery, or embezzlement.

Chapter Eleven, *An Ounce of Prevention* offers sixty-one specific recommendations to prevent family conflict and elder abuse. Preventive measures are suggested based on the stage of conflict, from the nascent state of undue influence to measures intended to bring the parties together after conflict has already broken out. The starting point to any prevention or reconciliation is to try to see things from an adversary's point of view; to walk in his shoes. Many a war has been started based on misinformation, misunderstanding, and the unwillingness or inability of the parties to see things from their adversary's point of view. Whenever possible it is better to reconcile; to put the past behind. Obviously, it is much easier said than done, as the feelings that precipitate family conflict run deep. It also takes at least two to reconcile. One party may come to a place where he is at peace with the past, but others in the family are not. We truly only have the power to change ourselves - to do our best to filter out family dysfunction so as to not pass it to our progeny. Nonetheless we should never stop trying to preserve family, our most cherished inheritance.

The discussion of *How We Got Here: A History of Inheritance* in the Appendix is an admittedly ambitious attempt to summarize a vast topic in relatively few pages. The history of mankind is long and its peoples diverse. Despite the perils of the task, I believe that an historical view of inheritance laws and customs adds perspective to the current state of the law. It also shows how inheritance laws have evolved to meet the needs of the changing family, and how they influence the expectations of individual beneficiaries.

Regrettably, many funerals are a requiem for family cohesion and harmony, with family members vowing never to speak to one another again. Despite the tension and rivalries that naturally exist in all families, family conflict is not inevitable. The hope of *Blood & Money* is that, armed with a new understanding of why families fight, you will be better equipped to prevent fighting in your family and leave a legacy that preserves the precious commodity of family. We can all aspire to be like Alfred Nobel (whose story is told in Chapter Four), who changed his life and legacy after reading his own erroneously reported obituary.

PART I

WHY FAMILIES FIGHT

BEHAVING LIKE ANIMALS 1

"The affinities [relations] of all the beings of the same class have sometimes been represented by a great tree. I believe this simile largely speaks the truth. As buds give rise by growth to fresh buds, and these, if vigorous, branch out and overtop on all sides many a feebler branch, so by generation I believe it has been with the great Tree of Life, which fills with its dead and broken branches the crust of the earth, and covers the surface with its ever branching and beautiful ramifications."

- Charles Darwin, *On the Origin of Species,* 1859

"Arguably the most culturally jarring theory in history, the theory of natural selection gave rise to the Darwinian revolution that changed both science and culture in ways immeasurable."

- Michael Shermer, *Why Darwin Matters* Prologue, 2006

Charles Darwin

Cinderella

INTRODUCTION

Humans are among only three percent of species that are organized into families.[2] Our family structure, parental instincts and long-term commitment to children allow children an extended period of dependency in which to focus their energy on personal and intellectual development. Blessed with the largest brains on the planet relative to our size, humans have developed language, agriculture, science, medicine, computers, law, and the fifty-five gallon trash bag with a built-in draw string.

Yet, despite our wonderful qualities, we still act in curious and self-destructive ways. We fight with our little brothers, our parents, kids at school, our neighbors, and neighboring countries. Why do we do this? What is it about us humans that, despite our incredible capacity and achievement, we have retained behaviors that resemble lower life forms? Why, for example, do we maintain a sandbox mentality about our material possessions, our stuff? Why do families fight, and why do we have a propensity to fight over matters of inheritance? In short, despite our great civility, why do we sometimes behave like animals?

This Chapter discusses the primeval forces within us that if not curtailed, cause us to fight with others including our own family. Later, we will show that these forces need not rule us, and that family fighting is preventable.

The starting point in understanding why families fight in matters of inheritance is the relationship among the principal actors in most inheritance conflicts: parents, children, siblings, stepparents, and stepchildren. But, our discussion begins with a different form of inheritance – the biological inheritance of our genetic code or genome.

Scientists have long accepted Charles Darwin's theory of evolution as the unifying theory of the organic world.[3] Darwin's theories have had a profound impact on many of the sciences, including geology, biology, zoology, entomology, physiology, and genetics. The basis of Darwin's theory is that all organisms, including man, have evolved over billions of years into diverse species peculiarly adapted to their local environments.

A new branch of science known as *evolutionary psychology* has recently emerged. It combines principles of traditional psychology and biology to help explain *human behavior*. Applying Darwinian principles, evolutionary psychology explains human behavior on the basis of how it is (or was) adaptive to the basic principles of natural selection: survival and reproduction. Behaviors that promote survival and reproduction are said to be *adaptive* and are therefore maintained, while behaviors that are not adaptive eventually become extinct. Evolutionary theory and evolutionary psychology are the starting point to understanding human behavior within the family dynamic and, more specifically, inheritance conflict.

EVOLUTIONARY THEORY

Darwin perceived that organisms change or evolve over time through a process called *natural selection*. Nature "selects," i.e., rewards or propagates, those features of organisms, human or otherwise, that are best adapted for survival and reproduction. Features which promote survival and reproduction of the organism, like size, color, shape, strength, and cunning, raise the odds of successful survival of the individual, and are thus more often passed on to the next generation. Variations that are not adaptive fail to promote survival, and eventually become extinct.

A reptile with colors that blend with the local vegetation is less likely to be eaten by predators. A bird with a beak of a size and shape that allows it to crack open indigenous nuts or access local insects will eat when others starve. Organisms with adaptive features survive and reproduce in greater numbers, an event termed *differential reproductive success*. When this process is repeated generation after generation, the result is the formation of a new species.

Genetic success, however, is not just about surviving; it also requires that the organism produce offspring. Characteristics that lead to higher rates of *reproduction* are also passed down to future generations at a greater frequency. Darwin was originally confounded as to why certain organisms possessed traits that did not promote survival. For example, why did the peacock evolve to possess such brilliant colors and the stag to have such prodigious antlers? Wouldn't such conspicuous traits make the peacock or stag more vulnerable to predators? Darwin also wondered why there was such a great disparity in size, shape, and color between the sexes of various species, including humans. Didn't both sexes face the same survival challenges?   Darwin ultimately answered these questions with a second evolutionary theory: *sexual selection*.

Just as natural selection rewards traits that are adaptive to survival, sexual selection rewards adaptations that increase the likelihood that an organism will mate and produce offspring. As with natural selection, the genes of the winners are passed to the next generation while those of losers are not. Sexual competition for reproduction occurs both within a gender and between genders.

Same sex contestants, most often males, battle for the right to mate with the opposite sex. Stags lock horns, rams butt heads, and male lions do battle for supremacy. The winners eat first and earn the right to mate. The losers are either killed or move to the next herd or pride. The traits of winners (size, strength and cunning) are in this way passed to offspring in a recurrent process, generation after generation, epoch upon epoch. This explains why males in many species, including humans, are often substantially larger and stronger than their female counterparts.

Today, lying beneath the civilized veneer of our twenty-first century lifestyle, are characteristics of our mammalian ancestors. We can see, for example, a reenactment of intra-sex natural selection in modern day sports. It is no wonder that there are very few co-ed sports. Virtually all adolescent, adult, and professional sports, team or individual, are direct same-sex contests. Some, like hockey, football, boxing, and wrestling, involve direct and sometimes brutal physical contact. Played by rules with on-field officials to minimize mayhem, carnage, and even death, these intense same-sex contests have clear winners and losers. Opposite-sex cheerleaders on the sidelines eagerly await the outcome, bouncing up and down, kicking their legs high into the air.

Sexual selection is not limited to same-sex contests. To breed, it is also important that an organism be desirable to the opposite sex. Certain traits of one sex are desired by the opposite sex and are thus perpetuated through successful reproduction. Vivid colored plumage in birds, large antlers in stags, as well as personality traits such as industry, fidelity or commitment to raising offspring make a breeder more attractive as a prospective mate. Traits that are desirable to the opposite sex are thus adaptive in the process of sexual selection and will therefore survive. In humans, traits of females that are an indication of fertility, like body shape and skin tone, are generally preferred by men.[6] Women tend to favor traits that indicate a man's likely ability to provide and protect, like height, muscularity, and financial success.[7] Due to the extremely long period of dependency of human offspring, each sex also favors loyalty, commitment, and parental involvement, which likely explains the human tendency toward a lifelong marriage commitment.[8]

But what does Darwin have to do with human inheritance conflict of the type discussed in *Blood & Money?* We don't live in the jungle and we bear little resemblance to prehistoric man. Evolutionary psychologists contend that much of twenty-first century human behavior is explainable using evolutionary concepts. While some behaviors may not be currently adaptive, they nevertheless survive as a carryover of behaviors that at one time were adaptive. With respect to certain maladaptive behaviors, modern man suffers from *evolutionary lag*.

Evolution is an extremely slow process that continually lags behind changes in the physical environment. The result is that some behaviors are vestiges of behaviors which were adaptive at one time, but which may not be currently adaptive. The delay explains why we continue to crave sweet and fatty foods, and why we fight with each other as if our lives depend on it. Some of these behaviors are distinctly *not adaptive* today, yet they persist.[9]

EVOLUTIONARY PSYCHOLOGY

A scientific and academic leap occurred in the late 1970s when biology and psychology combined to form a new way of explaining human behavior. The premise of the new *evolutionary psychology* is that man has evolved both *physiologically* as well as *behaviorally* to adapt to his environment. Virtually every human behavior – how we dress, eat, work, play, interact, choose a mate, raise children, cooperate, fight, save, and spend – can be explained on the basis of natural selection. Their success and continuance depends on whether they are ultimately adaptive to survival and reproduction.

Evolutionary psychology is the model for understanding the subjects central to this book: parenting, sibling rivalry, greed, kinship, aggression, favoritism, forgiveness, fear of exclusion, and altruism.

Psychologist and author David M. Buss explains the application of Darwinian principles to human behavior in his 2008 book, *Evolutionary Psychology: The New Science of the Mind:*

> Humans, like most organisms, face a large number of adaptive problems: survival, thermal regulation, avoiding predators, selecting and attracting a mate, attending to the needs of children, investing in kin such as siblings and more distant relatives, dealing with social conflicts and social hierarchy. Just as our bodies contain thousands of specific mechanisms, the mind also contains hundreds or thousands of specific mechanisms for addressing these problems.[10]

Sibling rivalry, a key component of family and inheritance conflicts, can be explained as part of the evolutionary struggle for survival. It is an evolutionary fact that organisms naturally produce more offspring than can be supported. According to biologist Douglas W. Mock in *More Than Kin and Less Than Kind: The Evolution of Family Conflict*, organisms over-reproduce "knowing," in an instinctual sense, that not all offspring will survive. Extra offspring are produced as insurance against the vagaries of survival, which include drought, disease, and predators. Birds lay two eggs in the event the first egg does not produce a healthy progeny. In cases where both eggs hatch, intense sibling rivalry for scarce resources ensues. Likewise, in the context of human families, the production of "extra" offspring increases the chance of successful gene propagation.[11] Although humans are decreasingly subject to drought, disease and predators, sibling rivalry persists either as an evolutionary lag or as an adaptation to survival in the competitive modern world.

According to Mock, siblings engage, even to the point of death, in two different forms of competition: *scramble* and *interference*. Scramble competition occurs when siblings fight for their share of limited resources, like baby birds fighting over worms brought back to the nest. Interference competition occurs when one sibling excludes, neutralizes, or kills the competition, or in Mock's words, when: "one diner makes another diner its dinner, thereby reducing the number of diners and stretching the non-diner dinner."[12] This competition continues even when food is not in short supply. Mock points out that humans are not above killing a sibling to accede to power, pointing to Edward II (the Martyr) who in 978 A.D. was fatally stabbed as a teenager so his half-brother Aethelred (the Unready) could ascend to the throne of England. A generation later, Edmund, Aethelred's eldest son, was murdered by his younger brother Knut for the same reason.[13]

Although population culling may seem to be a barbaric remnant of man's distant past, it continues in humans to this day. The average number of children born to the modern western family is currently about two – the minimum number necessary to maintain the species. In the most destitute parts of the world, the average number of children per family is much higher. Watching the evening news we wonder why such destitute mothers have so many children. The answer is that from a genetic point of view, having more children in difficult times is adaptive. Fertility rates (the average number of offspring per family) are directly connected to prevailing mortality rates. The higher the mortality rate, the greater number of children a family must have to insure survival of the parents' genetic code. Today, fertility rates in the poorest regions of the world continue to be high. In 2010 the estimated fertility rate in Niger was 7.75; in Mali, 6.62; Somalia, 6.52; Uganda, 6.77; Afghanistan, 5.60, and Yemen, 5.0. The opposite pattern presents in countries where the mortality rate is low. In the United States, for example, mortality rates have steadily declined throughout our history. The average number of children per family in the U.S. has also steadily decreased from 7 in 1800, to 3.5 in 1900, to about 2.05 in 2010.[14]

INCLUSIVE FITNESS

If evolutionary theory is correct, how do we account for *true love,* affection, or caring for others? How can such altruistic behavior be explained within the context of dog-eat-dog evolutionary theory?

Critics of Darwin's theory, and even Darwin himself, asked the same question: If it's all about survival and reproduction, why would we do anything to help our fellow man? Why, for example, would a squirrel alert his fellow squirrels of an approaching predator? Doing so would surely alert the wolf or fox to his own location and increase his likelihood of being eaten. So why would he risk individual survival for the benefit of others? Biologist William D. Hamilton answered this question in the early 1960s with the development of *inclusive fitness theory,* sometimes called the *Hamilton rule.* Inclusive fitness theory can be summarized as follows: "Reproductive success is the sum of an individual's own reproductive success (classical fitness) plus the effects the individual's actions have on the reproductive success of his or her genetic relatives."[15]

Aided by scientific advancements in genetics and mathematics, Hamilton postulated that we have a stake not only in our own survival and reproduction but also in that of our closest relatives. In what is now considered scientific fact, he theorized that the closer someone is related to us the more common genes we share and therefore the greater stake we have in their survival.

Hamilton's rule is essential to understanding the human family dynamic.

We are most likely to act altruistically toward those with whom we are most closely related. First, we are most related to ourselves. Therefore, we are most likely to act in ways that benefit us personally. This fact alone goes a long way in explaining inheritance disputes. Our next closest relations are our children, parents, and siblings, all of whom are fifty percent related to us. Despite the fact that we are equally related to these three groups, we are likely to do more for our children than for parents or siblings because children have the greatest reproductive value, that is, the greatest likelihood of passing our genetic code to the next generation.

Hamilton asserted that evolution was best understood by viewing natural selection from the gene's perspective. Genes pass to the next generation both through their own survival and through survival of organisms to which they are most closely related. Individual genes can increase their relative reproduction by helping brothers, sisters, nieces, or nephews who carry the greatest number of common genes.

Hamilton's formula takes into consideration the cost to the doer of good acts, the ability of the recipient of the good acts to benefit from them, and the degree of relatedness between the doer and the recipient. When a squirrel cries out that a predator is approaching, he decreases his individual chance of survival. However, his warning increases the chance of survival of all of his brother squirrels, many of whom carry his genes. Instinctively he will risk his life when the benefit conferred upon his offspring and kin is greater than the cost or risk to himself.

The components of cost, benefit, and degree of relatedness in Hamilton's inclusive fitness theory are the basis for understanding parent-child conflict, parental favoritism, sibling rivalry, and the troubled stepparent-stepchild relationship discussed in the balance of this Chapter.

LIMITS OF EVOLUTIONARY PSYCHOLOGY

Evolutionary psychology is only the starting point in explaining human behavior. Our ability to think, reason, feel, and believe allows us to regulate our instinctive behavior. We cannot use evolutionary theory as an excuse for bad behavior. All members of society are held accountable for their actions and to an understanding of the difference between right and wrong. To live in society, each member must subjugate to the common good his own instinctive drive for sex, power, greed, and dominance; we cannot steal, kill, rape or pillage in a civilized world without serious consequences.

Nor do the principles of evolutionary psychology resign us to an involuntary future. Our lives are not predetermined. As humans, we have a soul, a mind, and a free will. We are thinking creatures that can affect our own behaviors and our future. Just because we have evolved to fight with our parents and our siblings doesn't mean that we must. Just because it is our nature to look after "numero uno," doesn't mean that we are not capable of tremendous acts of generosity and altruism.

Geneticist Steve Jones cautions against over-application of evolutionary theory. In his 1999 book *Darwin's Ghost: The Origin of Species Updated* he states that "Behavior comes from brains; and brains, like heart or kidneys, are made by genes." But, he observes so too are culture, habit, and custom built on "what evolution has provided."[17] Jones posits that Mozart learned to play the piano at three because of his genetically provided genius. The fact that he expressed his genius on the piano and in the particular music he played was the product of a number of non-evolutionary phenomena such as style and culture.[18] Our large brain makes us human, but as a species we are defined by what we have been able to learn and accomplish with it. A rocket to the moon is not a product of evolution, but the highest accomplishment of evolved man.

What distinguishes humans from the rest of the animal kingdom is our ability to understand right from wrong and to imagine the future. These special attributes can be traced to the rather precipitous evolution of the human brain which began about three million years ago. During a relatively short (by evolutionary standards) two million year period, the human brain doubled in size and developed frontal lobes. The change is evidenced by the change in the shape of early man's head from the sloping brow of *Homo habilis* (referring to man the *handyman* for his use of stone tools) to the more vertical forehead of modern man; a change necessary to accommodate man's new frontal lobes located directly over the eyes. Modern *Homo Sapiens* refers to man *the knower,* a moniker that carries with it the responsibility to *know better.*

Unique to humans, frontal lobes changed the course of human history. This new body part gave us the ability to wonder about the future, to foresee our own death, and gave rise to man's existential dilemma discussed in Chapter Three, *Terror Management*. Frontal lobes are also responsible for the ongoing dialog between the much older part of our brain prone to instinctive behavior (the proverbial devil on one shoulder) and the new part of our brain (the angel on the other) that reminds us of the consequences of our actions. The frontal lobes are the last part of the human brain to evolve (explaining teenage behavior), and the first to deteriorate as we age[19] (resulting in the difficulties and vulnerabilities described in Chapter Six, *Vulnerability In The Twilight of Competence*).

Fortunately, evolutionary forces promote cooperation as well as conflict. Man's survival depends on cooperation, and cooperation requires that there be a way of resolving conflicts that naturally arise. The mechanism of *forgiveness* serves this function; organisms that are able to forgive are better able to cooperate and survive.[20] According to Michael E. McCullough in his book *Beyond Revenge: The Evolution of the Forgiveness Instinct*, "Forgiveness is … evolutionarily vital … because there has to be a way to restore people to good standing so that they'll be motivated to return to cooperation … If forgiveness weren't available, the average gains of cooperation would slowly decline in the population with each successive generation."[21] There are a number of factors that promote forgiveness, perhaps the most important of which is the ability to empathize, to see things from our adversary's point of view.[22]

The point is that although many families fight, they cannot blame their bad behavior on Darwin. Although the origins of family conflict can be identified, family fighting is not inevitable. By understanding that rivalries and conflict exists in *all* families, you can prevent conflict in *your* family.

PARENT-CHILD RELATIONS

Mating and birthing are only the beginning of the process of assuring the propagation of the species. Genetic success also requires the survival and the reproduction of offspring. The long maturation process of human infants makes human parenting unique in the animal world. Extended parental care and involvement are critical for the survival of human infants who are completely dependent on their parents for a number of years after birth. Evolutionists speculate that this extended period of dependency is necessary for the human brain to develop. By contrast, some species, like sharks, are fully self-sufficient at the moment of their birth (in fact they have likely already eaten a couple of their brothers and sisters while still inside their mother).

Natural selection favors strong parental love and commitment. The extended dependency of infants carries a high cost to parents, who must risk their own survival, mate finding, and further reproduction. Parents who make such commitments have successful offspring. Infants too have adapted to attach to their mother in order to protect themselves from predation, facilitate learning, and provide comfort from stress.

The happy parent-child image is not without its stresses. In Hamiltonian terms, a child is *one hundred percent* related to itself and therefore favors its needs above *all* others. Children have a bond with their immediate family, but will be most sensitive to their own needs. Thus begins a lifetime of love, nurturing, and conflict between parents, children, and siblings, with each instinctively placing his or her interests above all others. It is natural for children to desire a larger portion of a parent's resources than the parent is willing to give.[23] In turn, parents encourage children to value their siblings more than children are naturally inclined to do.[24] For the good of all children, parents tend to reward cooperation and punish conflict between siblings.

Hamilton's rule provides the building blocks for understanding both family harmony and family conflict. Family members are our closest genetic relations; we are most likely to love and protect them above anyone else as they are genetically part of us. Although humans usually bear only a remote genetic relationship to their spouse, the common cause of raising successful offspring creates a genetic bond. Despite all the warmth and fuzziness of their genetic connectedness, however, spouses, parents, children, and siblings also compete for precious resources to ensure their own survival. This is the nature of the ambivalence which naturally exists between spouses, siblings, parents, and children.

The relationship of ambivalence between generations is characterized by mixed feelings of both love and hate. According to German sociologist Kurt Lüscher, "[p]arents and children want to be independent of one another, knowing all the while that they are still mutually dependent."[25] With shared values and common genes, parents and children have common goals. However, parents and children conflict over resources and control. Parents control resources and are the upholders of the prevailing social norms. Early in life, children desire freedom from parental authority; later in life from obligation. Despite these stresses, researchers still point to strong continued importance of the parent/child relationship. The increase in human lifespan has increased the opportunity for both continued involvement as well as conflict between parents and children.

Psychologist and human development expert Harry G. Segal discusses the nature of parent-child ambivalence:

> Being with parents can be satisfying or boring, joyful or depressing, but there is often a divided quality. It may seem as though psychologically one foot is in the past and the other in the present. For those whose early experiences with their parents reflected as secure loving attachment, that double quality may be a pleasant echo, a subtext or ghost of early trust. For others, depending, frankly, on how bad or troubled it was, the echo can be so loud as to drown out the real conversation of the present.[26]

While we may love our parents, their death also frees us from the insecurity of wondering whether they approve of us. Children with particularly conflicted relationships with their parents sometimes marry only after the death of a parent who never saw their child's love interests as worthy. Jeanne Safer, Ph.D, in *Death Benefits* said it well: "I have found that the death of a parent – any parent – can set us free. It offers us our last, best chance to become our truest, deepest selves. It creates unique opportunities for growth – possibilities unimaginable before and not available by any other means. Nothing else in adult life has so much unrecognized potential to help us become more fulfilled human beings – wiser, more mature, more open, less afraid."

Sensing instinctive impulses at play, the late William F. Buckley described Philip Marshall's act of turning in his father to authorities in the Brooke Astor case in Chapter Five as a *"parricidal intervention."* Anny Sadrin explains the absence of the father authority figure as both limiting and freeing when she observes that all of Charles Dickens' heroes - Oliver Twist, Nicholas

Nickleby, Martin Chuzzlewit, David Copperfield, Richard Carstone, Arthur Clennam, Charles Darnay, Philip Pirrip, Hohn Harmon, Edwin Drood – were orphans:

> Such is the rule: fathers must die that their sons shall live. The father's death is vital, necessary to the self-fulfillment of the son whose bereavement is his true birth. He can now take his stand in the order of succession, in the great chain of being, an innocent heir at long last, cleansed of sinful desires, delivered from temptation... For, as long as the father lives, how can the son be entirely free from expectations and parricidal yearnings?[27]

The competition between parents and children isn't limited to material resources. Children also compete for intangibles like love, attention, and validation. Psychoanalytic theory suggests that a child's early sense of self is established in the context of the parent-child relationship and that parents play a central role in the child's budding sense of identity. Offspring continue to crave their parents' approval until the end of life. Conversely, parents derive a sense of accomplishment through the successes of their children. Evidence demonstrates the continued importance and influence of these relationships throughout the lifespan of parents, children, and siblings.

The value of children as gene carriers grows over time as parents age and their own ability to reproduce declines. Children continue their importance to parents as gene carriers as they bear grandchildren. The intensity of the grandparent/grandchild relationship is to be expected, as grandchildren represent a second wave of gene carriers.

Conversely, as parents age, they become less valuable to their children, as they are no longer necessary for the child's survival and reproduction.[28] In fact, parents become a burden as they age and need care. Thus, while parents have an evolutionary incentive to care for, love, and be involved with their children and grandchildren for the rest of their lives, these same parents begin to lose their utility in their children's teenage years, when children mature sexually and begin to focus on their own reproduction.

Elder abuse, including the type suffered by Brooke Astor at the hands of her son Tony Marshall, is the unfortunate but foreseeable product of the increasing dependence of parents on their increasingly independent children. Having outlived their utility, parents are not only expendable but in many cases stand in the way of their children's psychic emancipation and financial inheritance. While in raw numbers relatively few elders are abused, evolutionary psychology helps explain why abuse occurs, especially in families with a history of dysfunction or mental illness.

Parents historically have offset their children's waning interest in them with the promise of a future inheritance. But this promise may not be enough to maintain filial loyalty. As we will see in Chapter Six (particularly see the graph on page 115), the incidence of elder abuse rises sharply as parents age and begin to decline cognitively. This phenomenon is even reflected in our language. The prefix *ab* in Latin means to move away from; it is perhaps no coincidence that the incidents of *ab-use* increase as parents become of less use to their family.

FAVORITISM

Parents will tell you that they love their children equally. From a genetic perspective, parents are equally related to all of their children and in theory should show no favoritism. Nonetheless, favoritism, no matter how subtle, is a factor in virtually all families.

Favoritism occurs naturally and benignly as parents promote the best qualities of each of their children in an attempt to make each child feel special. Despite their best efforts, children often feel slighted. At some level, children want it all. As with other resources, children are genetically hardwired to seek *all* of a parent's favor. Adding to the problem is the extreme sensitivity we all have to the slightest hint of personal rejection inherent in favoritism. The end result is that parents can't seem to win; no matter how hard they try to treat their children equally and praise each child's special qualities they are forever defending accusations of favoritism.

The reality is that not all offspring are equal when it comes to transporting their parents' genetic code. Some are better at survival, and some have more promising mating prospects making them better reproductive bets. Natural selection favors allocating precious parental resources to offspring who have the highest likelihood of reproducing, or, in modern parlance, children who provide the *"biggest bang for the buck."*

According to evolutionary theory, parents will invest more in, and thus show favoritism towards, older children, healthier children, and boys. The probability that a child will reproduce increases from birth to puberty. Therefore, younger children are lower in reproductive value than older children. Reproductive value increases with age primarily because some percentage of children, especially infants, will die, thereby lowering the average reproductive value of that class.[30] Parents naturally favor healthy children over unhealthy children as healthier children are more likely to benefit from parental resources.[31]

Parents favor sons over daughters because of their ability to create an unlimited number of genetic copies. Reproductive success with women is akin to *"putting all of your eggs in one basket."* The reproductive success of a daughter is limited to the number of fertile eggs she can produce in a lifetime – a finite number – and is further impacted by her health during her limited period of fertility.

It is perhaps for these reasons that the inheritance system of *primogeniture,* predominant in the Middle Ages (discussed more in the Appendix), favored oldest sons. In a period of history where survival was less certain, family lands and possessions had to be allocated to the offspring with the highest chance of survival and reproduction. An eldest son had the greatest chance of survival and reproduction: he had already survived his youth and was the most likely to create the greatest number of genetic copies.

Favoritism is also affected by the inherent parental uncertainty of fathers. Mothers are certain that they are the parent of the child since they witnessed the birth. Men – with the exception of very recent genetic testing – can never be sure.[32] This uncertainty impacts the parenting commitment of fathers (and as will be seen in Chapter Two, the inheritance rights of children born out of wedlock). The greater a man's belief that he is the father, the more he is willing invest in that child. Mothers and their families promote acceptance by the father by promoting the belief that the child resembles the father. Studies have shown that although children should resemble one parent roughly half of the time, mothers and their families are about four times more likely to comment that a child resembles the father than the mother.[33] Studies also show that men have more positive relationships with children they believe resemble them.[34] By contrast, fathers are more likely to physically abuse their partners in cases where they question the genetic link to their children.[35]

Physical resemblance as a measure of parental acceptance is reflected in our speech. The term *"black sheep"* connotes an offspring that might not be "one of us," increasing the likelihood that it will be ostracized. The colloquial expression *"red-headed stepchild"* has multiple significance. Being unlike the rest of the family (red hair), and having no genetic connection (stepchild), the expression, used jokingly, implies that there is no reason to invest in such child and may even be a cause for abuse.

SIBLING RIVALRY

Sibling rivalry is as old as the sibling relationship itself. In the Book of Genesis, Cain and Abel were the first and second sons of Adam and Eve. Cain, the older of the two, commits the first Biblical murder by killing his brother Abel in a fit of jealousy after God rejects Cain's sacrifice but accepts Abel's. When the Lord says to Cain, "Where is your brother Abel?" Cain replies "I don't know," and "Am I my brother's keeper?" Seeing through Cain's deception, and hearing "the voice of Abel's blood ... screaming to God from the ground," God curses Cain to wander the earth alone.

The truth is that we are our brother's keeper. Apart from our moral or ethical obligations to our siblings, we have, as Hamilton recognized, a genetic stake in our siblings' well-being and survival. Nevertheless, the relationship of siblings is often characterized as ambivalent. With half of our genes in common, siblings are at once among our closest relations and our fiercest rivals. Siblings are major competitors for parental resources. For modern humans, the competition is not necessarily for food and shelter but for love and recognition. It is a competition that lasts a lifetime, with each child seeking special recognition of their unique qualities.

Psychologists and psychiatrists have long understood that parental love, attention, and approval are the building blocks of self esteem. Parental love is essential for the development of a child's feelings of safety, worth, and acceptance. As one practicing psychologist team put it: "To survive psychologically, we must feel that we fit somewhere, that we are somebody, a person of substance to whom attention must be paid."[36] In a perfect world, children would receive all the love they need to grow into perfect parents who would in turn continue the cycle of perfect love with their own children. Unfortunately, that isn't how it works; parents have their own problems: they die, they divorce, they are mentally ill or have addictions, and they must divide their attention among many competing interests, including their spouse, boss, clients, and other children.

For all the negative qualities ascribed to it, sibling rivalry has its benefits. We learn to compete by knocking heads with our siblings. We hone our social skills with our siblings, forming our first alliances and suffering our first betrayals. Longer in duration than any other relationship, the history we share with our siblings endures a lifetime. Siblings are part of our permanent fiber. The importance of the relationship magnifies not only the love but the hurt, and anger we feel towards them. Siblings know our secrets and our hot buttons. Sometimes a simple look or an imperceptible slight can send siblings into an emotional tailspin. Given the competition for parental resources, it is not surprising that sibling relationships are often riddled with conflict. As Charles Chincholles observed, "That all men should be brothers is the dream of people who have no brothers."

Siblings are keen on drawing their parents into their quarrels. According to biologist Mock, acting up and acting out can be adaptive behaviors. Displaying behaviors that any parent of young children will immediately recognize, baby birds and other mammals exaggerate their needs in order to receive preferential treatment.[37] Nestling birds react frantically when parents arrive with food. Their screams and begging serve a number of purposes. Begging induces the parent to provide more food than it would otherwise provide. It also communicates to siblings the intensity of the beggar's desire for food and their willingness to fight for it. Because begging is noisy, parents will give the squawker what it wants so that the sound of the begging doesn't attract predators to the nest. Increased begging by one offspring also escalates the begging of all other chicks in the nest, resembling, by no coincidence, the sounds of squabbling heirs.

Birth order is a significant element of the sibling relationship. Eldest children receive all of their parents' investment early in life before other children are born. They are bigger and stronger than their younger siblings and are therefore able to dominate. As adults they may continue to expect to be in charge. Of course, this assumption may lead to conflict later in life as old roles may no longer fit with each child's real-life achievements.

In contrast, youngest children must always share with others, because there is never a time when other siblings are not around. As a result, they often feel inferior. They are eternal underlings that yearn for respect, glory, and independence, but at the same time are filled with self-doubts, looking for others to take the lead. Middle children, often labeled "troubled," are somewhere in-between and must figure out where they fit in the family hierarchy.[38]

Children are often assigned roles based on their perceived strengths and birth order. Roles help define our place in the family, and once assigned are resistant to change. In fact, we tend to carry our childhood roles to the workplace, to marriage and to friendships. According to Drs. Hapworth, oldest children tend to be leaders or caretakers, middle children tend to be mediators, while youngest children tend to assume the role of the family rebel or comedian.

Parents must be respectful of their children's roles when allocating responsibilities. Failure to do so will be perceived as a slight that will cause deep hurt and resentment. Appropriately recognizing a child's strengths is an affirmation of a child's value, and is every bit as important as who gets what in terms of inheritance. Failure to properly allocate such recognition is a form of disinheritance.

As relatively few children in the United States starve for lack of food and shelter, sibling rivalry in the twenty-first century is largely a competition for the parental prizes of love and recognition. Competition is natural; all families, no matter how wealthy or urbane, suffer through feelings of competition and jealousy.

The illness or death of a parent breathes new life into old and perhaps dormant rivalries. Resentments over past inequities or transgressions are rekindled as siblings jockey to determine who will be in charge of aging parents and who will inherit prized possessions. The rivalries of the sandbox are reincarnated in the struggle over who will be the leader or who will get dad's gold watch. These disputes are really not about who is in charge or who gets the watch, but who is bigger and more worthy. Losing the battle for superiority leaves the loser feeling insignificant and unwanted. With the stakes so high, it is not surprising that inheritance and other family disputes are felt as life and death struggles with the potential of turning into scramble competitions where nobody gets anything.

STEPCHILDREN/STEPPARENTS

Stepchildren add a new dynamic to the already complex family structure. Step-relationships are often characterized by tension and mistrust, a predictable consequence of putting people together who have no genetic connection. Although many step-family members are able to develop positive caring relationships, the incidence of problems and tensions are much higher than in traditional nuclear families. For example, studies show that step-parenthood is the single most significant risk factor for predicting child abuse.[39] Stepchildren are abused much more frequently than natural children, and infanticide of stepchildren – although rare for both natural and stepchildren – is as much as one hundred times more likely than infanticide of natural children.

The instinctive conflict between stepparents and stepchildren has a brutal outcome in the animal kingdom. The treatment of nursing lion cubs by newly dominant males is a perfect example. The typical lion pride is matrilineal: females are born and eventually breed in the group into which they are born. By contrast, males leave the pride at maturity and seek, either alone or in a group of other young males, to unseat the males of other prides. Young males who succeed in unseating the established male will themselves reign only a few years before they in turn are displaced. Like other mammals, a lioness does not ovulate during her gestation period (about 110 days) or while nursing (about eighteen months). Therefore, a pregnant lioness will be unable to produce a new litter for approximately two years unless her cubs die prematurely. In the latter case, lactation ceases and the lioness' pregnancy can occur sooner.

With no time to waste, the new dominant male must immediately reproduce in order to ensure that his genes survive. Natural selection weeds out male lions that are willing to help raise other's young. The genes of patient and altruistic lions would soon become extinct as they would fail to reproduce. It is for this reason that the first act of young males that succeed in taking over a pride is to kill all of the nursing cubs. This gruesome practice serves the genetic purpose of promoting the new dominant male's genetic code over that of his rival. With his rival's offspring out of the way, he can then begin to promote his own reproductive success.

The good news is that humans do not systematically dispose of their predecessor's young. Most stepparents derive some pleasure from helping raise their partner's children, and many stepparent households are nearly as loving and nurturing as natural ones. On the other hand, raising step-children can be an onerous commitment. Based on what we know about evolutionary processes, it would indeed be surprising if parental feelings could be fully engaged merely by hooking up with someone with children. Stepparents do not, on average, feel the same love as genetic parents, and therefore are less inclined to invest in their new mate's children either during life or at death.

This is not to say that stepparents and step children can never develop loving relationships; it is just that the genetic cards are stacked against them. The odds that a blended family can happily co-exist are much higher when both parent and stepparent are alive. During the marriage, stepparents will be on their best behavior in order maintain good relations with their mate. Studies show that men in particular will invest more in children, both natural and step, when the child's mother is their current mate. Although these studies were limited to male behavior, the inference may logically be made that women too are on their best parental behavior when the natural parent is alive.

The death of a parent fundamentally changes the tacit agreement of cooperation among members of the stepfamily. Brought together by the relationship between the deceased natural parent and the surviving stepparent, children are left with no genetic connection or direct bargain with their surviving stepparent. A blended family that may have tolerated each other while both parents were alive may quickly dissolve into disharmony and disaffection. In the inheritance realm, stepparents are pitted against stepchildren for the inheritance spoils, both economic and emotional, of the decedent.

The stepparent/stepchild relationship frequently fractures on the death of the natural parent. From the stepparent's perspective, stepchildren do not carry their genes and therefore do not merit continued parental involvement.[40] Conversely, stepchildren often view stepparents as tricksters or sexual predators who have usurped their parent's bounty. They fail to appreciate that their deceased parent had his or her own emotional and physical needs that the stepparent satisfied, or that the surviving stepparent may legitimately depend on inherited assets for their economic survival. For stepchildren to even entertain the thought that their parent wished to provide for their surviving spouse is to concede their importance. These evolutionary forces are played out in the classic fairy tail, Cinderella.

CINDERELLA

Predating the field of evolutionary psychology by centuries, the Cinderella story reflects man's instinctive understanding of the connection between parents and their natural children. With no genetic connection to her stepmother, Cinderella had no value and was as dispensable as spent coals -thus the name *Cinder-ella*, or *little cinder*. Worse, with her natural beauty and the potential for attracting a suitable man, Cinderella threatened the economic future of her stepmother and her less attractive stepsisters.

Cinderella is more than a bedtime story or Disney movie. Her story is a fictionalized tale of life in the Middle Ages that was used to entertain as well as educate. For our purposes, the story of Cinderella, like the saga of Brooke Astor in Chapter Five, exemplifies human behavior that bears upon our discussion of inheritance and family conflict. It describes the harsh realities of life in the Middle Ages, and the Darwinian plight of stepchildren. Stripped of their happy ending, medieval fairy tales were stories of struggles for survival. Such tales allowed a largely illiterate population to pass on the important lessons of the day. Evil witches, abandoned children, and murderous stepmothers captured the attention of children and allowed parents to convey important life lessons. These stories survive as entertaining fantasies, but in their day, fairytales like Cinderella were used to educate children on the practical laws of survival while offering hope for a happy ending.

The first known version of the Cinderella story dates back to the first century BC. In the Greco-Egyptian version, Rhodopis, a Greek slave is mistreated and oppressed in her Egyptian master's household. In a plot similar to the 1810 Grimm brothers' version, the beautiful and talented Rhodopis is prevented from attending the Pharaoh's ball. While doing laundry at the shore, one of her slippers is stolen by a falcon and delivered to the Pharaoh. Seeing it as a sign from God, the Pharaoh searches his kingdom to find the shoe's owner. The Pharaoh ultimately finds Rhodopis, and in storybook fashion, they marry and live happily ever after.

The modern version of Cinderella is attributed to the German-born Grimm brothers, who in the early 1800s began to transcribe folktales that had been orally passed from generation to generation. In the Grimms' version, Cinderella lives with her stepmother and two stepsisters (her mother and father have passed away), and is treated quite callously by them. Her condition is desperate with no apparent salvation. But, alas, a fairy godmother appears and turns a pumpkin into a coach and Cinderella's tattered clothing into a fabulous gown with glass slippers. With the magic wave of her fairy godmother's wand, Cinderella is able to attend the ball where she meets a prince, whom she later marries.

Life expectancy in the Middle Ages was extremely short. Someone fortunate enough to reach the age of twenty could expect to live to only fifty-one.[41] Factoring in death from violent causes, life expectancy for this group reduces to forty-two; accounting for infant and childhood mortality the real figure is even lower.[42] As a result, parents in the Middle Ages rarely lived to see all of their children reach adulthood.[43] The severity of the living conditions of this period also mandated that a surviving spouse remarry as soon as possible after the death of their mate. We tend to think of stepchildren as the modern product of divorce, but the harsh realities of the Middle Ages made second marriages and stepchildren as common as they are today.[44] As in the story of Cinderella, the result was blended families with stepchildren fighting for recognition and survival.

The stakes were high for children, especially daughters and younger sons, since land was the principal form of wealth, and *primogeniture* was the principal method of inheritance. Under primogeniture, the eldest son inherited upon his father's death to the exclusion of the decedent's surviving spouse and other children. And it didn't matter that the eldest son was a minor; nearly half of the sons in medieval times inherited from their fathers while minors. Richard II (age ten), Henry VI (age nine months), and Edward V (age twelve), all became Kings of England while minors.

The characters in Cinderella bear a striking resemblance to their real life medieval counterparts. Cinderella's mother and father did not live to see her through to adulthood. Her stepmother—with little prospect of finding a husband (widowers remarried twice as frequently as widows during that period)—treated her cruelly. Her priority was to find landed husbands for her daughters in order to ensure their future as well as her own. With few eldest sons to go around, the young and beautiful Cinderella was a threat to her stepfamily's future security.

Cinderella, both a stepchild and female, did not have good prospects. Without the expectancy of an inheritance, daughters looked to marriage as the sole determinant of their future. A young girl's dream of a good life rested almost entirely upon the prospect of whom she married.

The prince in Cinderella, who was most likely an eldest child, inherited both his property and standing in the community from his parents. Land was the principal source of wealth, and virtually the only way to obtain it was through inheritance. A younger brother would be forced to join the military, the priesthood, or become a traveler looking for opportunity wherever it presented itself.[45]

CONCLUSION

Evolutionary psychology teaches us that family and inheritance conflict, far from being an aberration, is to be expected. The principles of evolutionary psychology are at play in all inheritance disputes and help explain the inherent ambivalence in our relationships with parents, children, and siblings. With no genetic connection, stepparents and stepchildren are natural competitors. Each views the other as thieves and interlopers with no purpose other than to deprive them of what is rightfully theirs. With no love, there is no love lost, and no reason to trammel the natural human instincts of greed, revenge, and predation. This is the nature of the love/hate relationship with our family and stepfamily and one of the principal reasons for inheritance conflict.

DISINHERITANCE

"The most egregious form of rejection that anyone can ever experience is parental rejection"
Hardy, 2002

INTRODUCTION

The disinheritance of a loved one is undeniably an act of rejection. Disinheritance by someone of importance like a parent can be so powerful as to be felt literally as life threatening. To be disinherited by a parent is to be disowned – to become an orphan retroactive to birth. Even to receive less than other beneficiaries who are similarly situated is exquisitely painful and can be disorienting.

From an evolutionary point of view, we have evolved to react strongly to any rejection, no matter how slight. In a primal sense, surviving in the wild required that humans stay with the pack. Without claws, fangs, a coat of fur, or great running speed, humans had to band together and rely on their collective resources and intelligence to survive. Ostracism from the group meant certain death. Marketers have long understood the heightened anxiety of feeling left out. Using scarcity as a motivator, they bark *"act now while supplies last," "quantities are limited," "the first five callers will receive this special offer,"* or simply *"call today."*

With our brain and nervous system highly calibrated to detect rejection, the opportunity for false positives is high. We often experience hurt or rejection from the slightest oversight or hint of rejection of others. Beneficiaries often see rejection or disinheritance where it doesn't exist. Virtually any showing of inheritance favoritism by the testator, or the suspicious actions of an inheritance rival, can activate strong anxieties among inheritance hopefuls.

The American legal system contributes to inheritance anxiety by granting testators unparalleled testamentary freedom, including (everywhere except Louisiana) the right to completely disinherit children, and to a lesser extent spouses. While it is not common to disinherit children, the right to do so is guaranteed by law. That disinheritance is a potential reality only feeds the innate fears of beneficiaries.

As with most freedoms, there are associated costs. With testamentary freedom, the cost is an increased potential for abuse. Although children are protected to a limited extent under state intestate schemes where the parent dies without a valid will, parents with toxic inheritance motives (Chapter Four) or who have been unduly influenced by others (Chapter Eight) are free to execute wills and trusts that disinherit.

In observing the American system, French historian and political commentator Alexis de Tocqueville (1805-1859) feared that untrammeled testamentary freedom would undermine the American family.[46] He speculated that if testators could, they would systematically forsake their children in favor of non-family. For the most part de Tocqueville was wrong; he underestimated the strong genetic connection between parents and their children. His concern, however, was not completely unfounded. Broad testamentary freedom opens the door to disinheritance by toxic testators and the selfish acts of influencers who impose their view of "what mom wanted," and who manipulate declining and vulnerable testators for their own gain.

Despite having the freedom to disinherit one's family, testators rarely do.[47] Studies of disinheritance since Colonial times indicate that disinheritance is relatively infrequent.[48] The vast majority of modern testators leave their estates to their spouses and children. Less than twelve percent of probated wills studied involve some form of disinheritance, and only about five percent involve some form of punitive motive. Non-vindictive reasons to disinherit include leaving less to children who received their inheritance during the life of the testator, gifting more to those with the greatest needs, bequesting to repay those who provided service during life, and excluding heirs who would use their inheritance to pursue an unhealthy lifestyle.

Will contests are also relatively rare, occurring in less than three percent of probated estates.[49] When they do occur, nearly seventy-two percent involve children and step-children, and over thirteen percent involve first or second spouses. Although inheritance disputes rarely end up in court, the relatively low level of litigated claims should not be equated with a low level of conflict. A number of factors explain the low level of litigation, not the least of which are its economic and emotional toll.

From a testator's point of view there may be very good reasons to disinherit. Disinheritance motives go hand-in-hand with the motives for *giving* an inheritance. Inheritance has long been used by parents to ensure the loyalty of their children, to secure the future services of children, as insurance against infirmity and old age (a primitive precursor to modern day pensions and social security), to influence future marriages, and to minimize family embarrassment and ostracism by securing compliance with societal norms. Violation of any of these tacit expectations can result in disinheritance.

Parents also tend to view reciprocity as a condition of inheritance.[50] Children are expected to return some amount of love to their parents. Although parents learn to expect a low return on their emotional investment during their children's teenage years, their expectations grow as their children age and start families of their own. A child risks disinheritance if he or she cuts off contact with parents or bars contact with grandchildren. Disinheritance may be a parent's only recourse against a child who has physically or emotionally abandoned them. A breach of reciprocity on the part of the child is more than just moving far away geographically or being busy with one's career or children; it usually involves more affirmative acts like not speaking to parents, barring access to grandchildren, or excluding them from holidays, birthdays and other important events.

Historically, certain conduct resulted in *legal* disinheritance. Such conduct included being born out of wedlock, criminal activity (the chattels of criminals were confiscated by the king), and entry into a religious order (which was considered a *civil death*).

Being born out of wedlock was cause for disinheritance for the reason that inheritance was *patrilineal* (passing through the father). Without a marriage contract validating the paternity of the child, the paternal blood connection was uncertain *("mamma's baby, daddy's maybe")*. A child born out of wedlock was considered a *bastard, illegitimate,* or a child of nobody *(filius nullius)*. Biologically, the mother is always certain *(mater semper certa est),* but the father, unless he himself was willing to be contractually bound by marriage, was not. A series of U.S. Supreme Court decisions in the early 1970s abolished most, if not all, of the common-law disabilities of bastardy as being violations of the equal protection clause of the Fourteenth Amendment of the United States Constitution.

The right to leave or receive an inheritance is not a constitutional right.[51] Although states retain "broad authority to adjust rules governing the descent and devise of property without implicating the guarantees of the Just Compensation Clause,"[52] they have historically been reluctant to do so. The result is that short of his killing the testator, a beneficiary may not be deprived of the right to inherit.[53] There is, however, a growing body of law in a number of states, including California, Arizona, and Illinois, which grants broad judicial discretion to disinherit *unworthy heirs* who abuse their fiduciary responsibility by engaging in financial elder abuse.

Despite the relative rarity of disinheritance, the angst and the underlying fears related to potential rejection, exclusion, and ostracism (discussed below in *Sociometric Theory and Disinheritance*) are likely to continue to generate family tension and conflict. The current state of American inheritance law, especially as it relates to children, does little to allay those fears. Family conflict activated by real or imagined disinheritance is as prevalent and as real today as it has ever been.

RIGHTS OF CHILDREN

Protections against disinheritance have existed at least since the Code of

Hammurabi, which granted a mandatory share to children.[54] Under Roman and civil law, children were protected by a device know as the *legitime*, which guaranteed children a portion of their deceased parent's estate. Protections against disinheritance were part of English law, but gradually disappeared with the emergence of individual rights. By 1724, *forced shares* for family members, expressly sanctioned in the Magna Carta, had vanished entirely from English law. England's emergence as an imperial power and the rise of economic and political individualism led to the demise of any restriction on free testation. In Edmond N. Cahn's words:

> "Men had burst forth from the mediaeval collectivism of the feudal system and had begun to learn of their inalienable rights, while forgetting their inescapable obligations."[55]

The freedom in the U.S. to disinherit one's children is perhaps without parallel in the western world. Testamentary freedom is so fundamental to our system of inheritance that decedents are free to disinherit even minor children. There is a limited exception in the State of Louisiana which protects the interests of incapacitated children and children under the age of twenty-three. Discussed more fully in the Appendix, Louisiana law is unique in our country in its reliance on the Napoleonic Code.

Other countries protect children through similar systems of guaranteed shares. In Sweden, Finland, and Greece, for example, children must receive at least one half of what they would have received under rules of *intestacy* (the default provisions of state law that govern cases where the decedent died without a will). In Switzerland, children are entitled to all of their parent's estate if a parent is unmarried at the time of death, and three-quarters of the estate if the parent is married. In France, the amount required to be left to children depends on their number: one child receives half; two children receive two-thirds; and three or more children receive three quarters of their parent's estate. In Islamic countries children are also entitled to a forced share.

In the United States, there are limited protections to children who are mistakenly omitted from the testator's legacy. Children of all ages are protected from *inadvertent* disinheritance under state *pretermittance* statutes.

Such statutes protect children unless there is convincing proof that the decedent intended to disinherit them. Some pretermittance statutes protect only children born or adopted after the execution of the will, while others protect any child not provided for in the will whenever born or adopted. The share of a pretermitted child varies from state to state, but inadvertently omitted children are typically entitled to receive an intestate share. Testators are advised to specifically state that they are disinheriting a child to avoid application of pretermittance statutes. The practice of leaving "one dollar" to disinherited heirs, though not the most legally sound approach, has found its way into Hollywood movie folklore and perhaps a will or two. Instead, testators are advised to simply state that "for reasons best known to me I make no provision for my son, Jerome."

Leaving everything to a surviving spouse is a form of disinheritance that children of first marriages readily accept. In first marriages, leaving everything to a spouse typically does not raise anxieties since children appreciate the needs of their surviving parent and trust that they will inherit on the surviving parent's death. Children do not have the same comfort when the surviving spouse is a stepparent. With no biological connection, children are rightfully concerned that the stepparent will disinherit them in favor of either the stepparent's natural children or a subsequent spouse. The high incidence of divorce and re-marriage requires special planning to ensure that everyone is treated fairly in multiple-marriage families and to allay the anxieties of all involved.

With few protections in the United States for non-spouse beneficiaries, the potential for abuse is high. Disinheriting a child where there has been a breakdown of the relationship or in situations where an inheritance would allow a child to continue a self-destructive lifestyle is a legitimate exercise of free testation. It may even be an acceptable risk of free testation to allow spiteful and arbitrary testators to disinherit their children. But disinheritance is tragic when confused and even demented testators disinherit their children as a result of delusional thinking or undue influence. It becomes criminal when ill-intentioned stepparents, evil siblings, or other predators coerce or defraud testators into disinheriting children in favor of themselves.

RIGHTS OF SPOUSES

The conjugal role of spouses is evolving. Today, there is a greater financial partnership between husbands and wives during life, and a greater responsibility to one another in death. One's surviving spouse has become a deceased spouse's overwhelming choice as primary beneficiary, even enjoying priority over children. This development is remarkable in light of the fact that widows were an afterthought in the Western inheritance scheme until the mid-1800s. A surviving wife was perceived as a threat to the continuity of the family, and for that reason rarely inherited anything save for items of personal property. The medieval practice of *quarantine* provides insight into the evolution of women's rights. While today we associate the term quarantine with isolation aimed at preventing the spread of disease, it derives from the Latin word *quadraginta* literally meaning "forty," and originally referred to the limited period of forty days in which a widow had the right to remain in her dead husband's home. In a little more than a century wives have gone from a peripheral, or minor, legatee to a husband's primary beneficiary.[56] Today, married decedents tend to leave everything to their spouse, and appoint each other to trusted *fiduciary* (a term that identifies a position of trust derived from the Latin word *fiducia,* meaning trust) roles such as trustee, personal representative, and holders under powers of attorney.

The growing entitlement of spouses can be attributed to the growing interdependence of spouses, and to the increasing independence and mobility of children. Today, children no longer need an inheritance to survive.[57] Family lands are no longer the primary means of support, as education and social contacts have become the new ingredients of a successful future. The extended childhood of children obligates parents to dedicate a much larger portion of their personal resources to raising their children, leaving them less time to secure their own financial future. The geographic mobility of children and the demands of raising their own children dictate that aging parents must focus on their own survival without any expectation that their children will be available to support them.

Modern pension laws have likewise adapted to accommodate the needs of surviving spouses. For example, the Employee Retirement Income Security Act of 1974 (ERISA) and the Retirement Equity Act of 1984 protect spouses by requiring that they receive a spousal annuity which can only be waived with the surviving spouse's consent. Prior to 1984, a working spouse could elect a larger lifetime pension that would end at his death. The Retirement Equity Act of 1984 changed the law to require that a worker's surviving spouse receive at least one-half of the monthly pension received by the working spouse unless the non-working spouse waives such right.

Today, in one way or another, every state protects a surviving spouse from disinheritance. State laws regarding the marital rights of surviving spouses break down into two groups: *community property* states and non-community or *common law* states. In the nine community property jurisdictions, surviving spouses are protected against disinheritance by virtue of their deemed ownership of half of the couple's community property, even if title is only in the deceased spouse's name. Generally, community property consists of all property acquired by the efforts or industry of either spouse during the marriage. Property acquired by gift or inheritance is not community property, nor is property brought into the marriage. These later items are considered *separate property* to which the surviving spouse has no entitlement (other than perhaps intestate rights described below). Community property laws also protect spouses in the event of divorce.

In all non-community property or *common law* jurisdictions, except Georgia (which only grants a one-year living allowance), surviving spouses are protected from disinheritance through a mechanism known as a *statutory share* (sometimes called *forced share, elective share,* or the right to *elect against the will*).[58] In such non-community property states, a disinherited spouse may elect a statutory portion of the deceased spouse's probate estate (and, in many cases, non-probate assets as well) regardless of the terms of the decedent's will. The size of the spouse's forced share varies considerably among the states. Frequently it is one-third of the decedent's probate estate (some states include non-probate property in the calculation in what is referred to as the *augmented probate estate)* to one-half of the probate estate if the decedent is not survived by descendants.[59] Whether non-probate assets are used to augment the spouse's elective share varies from state to state and case by case.

In addition to his or her spousal share, a surviving spouse in both community and non-community property states may also be entitled to a *homestead allowance* (either a small dollar amount or the right, subject to a mortgage, to occupy the family home for life), a right to the deceased spouse's automobile (subject to liens), household furniture, personal effects, and a family allowance to provide support during the administration of the estate. These rights are intended to maintain the surviving spouse during the administration of the estate and are not part of the division of marital assets. In Georgia, the family allowance is the amount needed for one year of support. A few states, like Michigan, still recognize *dower* rights. Generally provided to a widow, dower is a lifetime right to the income from one-third of her deceased husband's real estate. Dower rights lapse at death and do not allow the widow to direct who shall enjoy the remainder. *Curtesy* is a similar but much rarer protection granted to widowers. Curtesy provides a surviving husband with a life estate in all of his deceased wife's real estate, but only if there were children of the marriage.

Some non-community states also have *pretermitted* will statutes that allow surviving spouses to elect against a will that was executed before the marriage which omits them. Pretermittance statutes are intended to protect spouses disinherited by mistake or inadvertence. Under typical pretermittance statues, spouses may choose whether to take an elective share or a modified intestate share. Pretermittance statutes apply only when the omission is unintentional; a statement disinheriting one's spouse would preclude protection under such statutes.

The Uniform Probate Code (UPC) has perhaps the most progressive protections for surviving spouses. The UPC is a statutory scheme of model laws created by national legal experts to promote uniformity of laws around the country. The UPC is significant in that it represents the most current and informed thinking on matters of inheritance. Borrowing concepts from both community and non-community property states, the UPC views marriage as an *economic partnership*[60] under which all property acquired during the marriage and even property brought into the marriage is considered part of the marital estate. In a novel approach, the UPC first creates a *super-augmented estate,* pulling into the marital estate not only separate property but also life insurance and property gifted by the decedent within two years of death.[61] The spouse's share is determined by multiplying the super-augmented estate by a factor which is based on the length of the marriage. Under the UPC formula, the longer the marriage the larger the survivor's entitlement.[62] Factoring in the length of the marriage recognizes the fact that the longer the marriage, the fewer remaining years the survivor has left after a spouse's death to accumulate assets sufficient to support him or herself.

SOCIOMETRIC THEORY AND DISINHERITANCE

The human need to belong is as fundamental to survival as "air, water, and food."[63] *Belongingness* is adaptive as humans have evolved to depend on group cooperation as their principal survival strategy. Without fangs and claws, and burdened with an extended childhood that makes humans vulnerable to predators, primitive man was not well suited to living alone in the hostile early world. To compensate, our earliest ancestors relied on cooperative living for food, protection, and securing a mate.

To be excluded from the group – whether due to mental or physical illness or misbehavior – was an early death sentence. Alone, the excluded were left to fend for themselves, soon becoming weak with hunger and exposure. They would either starve to death or become easy prey to roaming bands of hungry predators. With early man's very survival dependent on maintaining membership in social groups, it is not surprising that we have evolved to have such sensitive antennae for detecting rejection and that we react so strongly to rejection, real or perceived. Reverend Martin Luther King, Jr. placed a high value on the friendship, acceptance, and cooperation of his fellow man. Reverend King expressed the significance of belonging when he said: "In the end, we will remember not the words of our enemies but the silence of our friends."[64]

In addition to satisfying our physical needs, belonging satisfies our very real psychological needs. The early attachment experiences of infants help them form early perceptions of themselves as worthy and lovable. These early relationships carry over into our adult life, and influence our need for intimate contact in our adult relationships (*adult attachment theory*).

Humans are social animals by nature; we require social interaction to keep us happy, stable and sane. Involvement with others minimizes anxiety and depression, and gives meaning to our life. As discussed more fully in Chapter Three, *Terror Management,* we also rely heavily on belonging, friendship, and the company of others to combat our inner terror of death. Intellectually, we rely on the information obtained from others to validate our perception of reality. Emotionally, our level of self-esteem is directly impacted by our relationships, our family, and our associations. As Walt Whitman said in *I Sing the Body Electric* in 1855: "There is something in staying close to men and women, and looking on them, and in the contact and odor of them, that pleases the soul well...."[65]

Humans have evolved to feel *social pain* in response to rejection. Experienced physiologically much like physical pain – including anxiety, hurt, upset stomach, and panic - social pain motivates us to end exposure to the dangerous stimulus. Social pain also alerts us to alter our behavior to either avoid exclusion or to regain entry into the group if already excluded. Social pain as a physical phenomenon is reflected in expressions like *"broken heart," "hurt feelings," or "getting burned."*

The danger of any ultra-sensitive detection system is the potential for false positives. Who hasn't perceived a slight of another that on further examination was misinterpreted? It often happens that person "*A*" perceives rejection or what he or she believes to be dismissive behavior from person "*B*". Experiencing social pain, *A* begins to avoid or act in a hostile manner toward *B*. Feeling the *chill* (an expression that may derive from the sense of being separated from the warmth of the pack) from *A*, and unaware that *A* is reacting to something *B* said or did, *B* feels social pain and likewise returns the chilling or aggressive behavior. The parties are soon engaged in a conflict that neither can explain. Kristin L. Sommer and Yonata S. Rubin explain why we might be quick to pull the trigger when we feel a chill from others:

> By rejecting others before others have had the opportunity to reject them, people can generate alternative, nonthreatening attributions for their treatment and also stave off the feelings of worthlessness and anxiety that accompany feelings of being unwanted. From a cognitive and emotional standpoint, then, antisocial behaviors may protect the self from future harm.[66]

This explains in part why we are often conflicted in our relationships. Our profound need for acceptance combined with hyper-sensitivity to rejection make us psychotic social creatures; afraid that the social acceptance we so desperately need will be taken from us. Eerily, entire countries - through their all too human leaders - suffer from the same need for alliances and hyper-sensitivity to rejection.

It would seem adaptive for an excludee to alter his behavior to regain acceptance into the group. Several studies, however, have shown that people will regulate their behavior only if they believe there is a realistic chance that they can regain acceptance. If they believe that their efforts will be futile, they become aggressive, self-defeating, and self destructive.

We are able to live freely in society as long as we agree to regulate our biological urges and play by the rules. Most of us have the ability to understand the bargain and abide by it. We consider self-restraint to be a reasonable price for membership. However, that bargain ends when a member feels excluded with no possibility of re-entry. The result is that those who feel rejected or ostracized end self-regulation and act out. Recent school killings in North America and in Europe show a consistent pattern of social alienation. There were more than thirty such shootings in North America between the mid-1990s and 2005. Studies show that in more than eighty-five percent of those cases the perpetrators previously experienced chronic or acute social rejection.

The permanent nature of disinheritance touches disinherited's psychic core, upsetting his or her deepest sense of belonging and concept of self.[67] The very belief that one will be excluded from an inheritance can in and of itself lead to disregulation and preemptive acts against rival heirs or to elder abuse. With the possibility of resurrecting or repairing the relationship with the deceased slipping away, there is no longer any reason for the disinherited to regulate his or her instinctive urges. Fears are heightened and disregulation becomes more common as death approaches. Not surprisingly, and as will be seen in Chapter Six, the incidence of predatory acts against testators grows at an exponential rate as their target fails and death nears.

CONCLUSION

The permanent nature of disinheritance adds to the intensity and emotional reaction that any form of rejection evokes. The human fear of rejection is also magnified when coupled with reminders of our own mortality. Chapter Three, *Terror Management*, explains why the fear of death plagues man throughout life, and how it is activated by the death of a loved one. As we will see in Chapter Five, all of the key players in the Brooke Astor drama suffered from the social pain of real or perceived exclusion.

TERROR MANAGEMENT | 3

"One cannot look directly at either the sun or death."
- Francois La Rochefoucauld (1613 – 1680)

"Fear is the path to the dark side. Fear leads to anger; anger leads to hate; hate leads to suffering."
- Yoda, Star Wars, Episode One: The Phantom Menace, 1999

INTRODUCTION

One cannot understand inheritance conflict without considering the emotional and psychological impact of death itself. The death of a loved one is one of life's most profound and painful experiences. Beyond sadness and other powerful emotions it may invoke, death activates the inner terror of those left behind.[68]

By its nature, the final severance of a relationship with someone close to us touches both our sense of security and the fear of our own mortality. It conjures insecurities similar to those activated by lifetime rejections discussed in Chapter Two. Being separated from a loved one or from the pack leaves us feeling vulnerable, exposed, and afraid. Because of its permanence, death also "presents one of the most formidable challenges to the idea that human life has meaning and purpose."[69]

The death of a loved one shakes our psychological and emotional foundation in two basic ways: First, in cases where the departed was a parent or parent figure, we are deprived of an important source of our original sense of safety and security. Second, it awakens the subconscious terror of our own mortality that social scientists say resides in all humans from an early age. Given these facts, it should not be surprising that fear, even terror, is the most commonly expressed emotional response to death.[70]

Because death activates our innermost fears, it causes us to act in ways that are a departure from our usual, rational, thoughtful selves. Those left behind scramble to assuage their fears, attaching themselves to the things that bring them comfort, like their faith, relationships, work, their appearance, health, money, and possessions. They may also crave symbols of the decedent, like dad's watch, mom's jewelry, or other objects that symbolize their lost loved one.

Conflict often ensues as each child competes for a piece of the deceased parent, both to feel special and to allay the fears that the decedent's death conjures. Quarreling beneficiaries are universally mocked as being greedy, foolish, petty, and absurd. But what may appear to outsiders as raw greed and child-like behavior is in reality the desperate acts of survivors seeking to hold on to the symbols of the decedent and other items like money and wealth that they hope will bring them security against their repressed inner terror.

In matters of death, fear and terror abound. The sick and dying fear the unknown of what awaits them on the other side. Their survivors, having witnessed their loved one's passing, are left feeling naked and reminded of their own mortality. Both sides grab desperately for the symbols, beliefs, and ideals that calm their fears and assure them that they will survive beyond their finite days on earth in some fashion. Nothing brings comfort and the apparent ability to control life's contingencies like money and wealth. It is this combustible union of terror and money that activates inheritance conflict. Once begun, the conflict takes on a life of its own as the combatants are propelled by a subconscious inner terror of which they are not aware.

TERROR MANAGEMENT THEORY

A widely-accepted psychological theory contends that humans live with the ongoing existential terror of death. Such terror derives from man's unique ability to observe that, like all living things, we are destined to die. When combined with our instinctive desire to survive and procreate, the capacity to contemplate our mortal fate creates "an irresolvable existential paradox."[71] Hardwired for survival, we are aware that our struggle is ultimately a losing battle.

Unable to comprehend that our life simply dissolves into static nothingness, like 1960s television programming at 2 a.m., we push the problem of death into the unforeseeable future. When confronted with our mortality we trick ourselves, through what psychologists call *cognitive distortions,* into believing that death isn't something we need to worry about anytime soon.[72] We defer thoughts of death by focusing on our good health or the longevity of those like Winston Churchill who lived to age ninety despite a lifetime of bad habits including heavy smoking, drinking, and a sedentary lifestyle (he was known to work from bed). "Hell!" the thinking goes, "if he can live that long with his bad habits, I should have nothing to worry about!" If for health reasons or advanced age our death is less deniable, we focus on possible new medical research or promise ourselves that we'll go on a diet or start exercising. All such distortions create the illusory expectation of continued life. Too disturbing to be allowed to reside among our *conscious* thoughts, we repress thoughts of death.

From an evolutionary point of view, the conscious denial of death is adaptive. It helps us avoid the paralyzing terror that would ensue if we fully appreciated our dismal mortal fate. However, to not fear death at any level would be equally dangerous. Long ago, evolution weeded out those who did not fear death, as they were eaten by predators or died from exposure. Thus, fear of death promotes individual survival and social order.[73] Yet despite its utility, fear plagues us, making us anxious creatures prone to conflict with those with whom we feel we compete for love, importance, and survival.

Though driven from consciousness, the terror of our potential non-existence cannot be totally denied. Many psychologists believe that the terror of death continuously resides in our subconscious where it affects our everyday lives in dramatic ways. According to modern psychological theory, the *subconscious* fear of death is the motivating factor behind much of human behavior. Social scientists have come to this conclusion by demonstrating through hundreds of studies that reminders of our mortality *(mortality salience)* push us to adhere even more passionately to our particularized view of the world *(worldview)*.

The illness and death of a loved one, and sometimes even of someone we do not personally know like Elvis, Michael Jackson, Princess Diana, or Pope John Paul II, touches our subconscious awareness of our own mortality.[74] Scientists have documented the effect of mortality salience on human behavior and have consistently found that such death reminders cause us to adhere to the every day things we use to manage our subconscious terror – things like spirituality, work, exercise, wealth accumulation, and relationships.

Terror management theory (TMT), clearly enunciated for the first time in 1986, was inspired by the works of Otto Rank and cultural anthropologist Ernest Becker, both of whom believed the fear of death to be universal. Sigmund Freud's colleague Rank argued that mortality anxiety is the fundamental human fear. He attributed religiosity and the development of societal structures to man's awareness of his personal finitude. Similarly, Becker observed that, "the idea of death, the fear of it, haunts the human animal like nothing else; it is the mainspring of human activity – activity designed largely to avoid the fatality of death, to overcome it by denying in some way that it is the final destiny for man."[75]   Freud himself believed that man has devised sophisticated ways of denying his own death: "Our own death is indeed quite unimaginable, and whenever we make an attempt to imagine it we can perceive that we really survive as spectators.… [A]t bottom no one believes in his own death,… in the unconscious everyone of us is convinced of his own immortality."[76]

"Everyone wants to go to heaven, but nobody wants to die."
Blues guitar legend Albert King

LITERAL AND SYMBOLIC IMMORTALITY

Terror management theory suggests that we have learned to cope with our *subconscious* fear of death through the belief that we live on in some way beyond our death. Faced with the potential finality of life, we seek beliefs and social structures that give meaning to our life and allow us to psychologically transcend death. We either believe that we literally survive our death in some form of afterlife *(literal immortality),* or that we survive symbolically through our children, the lives we touch, or through our works, deeds, and accomplishments *(symbolic immortality).*[77] Pop icon Michael Jackson (1958 – 2009) understood symbolic immortality at a young age when he said, "I give my all in my work because I want it to live." Woody Allen has his own twist on immortality: "I don't want to attain immortality through my work; I want to attain immortality by not dying."

Each of us adopts an individualized version of the world which provides the promise of literal or symbolic immortality if we live up to prescribed standards. Those of faith believe that their spirit, body, or both survive in the afterlife if they are a good Christian, Jew, Muslim, Hindu, or soul. Others, including those of faith, believe that the secular world is a meaningful place that survives their death. They believe that by being a good parent, friend, doctor, businessperson, artist, athlete, Republican, Democrat, plumber, Rotarian, or sports fan they are making a valuable contribution to a meaningful world that survives after they are gone. Perhaps the most common form of symbolic immortality is the belief that we survive genetically through our children, grandchildren, and relations. Religious historian Milton McC. Gatch observed: "Like his predecessors, the man who dies becomes one of the fathers, a name in the genealogical list; and as such he never ceases to be part of the continuing story of the People."

The pursuits of literal or symbolic immortality are interchangeable means of dealing with death-related concerns. TMT studies have shown for instance that the stronger the belief in an afterlife (literal immortality), the less important one's place in the world (symbolic immortality) becomes.[78] Whatever one's worldview, we each adopt our own individualized vision of the world with its own reality, meaning and permanence. Also, we each have our own vision of the world after we are gone – our "post-self."

Belief in *literal immortality,* or the afterlife, is older than the human race. Neanderthal man left flowers, grain, and other grave goods in his burial places. The belief that the dead survive in the form of spirits, both good and evil, has been pervasive ever since. Interestingly, the association of heaven with immortality was originally Egyptian, occurring thousands of years before it became part of Biblical or Greek tradition. The *akh* (transformed spirit) of mummified ancient pharaohs were believed to travel to heaven on pyramids built as giant compasses that pointed to the stars which were to be their resident's permanent resting place.[79] Belief in the afterlife continues today; recent surveys show that the vast majority of the world's population believes in some form of life after death.[80] Ironically, in the United States, more Americans believe in an afterlife than believe in God.[81]

In the face of our mortality, we seek that which does not die. Cultural institutions like business, government, education, and sports, confer a form of symbolic immortality that allows their participants to feel part of something larger, more significant, and lasting. Such institutions define what is important and revered. Behaviors like finding a cure for disease, scientific discoveries, sports, and educational achievements are elevated as important goals, giving achievers special *hero* status. Being a good American, a caring parent, a devout Yankee fan, a church elder, and by believing in the ultimate importance and value of such pursuits, allows us to feel part of something eternal. Such informal systems make for a better world. They also give human life meaning and purpose, allowing less time for busy achievers to feel their inner terror.

We strive to succeed in the world as we each define success. The things we strive for our entire life, what we want to be when we grow up, or how much money we want to make, all give meaning to our life. Such hopes and dreams help us deal with our subconscious death terrors including fear of being insignificant, not being remembered, or not making an impact on the world. We dream of becoming a CEO, a rock star, a professional athlete, or we aspire to a big house, an attractive spouse, or to drive a fancy car. We feel good about ourselves when we meet the standards of what we believe is important. We are secure in the belief that we are a valuable participant in something meaningful.

According to Becker, human accomplishments empower the achiever giving him or her the feeling that he or she can better deal with the unknown: "They earn this feeling by carving out a place in nature, by building an edifice that reflects human value: a temple, a cathedral, a totem pole, a skyscraper, a family that spans three generations. The hope and belief is that the things that man creates in society are of lasting worth and meaning, that they outlive or outshine death and decay, that man and his products count."[82]

According to TMT theorists, "…[E]ach individual human's name and identity, family and social identifications, goals and aspirations, occupation and title, are humanly created adornments draped over an animal that, in the cosmic scheme of things, may be no more significant or enduring than any individual potato, pineapple, or porcupine. But it is this elaborate drapery that provides us with the fortitude to carry on despite human awareness of our mortal fate."[83]

Living up to societal standards creates a sense of personal value and self-esteem. It gives us the feeling that we are a valuable contributor to a meaningful universe, and that our life has meaning and value. Perhaps we also believe that our success or mastery in the temporal world will somehow prepare us for success in the next.

Money and wealth are central to self esteem and terror management. Wealth is how we keep score, how we measure our worth, value, and importance. Nearly every culture accords special status to the wealthy, especially those who achieve wealth through their industry, ingenuity, ambition, or savvy. Wealth is the most recognizable and universal measurement of how well we have adhered to the structures of our culture, conferring on its owners special status and power. Wealth also buffers us from life's contingencies, providing us access to the things we need.

Wealth insulates us from the things in life that scare us. Wealth allays our fears of the unknown as it gives us the confidence that we can obtain what we need to protect and sustain ourselves. Wealth takes on special importance for aging citizens whose declining physical abilities and cognition leaves them feeling vulnerable. Yet, despite its allure, wealth creates its own impossible dilemma with regard to the fear of death: how much do we need to protect us from that which is unquantifiable?

Death is the greatest and most terrifying unknown. Not knowing how much money is needed to fight such a terrifying beast, we grab for as much wealth as we can lay our hands on.[84] Many risk everything, including their health and relationships, to get more. Perhaps this is why many are never satisfied with what they have. Never feeling big enough to defend themselves against their inner terror, they endlessly pursue wealth to make themselves feel bigger and less vulnerable.[85]

ATTACHMENT THEORY

Another force underlying inheritance conflict is what psychologists term "attachment." Healthy humans are born with an attachment mechanism geared to maintaining proximity to significant others.[86] It begins as helpless infants instinctively attach themselves to their parents for survival. Infants seek the love and protection of their parents to satisfy their physical needs and to ward off their innate fear of being alone in the world. The terror expressed by infants at the slightest separation from their parents is evidence of the power of this attachment. Such *separation anxiety* is the purest unadulterated expression of terror.

The attachment system is active throughout our life.[87] What starts with our parents and immediate family, expands to the larger world as we leave the nest and form our own identity. Our relationship with others, and for some, God, gives our life meaning and pacifies our ongoing terror of death. The greater our sense of being loved and valued, what might be called self esteem, the safer we feel. The sense of being loved assures us that we are worthy, loved, and will be protected in times of need and stress. We feel good about ourselves when we feel that we are accepted and valued by others. Conversely, we question our value when we feel rejected or excluded.

In times of stress we turn to our closest friends and family for comfort.[88] The importance of close relationships in alleviating fear and stress has found its way into the common vernacular. We find *safety in numbers* and *circle the wagons* against life's exigencies. Funerals themselves are a symbolic gathering of close family and friends intended to comfort those grieving the loss of a loved one. Awkwardly, we offer our help to the grieving with clichés like *"if there's anything you need don't hesitate to call."* What we are really saying is *"don't be afraid; we are here for you; you are not alone."*

The importance of human contact and attachment is evidenced in the degenerative effects of isolation. As discussed in Chapter Six, elders deprived of human contact quickly become vulnerable to the suggestion of others. Even well-adjusted healthy adults soon become disoriented when deprived of regular external stimuli. They quickly become delusional, psychotic, and experience hallucinations. Such hallucinations are a desperate attempt to restore contact with some "reality," even if it is only invented to cope with the crippling fear associated with coming face-to-face with the inner terror of isolation and death. As noted by psychiatrist, Reuven Bar-Levav, "Hallucinations may be jumbled, distorted, or confused pictures of reality, but even if they make only crazy sense, they are much more desirable to the one experiencing them than the absence of any sense at all."[89] Actor Tom Hanks portrayed this coping strategy well in the movie *Castaway*, when stranded on an island alone for four years he developed a conversational relationship with a soccer ball upon which appeared the image of a human face.

Close relationships are also an important source of symbolic immortality. In practical terms, close relationships help us find a mate and procreate. We survive biologically through our children and grandchildren, and to that extent solve the existential problem of our biological finitude. Close relationships also allow us to feel that we are part of a larger community that offers safety in numbers and strengthens our sense of connectedness to the world. Relationships also mitigate the fear that no one will remember us after we are gone.[90] For most, the most significant impact we make on the world is through the lives we touch.

The illness and death of someone of special importance, like a parent with whom we first attach and develop our first sense of security, causes particular angst.[91] We combat our fears by clutching onto the symbols that remind us of them. Prized possessions of the parent remind us of the safety we felt while under their protection early in life. Their possessions are a form of symbolic immortality to which we bond. As a *blankie* or thumb represent a parent's embrace or a mother's breast, dad's favorite watch and mom's wedding ring symbolize a parent's continued presence. To possess such items is to feel special and connected with the departed loved one. Contested items are typically those most cherished by the decedent. Such items may be of pure sentimental value; however, more often than not, sentimental items by their nature are the decedent's most valuable possessions. Such *"valuables"* were most cherished for the reason that they represented the decedent's successes, or were a symbol of such success. Dad's car, war medals, guns, stamp and coin collection, or mom's jewelry, fine china, and crystal are all trophies acquired from the fruits of their life's work and thus are the embodiment of symbolic immortality. Cherished items may also be items inherited from previous generations and thus represent symbols of family continuity and lastingness.

POST-SELF

The closest we come to conscious thoughts of our death is what Edwin S. Shneidman (1918 – 2009) termed our *post-self.* Shneidman theorized that each of us has a vision of the world after our death and how we will be remembered. He posits that one way we imagine our survival is through the passage of our property.

Shneidman views property as an extension of human personality on two planes: lateral and vertical. In the *lateral plane* or span of our life, property serves as a projection of self. Property is *"something I use," "something I do,"* and *"something I am."* Our home, possessions, business enterprises, and tangible accomplishments help define us. Existential philosopher Jean-Paul Sartre said, "The totality of my possessions reflects the totality of my being, I am what I have."[92]

The *vertical plane* spans the boundary between our life and death. The vertical adaptation of property and creations are a projection of our personality and existence beyond the present, into the future, and beyond our death in the form of our post-self. Leaving property at death bridges the gap between life and death. The continued existence of our property is our proxy and our *alter ego* in the post-world. Our property represents us when we cannot be physically present. In Sartre's view, our property creates a form of existential permanence: "If I turn away from it, it does not thereby cease to exist; if I go away, it represents me on my desk, in my room, in this place in the world."[93] Certainly the passage of our property through the process of estate planning is a key way to influence our legacy after our death.

SYMBOLIC IMMORTALITY AND WILL MAKING

Given the human avoidance of conscious thoughts of death, it is not surprising that more than half of the adult population regularly fails to prepare even a simple will. Like a horror movie, many choose to cover their eyes to avoid the scary scenes. Unfortunately, averting one's eyes provides little comfort as the fear of the unknown is often worse than the scenes depicted on the big screen. And, you miss the movie. Closing one's eyes to the apparent finitude of life doesn't make death any less terrifying, but it most assuredly results in missing the opportunity to live a more complete and meaningful life.

Memento mori is a medieval Latin expression which means *remember death*. As terrifying as it may be, our own death puts life into perspective. Things like recognition, money and possessions become trivial when held against death. And things like love, trust, honesty, generosity, and forgiveness - things that often take a back seat to our struggle to survive - shine through as infinitely more important. These truths would be more apparent if we more often had the courage to look death in the eye.[94]

The sad result of our lifelong struggle to buffer ourselves from thoughts of our own mortality is that many live their entire life without realistic contemplation of death. Pushing death from conscious thought and living as though one will never die may provide short-term psychic comfort, but the long-term effect of denying death extracts a high cost: we live thoughtlessly, overvaluing the things that bring us temporary worldly comfort while undervaluing things of lasting value. German philosopher Martin Heidegger viewed confronting one's finitude to be essential to living an *authentic life*. According to Buddhist scripture, the Dhammapada, "Those who are earnest do not die, those who are thoughtless are as if dead already."

Will making is one of our last opportunities to set things straight, to correct past wrongs, to leave one's heirs and the world in a better place, and to give voice to our post-self. Inheritance is thus the vehicle through which each decedent travels in his or her psychic journey to the post-self world. Thoughtful testators, like Scottish curlers, carefully deliver their stone. They strategically guide their legacy until the very last moment when they must loosen their grasp and let go. The curler then relies on his fiduciary sweepers and "skip" to deliver his plan to the intended target.

Making an estate plan confers a form of psychological immortality on the testator.[95] The maker influences and thus participates in the lives of his beneficiaries after his death.[96] Estate planning is one of those rare occasions when the testator consciously contemplates his death. Although many come to the task motivated to keep the government from intruding into their affairs in the form of taxes and probate, they also address who shall inherit their bounty and succeed them in authority.

American novelist Herman Melville understood man's capacity, through the making of his will, to live beyond the mortal boundary of his death. In *Moby Dick*, seaman Ishmael observes:

> It may seem strange that of all men sailors should be tinkering at their last wills and testaments, but there are no people in the world more fond of that diversion. This was the fourth time in my nautical life that I had done the same thing. After the ceremony was concluded... I felt all the easier; a stone was rolled away from my heart. Besides, all the days I should now live would be as good as the days that Lazarus lived after his resurrection.... I survived myself; my death and burial were locked up in my chest. I looked round me tranquilly and contentedly, like a quiet ghost with a clean conscience sitting inside the bars of a snug family vault.[97]

In contrast to those too afraid to face the notion of their own death are those who despite seeing the potential effects of their failure to plan nonetheless choose to do nothing. They say *"what do I care, I'll be dead."* As we will explore in the next chapter, these testators act willfully out of their own disabilities, distortions, and hurt, either intending that their heirs suffer, or being so indifferent to or depressed by the events of their life that they leave a legacy of self-negation: a post-self suicide. The depressed and disillusioned simply cannot muster the energy to visualize and facilitate their post-self. Without a plan, they invite turmoil, leaving their heirs with a legal and logistical mess.

Life does seem to go by in the blink of an eye. If we are too frightened to grasp the shortness of our existence, we are doomed to spend our finite years focused on day-to-day survival. Like the Greek mythological figure Sisyphus, we are condemned to spend all of our days rolling a stone up and down a hill only to awaken one day to discover that our life is over. If, however, we have the courage to acknowledge our existential terror of death and consciously contemplate the brevity of our years, there is hope that we can live a more purposeful life.

Legendary Italian actor Marcello Mastroianni in a simple but poetic way contemplates the shortness of life, confirms man's innate love for family, and muses about the possibility of his continued life in some form:

> I've finally realized that my mother and father were right when they used to say, life is too short. At 20, 30, or 35, you don't understand. But it's so true. When you get to my age, 72, and look back, you realize that life has flown by. It's awe-inspiring.
>
> I get the feeling I've only been around for a few weeks, that I've just arrived, and already I've got to leave. It's absurd. So tell me, why am I here? To continue the species, as they say? To reproduce, have children? That's wonderful, but it would be even better to be able to look after them, watch them for two or three hundred years. See what they're going to do, them, and their children, and my grandchildren's grandchildren. Then life would be beautiful.[98]

CONCLUSION

By "looking into the sun" we can reduce our anxiety and affect our immortality. We must have the courage to regularly and consciously acknowledge the reality of our death. Although it may sound macabre, understanding our biological finitude gives meaning to our life and helps us prioritize what is important. Such awareness motivates us to take time away from the pursuit of "more" and focus on our legacy. Survivors, in turn, would realize the futility of fighting with one another. Creating an estate plan is an important step along this path as it forces us to address the current state of our life; that is, who is important and what is valued. It also allays our fears by creating a form of symbolic immortality.[99]

We have so far examined the elements of human nature that affect and motivate *all* testators and beneficiaries. In Chapter Four we begin to examine the role of the mental health and motivations of *individual* testators and beneficiaries in the inheritance process. We all leave a legacy of some kind whether it is intentional or unintentional, altruistic or toxic. As we will see in the next chapter, our aura, character, and legacy bleed through to the next generation whether we know it, plan for it, or want it to. It is often this legacy that produces the seeds of inheritance conflict.

†OXIC AND AL†RUISTIC
INHERI†ANCE 4

"Money has always been the primary language of power, making it a logical tool for controlling parents. Many toxic parents use money to keep their children dependent."

- Dr. Susan Forward, Toxic Parents

"I bequeath all my property to my wife on the condition that she remarry immediately. Then there will be at least one man to regret my death."

- Last Will of German Poet, Heinrich Heine

| Alfred Nobel | Sigmund Freud | Bill Gates | Warren Buffet |
| Leona Helmsley | Sumner Redstone | Glenn Close | Ted Turner |

INTRODUCTION

The vast majority of testators have altruistic motives. Most work hard during their life to avoid favoritism and to invest time, energy, and money in creating an inheritance scheme that avoids conflict. Some wealthy testators go to extraordinary lengths to protect their children from excessive inheritances or invest in charity with a view to leaving the world a better place. Unfortunately, there are also a good number of unhealthy or toxic testators whose post-self vision is tainted by emotional difficulties, addiction or even mental illness.

The role of testators in family conflict is largely ignored, with the blame most often directed toward *"greedy beneficiaries."* Few, for example, inquired into the role played by Brooke Astor in the events which led to the trial of her son Tony. In her opening statement, lead prosecutor Elizabeth Loewy asked the jury in rhetorical fashion *"What is this case about?"* Her pat man-on-the-street answer was *"It's about greed."* In reality, testators are invariably key contributors to the mess they leave behind. Inheritance conflict follows as the logical conclusion of an unhealthy lifetime family dynamic played out after the decedent's death.

This Chapter explores how the mental health of testators and beneficiaries, especially those with Cluster B Personality Disorders or traits of such disorders, impacts the inheritance process, and how such mental and emotional traits cascade from generation to generation. Mental health, good and bad, is an inherited gift that keeps on giving: Whether it is biological or developed in early childhood (nature versus nurture), its origins are heavily influenced by parents. A rocky inheritance experience can be expected when either or both testators and beneficiaries have significant mental health issues. Although this Chapter divides inheritance between toxic and altruistic, no decedent or beneficiary is either all good or all bad; neither completely toxic nor completely altruistic.

"Someday, this will all be yours."

CLUSTER B PERSONALITY DISORDERS

In addition to the other causes of inheritance conflict discussed in previous chapters, families fight when one or more of their members has a personality disorder or significant traits of one or more disorders. Participants in family fights such as divorce, child custody, and inheritance disputes regularly attribute their problems to family members whom they claim are "nuts." According to Bill Eddy, author of *High Conflict People in Legal Disputes,* their complaints are well founded. He concludes that nearly half of all legal disputes are driven by mental illness. He posits that the most common illnesses that lead families to fight are listed as Cluster B personality disorders in the Diagnostic and Statistical Manual of the American Psychiatric Association (DSM-IV-TR).

The four Cluster B disorders are *borderline, narcissistic, antisocial,* and *histrionic* personality disorders. A principal characteristic of all such disorders is that those afflicted have little or no insight into their disease. They do not see their role in conflicts, and tend to blame others for their internal distress. Their problems, however, are no secret to those closest to them. As most personality disorders develop in early childhood, friends and family members of the afflicted have been suffering the effects of their illness for years.

Borderline personalities are plagued by alternate fears of abandonment and intimacy. To prevent feeling abandoned, they attempt to manipulate others to remain engaged with them, or they rage against those they believe will abandon them. Alternatively, they fight to break free when they feel that their relationships have become too intimate; they feel trapped, engulfed, put upon. Borderlines frequently vacillate between excessive intimacy and hateful distancing behavior, giving those closest to them the feeling of walking on eggshells, never knowing what the next moment will bring. They are prone to extreme mood swings and manipulative behavior, including threats of suicide which are rarely completed. They tend to engage in physical (superficial) self-cutting as a way to regulate their intense feelings, a practice which is highly disruptive to relationships. Approximately two percent of the adult population consists of borderlines, and approximately seventy-five percent of those are women. Glenn Close's character in the 1987 movie *Fatal Attraction* is often cited as an example of borderline behavior.

Physically or emotionally abused as children, *narcissists* (once known as *egotists or megalomaniacs*) develop a kind of false public or outside self to defend against their inner sense of worthlessness. They lack empathy, are exploitive, and see others simply as a feeding source for their insatiable thirst for attention. While full blown Narcissistic Personality Disorder is rare, affecting mostly males and at most one percent of the population, narcissistic traits are much more common.

The greatest fear of a narcissist is to be forgotten or ignored. According to Sam Vaknin, in his book *Malignant Self Love: Narcissism Revisited,* "If he cannot be loved, the narcissist would rather be feared or hated."[100] Narcissists thrive on attention, even if it is negative. They are also deluded by the belief that they are the center of desire; for instance, narcissistic testators believe that everyone is after their money. They dangle inheritance in their children's faces to garner their attention and then revile them for their greed. They create punitive estate plans in order to punish the "greed" of their loved ones and to perpetuate their position of power. Or, they may completely fail to plan so that their children will fight over them long after their death.

The DSM-IV-TR diagnosis of *antisocial personality disorder* combines the diagnoses of psychopathic and sociopathic personalities. To feel secure, antisocials try to dominate others. They are chronic liars, manipulators, and con artists who lack remorse for their actions. Their disregard for rules and laws leads many of the less intelligent to spend time in jail. The more intelligent are potentially quite dangerous; they are sensitive enough to know others' weak points and smart enough to avoid getting caught for the exploitation they visit upon their victims. As children, antisocials are typically involved in fights, property destruction, theft, and cruelty to animals.

Histrionics, like narcissists, are preoccupied with the fear of being ignored. To remain the center of attention, they dress outrageously, are sexually seductive, and present themselves in an exaggerated theatrical fashion. Addicted to drama, they fabricate facts to make their stories more interesting. They are overly sensitive to criticism and disapproval, and blame their failures on others. It can be difficult to disengage from a histrionic once she has your attention. Histrionics tend to be female.

There are a number of potential causes of personality disorders, including biological predisposition, toxic role models, and early life traumas such as child abuse, addiction, or abandonment. Invariably, those with personality disorders experienced some form of attachment difficulty when they were very young. Without proper or adequate attachment in their first relationships (usually parents, who are the prototypes of all relationships that follow), they are unable as adults to form trusting and intimate relationships. Predictably, their personality disorders are perpetuated in their own relationships including their relationships with their children. While less than ten percent of the U.S. population suffers from full-blown Cluster B personality disorders, experts believe that an additional ten percent possesses some traits of the disorders. Personality disorders are resilient, lasting a lifetime, and in the case of toxic testators, beyond.[101]

In Eddy's view, what drives conflict is not the size or value of the matter in dispute, but the level of internal distress of the personalities involved. High conflict people move from one controversy to another - at home, at work, with neighbors, their spouses, and their families - without any clue that they are the one with the problem. They distort facts and project their internal distortions onto others. They claim that it is their adversary, not them, who has the problem. They also project their motives on others: Liars believe others are lying, and thieves believe others are stealing. In inheritance disputes, abusers believe that other family members are stealing or will soon steal their loved one's money or estate if they don't get there first.

Rather than examine their role in the conflict, Cluster B personalities (or those possessing traits of such disorders) seek allies - including friends, family, the police, and the courts – to support their view. They use persuasion, manipulation, and distortion to bring people to their point of view. Efforts and suggestions proffered by others aimed at helping them solve their conflict are rejected as if any gesture of compromise is an admission of wrongdoing.

In the inheritance realm, *borderlines,* who fear abandonment, react badly to the death of a loved one, which they view as the ultimate abandonment; *narcissists,* who need to be the most important player, make equal division of inheritance and authority impossible; *antisocials* grab and run; and *histrionics* frustrate smooth estate settlement by creating drama that makes them the center of attention. In families that fight over inheritance, one or more family members - testators and heirs alike – likely suffer from some form of Cluster B disorders.

OUR ROSE-COLORED MIRROR

Before we convince ourselves that a family member, and not us, is the source of conflict, we need to wonder whether we are viewing ourselves through a *"rose-colored mirror"*.[102] Studies show that while our perception of others can be fairly accurate (at least when we are not in conflict with them), we tend to have an inflated view of ourselves. Our tendency to view ourselves in the best possible light may make us feel good but invariably leads to conflict with others. When conflict occurs, rather than acknowledging our contribution to the problem, we regularly attribute relationship difficulties to the jealousy, insanity, or pure evil of those with whom we conflict.

Our keen awareness of the faults of others, and blindness to our own shortcomings is an age-old curiosity. Buddha observed that "It is easy to see the faults of others, but difficult to see one's own faults."[103] Jesus queried "Why do you see the speck in your neighbor's eye, but do not notice the log in your own eye?"[104]

Psychologist Jonathan Haidt in *The Happiness Hypothesis* explores the source of our distortions. He concludes that our perception of ourselves and others evolved from the need to see through the deceptions of those who might harm us, and the concurrent need to see ourselves as trustworthy partners. We resist any suggestion that we lack virtue or value because, if true, we would experience the terrifying possibility of exclusion. To maintain a sense of psychological well being, we desperately need to see ourselves as desirable creatures deserving of love, protection, and membership.

When faced with information that challenges our favored self-image, we set out on a one-sided mission to bring back data that supports our virtue. In psychological terms, we use *motivated reasoning* to seek and find *pseudoevidence* that supports our rosy view of ourselves. Not surprisingly, when Americans and Europeans are asked to rate themselves on virtues, skills, and other desirable traits (including intelligence, driving ability, sexual skills, and ethics), a large majority of us say that we are above average.[105]   We also tend to overestimate our contribution in cooperative efforts. For example, when husbands and wives are asked to estimate their contribution to housework, their combined responses (expressed as percentages) regularly exceed 120 percent.[106]   When MBA students on group projects estimate their contributions, their combined estimates total and even more impressive 139 percent.[107]

We are so practiced and adept in our subtle distortions that we truly believe that we are rational and objective. A form of *naïve realism,* we believe that our version of the facts is self-evident. If others disagree, they either don't have all the facts or are blinded by their prejudices. While we acknowledge that we are shaped by our own background, we believe that such experiences only *enhance* our insight. Convinced of our own virtue, we are quick to justify our own selfish acts and "see the bias, greed, and duplicity in others."[108]

Our relatively accurate perception of others quickly dissolves when we begin to conflict with them. We distort the facts when our self-image is threatened, weaving a story in which our pure virtue collides with the pure delusion or evil of our opponent. Such rationalizations obviate the need to critically look at ourselves and exonerate us from blame. In reality we are rarely completely innocent and our adversaries are rarely purely evil. Alleged evildoers like Anthony Marshall in Chapter Five have their own story and motivations, and victims like his mother, Brooke Astor, are rarely purely innocent.

Psychologist Roy F. Baumeister postulates that people who do evil things rarely see themselves as wrongdoers; they believe that their actions are justified in light of injustices and provocations inflicted on them. In fact, they often see themselves as the victim. Conversely, Baumeister finds that victims are rarely without blame. He points out that most murders result from an escalating cycle of provocation and retaliation. In half of all domestic disputes, both sides use violence.[109] This is not to defend the acts of wrongdoers. The point is that each side in virtually any conflict has its own rationale or justification for their actions. As the old saying goes, there are two sides to every story, or perhaps three: his side, her side, and the unvarnished truth. The root of the difficulty in bringing warring parties together is that both sides are entrenched in their position, clinging to their allies and psychoevidence, and unwilling to see things from their opponent's perspective. To allow ourselves to see things from an opponents view, even momentarily, risks exposing our own distortions, and shaking our desperately held belief that we are perfect and lovable.

Having a somewhat inflated view of oneself would seem to be relatively harmless. In fact, studies show that people who feel good about themselves tend to be happier, healthier, and better liked. The problem is that along with an inflated self image comes a correspondingly high sense of entitlement. The effects can be seen in families, the workplace, and in inheritance disputes, where each party believes that he or she is entitled to more than his or her fair share. In such a world, there can never be enough to go around.

It is doubtful that the toxic testators whose stories are told in the pages that follow see (or saw) themselves as bad actors. If we hope to avoid following in their footsteps, we must learn to look at ourselves honestly and be willing to find fault with ourselves.

TOXIC TESTATORS

The blame for inheritance disputes invariably falls on the living, while the role played by the departed is mostly ignored. Death seems to confer a pardon on toxic testators, leaving their heirs to play out their sometimes comic and always tragic roles for all to see. In reality, decedents play a major role in the mess they leave behind. Favoritism, divorce, mental illness, and unhealthy family dynamics are accurate predictors of inheritance conflicts. Narcissistic testators like Leona Helmsley and Sumner Redstone (discussed below) on some level even invite inheritance conflict in order to remain the center of attention long after their death.

Are the dead innocent, or should they be held accountable for the mess they leave behind? It seems that quarrelling beneficiaries rarely ask themselves this question. They would rather focus on the bad acts of their inheritance adversary than place the blame on their common benefactor where it may more properly belong. Perhaps we let testators off the hook because they can't be punished. Whatever the reason for our leniency, quarreling beneficiaries would be well advised to consider the culpability of the departed. Focusing on the role of the decedent in inheritance battles has a salutary effect: it helps those left behind understand how they got to, and perhaps how they can move beyond, their present sorry state.

Do toxic testators know the damage they cause? It is unlikely; not seeing themselves for who they really are, they fail to recognize the damage they cause during life, or the toxicity of their legacy. There seems to be nothing more difficult than accurately seeing oneself. With eyes genetically pointed outward to detect danger, find food and a mate, and our tendency to view ourselves in the best possible light, we are notoriously challenged when it comes to personal insight. To compensate, we use external cues such as the people around us as reflecting pools, to aid in self-understanding. It is perhaps for this reason that we are so profoundly influenced by what people think of us, and, as discussed in Chapters Three and Six, why isolation and solitary confinement are so psychologically destabilizing.

TOXIC INHERITANCE

The term *toxic* describes a poisonous process capable of causing injury or death to healthy living. Toxic inheritance is family dysfunction passed from generation to generation. It tends to follow Sir Isaac Newton's law of inertia: "persist[ing] in a state of ...uniform motion unless acted upon by an external force."[110] Without an intervening force like personal enlightenment or an epiphany (such as that experienced by Alfred Nobel described later in this Chapter) or involvement of new players through marriage, dysfunction is transmitted from parent to child, from children to grandchildren, and so on. We refer to these testators as *toxic testators* for the reason that their illness poisons the potentially altruistic process of passing one's assets and legacy to the next generation.

Inheritance involves more than receiving money and property. We inherit our family history and ways of being. Our parents are our first role models. The mental health we inherit from our parents – both genetic and environmental - is the psychological baseline from which we build our concept of self. The life led, the deeds done, and the time spent with family all survive the corporal world. Memories of loved ones, especially parents, echo in the minds and hearts of children for a lifetime.

The mental health and parenting skills of parents vary widely. Most parents have the requisite mental health to do their job without damaging their children. However, others are unstable, have personality disorders, addictions, or are mentally ill. Parents' emotional DNA impacts their children's mental health. Parents who feel that they weren't loved can be stingy and vindictive toward their own children during their lives and at death.

Parents who have suffered childhood abuse, whether physical or emotional, are more likely to develop personality disorders and become abusive parents. For the most part, the emotional wounds of their early life never healed. Instead, they develop maladaptive behaviors, defense mechanisms, and even psychiatric disorders in response to their troubled past. Without intervention, their troubles go unresolved and impact their ability to parent.

Children of troubled parents suffer in proportion to the level of their parents' troubles. They develop their own mental health issues which affect their relationships with their parents, siblings, the outside world, and, ultimately, their own children. Children are pitted against one another for the scarce commodities of love and acceptance. Rather than banding together to fight against the toxic parent, dysfunctional families are at odds, each believing that the other - siblings and stepparents- received the love they didn't get. In reality, in such families no one gets what he needs. Thus, a cycle of unhealthy behavior is passed from generation to generation – a toxic inheritance.

Parents with narcissistic tendencies can be particularly damaging to family cohesion. Having received inadequate nurturing and love, narcissistic parents spend a lifetime seeking validation from anyone who will give it to them, including their spouses, co-workers, friends, and family. They see their children not as tender psyches in need of care and nurturing, but as a budding audience for their exaggerated claims of athletic, academic, or occupational accomplishment. Parents who may have never held a position of authority, become drunk with parental power, insisting that they are always right and will always be bigger and smarter than their children. Although they rail against the treatment they received from their parents, they treat their children in much the same way.

As needy parents grow old and become more dependent, they fear that they will be abandoned by their children. Plagued by the lifelong belief that they are inadequate and unlovable, they believe that their children are only interested in them for their money. They believe that, given the opportunity, their children will take their money and discard them.

Such parents, no longer able to physically or emotionally dominate their children, use their looming financial legacy to extort their children's allegiance. Using inheritance as the prize, the parent calls the tune to which their children must dance. Threatened by the prospect that their children will gang up on them, they play one off the other. To keep their children off balance, they flip-flop in their wishes, each time altering who is favored and who is disfavored. Or they refuse to clearly set forth their wishes or order their affairs, leaving their children to fight over their estate long after their death. By failing to clearly plan for their death, they are assured of being the center of attention long after their death.

Death breathes new life into old conflicts. The chronic shortage of love and validation in dysfunctional families inevitably carries over to the realm of inheritance. Children of dysfunctional families desperately fight to right the wrongs they believe they suffered during the life of the decedent. What appear to be hyenas fighting over money, lamps, dishes, and dad's old Ford, are in reality hurting children looking for love. Unfortunately, they cannot succeed; even the winners will not be satisfied, because an extra dollop of material inheritance cannot resolve a lifetime of pain.

In the inheritance realm, children from toxic families worry that they will once again be short-changed, forgotten. As noted in Chapter Two, tensions rise at the mere prospect of being snubbed and rejected. As parents age and the prospect of death becomes more real, anxious children take matters into their own hands. With so much at stake, they cannot emotionally afford to be left out once again. Their very sense of self is at stake; for to be forgotten or slighted by a parent or someone who was instrumental in their original concept of self, is to become in one's feelings, a non-being. We all want to be special in our parents' eyes. Instinctively we want all of our parents' bounty. We settle for our fair share only when our rational adult self convinces our internal feeling child that it wouldn't be fair if we were to receive our parents' entire inheritance.

ALTRUISTIC INHERITANCE

Certainly not all inheritance is toxic. The vast majority of families manage their instinctive tendencies and avoid conflict. Most testators sincerely hope to improve the lot of those they leave behind, and to leave the world a better place. Few of us will change the world in any significant way; instead, we are satisfied that we make a difference in the lives we have touched.

Emotionally healthy parents are careful to avoid favoritism. They know that any show of partiality or favoritism results in hurt feelings that damage the parent-child relationship and fuels sibling rivalry. Their effort to remain impartial carries over to their estate planning. Unless there are special circumstances, they are careful to leave to their children equally and to allocate fiduciary responsibility in a way that avoids hurt feelings.

In their later years, to assuage anxieties and secure peace, thoughtful well-adjusted parents may include their children in their financial decisions and discussions of their final wishes. Sensitive to growing anxieties, they assure their children that they will be treated equitably. They emphasize the importance of family unity and express their wish that their children remain close after their death.

For those of means, especially the super-rich, providing for their children during life and after death is not an issue. In fact, they realize that the size of their estate may in fact be a detriment to their children. They rightfully fear that by over-endowing them they will encourage sloth and self-indulgence.

Thoughtful parents of wealth are cautious not to deprive their children of the joy of self discovery and personal achievement. Although they could easily afford to provide all of their children's material needs, and virtually all of their wants, they understand the dangers of doing so. They understand that their children's self worth, self respect, and healthy self image require that they make their own way in the world. As their children's metaphorical personal trainers, enlightened parents know that their children cannot build strength and character if they buy them a fitness center or have someone lift their weights for them. That success and family wealth can sap the motivation of inheritors has long been understood. Nineteenth Century industrialist Andrew Carnegie (1835 – 1919) wrote, "The parent who leaves his son enormous wealth generally deadens the talents and energies of the son and tempts him to lead a less useful and less worthy life than he otherwise would."[111] Albert Camus (1913- 1960) observed simply: "Without work all life goes rotten."

History is replete with stories of successful entrepreneurs like the original Astor who amassed a fortune only to have it wasted within one or two generations after his death. The aphorism *"shirt sleeves to shirt sleeves in three generations"* describes this phenomenon and is said to derive from an old

Lancashire (England) proverb *"there's nobbut three generations atween a clog and clog,"* believed to have been imported to America by Andrew Carnegie. Other cultures take a similarly negative view of excessive inheritance. The Italians, for example, in their classic lyrical style have an old expression: *"Dalle stalle alle stelle alle stalle"* ("from stalls to stars to stalls").

Bill Gates, founder of Microsoft, intends to leave his children only a modest portion (reported to be ten million dollars per child) of his multibillion dollar fortune. The rest will pass to the Gates Foundation, already the largest charitable foundation in the United States. Warren Buffet shares his friend Gates' views on inheritance. Buffet has said that the perfect inheritance for his children is "enough money so that they would feel they could do anything, but not so much that they could do nothing." Leaving the bulk of his wealth to charity, Buffet does "not believe in inheriting your position in society," and does not promote membership in the "lucky sperm club."[113] He views setting up his children "with a lifetime supply of food stamps just because they came out of the right womb," to be "harmful" for them and "an antisocial act."[114] He reportedly intends to pass on his charitable vision by leaving one billion dollars to each of his children's individual foundations.

Gates and Buffet are not the only wealthy parents who have decided to promote charity rather than leaving everything to their children. Hong Kong actor, Jackie Chan, intends to give half of his wealth to charity, and Asia rich man, Li Ka-Shing, has announced he will donate a third of his wealth to charity. In deciding to leave a substantial portion of his wealth to the arts, Broadway composer Andrew Lloyd Webber stated that "I don't think it should be about having a whole load of rich children and grandchildren."[115]

But wealth does not inevitably spoil, and parents sometimes underestimate their children. Such is the story of American media mogul and philanthropist, Ted Turner. Just days before his father committed suicide in 1963, the senior Turner arranged for the quick sale of his one million dollar Atlanta billboard business, Turner Outdoor Advertising, to businessman Curt Carlson. Carlson was unaware of Turner's plan to kill himself: "He told me he wanted to have some money to leave his wife when he died, but that everything he had was tied up in the business. He said he was sure if Ted got his hands on the business, he would run it into the ground."[116] Soon after Turner's death,

Carlson got a call from his widow, and a visit from Ted, then age twenty-four. "His mother wanted Ted to have the business back, and Ted, who can be very convincing, talked about how this was his one chance to get going in life."[117] Carlson agreed to sell the business back, and the rest is history. Ted used his one chance, to say the least, wisely. He went on to become a media pioneer, founding cable news network CNN and Superstation WTBS. He also went on to become one of the world's most generous philanthropists, donating one billion dollars for the creation of the United Nations Foundation, and founded the Goodwill Games. Despite having five children, Turner intends to leave most of his estate to charity in the form of the country's largest land conservatory.

Wealth beyond that which can be spent in a lifetime gives wealthy testators the luxury of contemplating their legacy. In addition to the societal benefits, philanthropy creates social currency that perpetuates the benefactor's family name. Viewed this way, philanthropy is not a form of disinheritance but creation of wealth in a different realm. Philanthropy replaces direct and immediate access to inherited wealth with a long-term legacy and family name recognition. The charitable works of the Astor family, Bill Gates, Ted Turner, Sebastian Kresge, Henry Ford, Andrew Carnegie, W. K. Kellogg, John D. Rockefeller, and Alfred Nobel perpetuate the memory of their family name long after their monetary legacy has been spent. Philanthropy also helps the benefactor fulfill his or her philosophical and existential vision of the world.

The stories of Leona Helmsley and Sumner Redstone below are examples of wealthy but toxic testators. As public figures, their lives have been widely covered in the media and offer us a thorough insight into their family dysfunction. In contrast, the story of Alfred Nobel that follows is a story of hope and redemption. Through his invention of dynamite and other advances in the technologies of warfare, he was on course to leave a tarnished legacy. His late-life epiphany changed the course of his life and legacy, as well as the worlds of science, literature, and peace.

LEONA HELMSLEY

"Throughout her life, Leona left a trail of ruin – embittered relatives, fired employees, and fatefully, unpaid taxes" wrote Jeffrey Toobin of *The New*

Yorker in 2008. Born Leona Mindy Rosenthal in 1920, Leona married her third husband, real estate and hotel magnate Harry B. Helmsley in 1972. Leona met Harry when she joined his real estate firm in 1970. He soon divorced his wife of thirty-three years to take up with Leona.

Leona, alternately dubbed the *"Queen of Mean"* and *"Rich Bitch,"* had one child, Jay Panzirer, who died in 1982 at the age of forty. He was survived by his wife Mimi and four children. For reasons that escaped the young widow, Leona hated Mimi. Following Jay's death, Leona and Harry immediately moved to evict Mimi from her home. The Helmsleys also filed a number of lawsuits in a five-year effort to obtain the proceeds of Jay's relatively modest $231,000 estate. Ultimately they won more than half of the estate. As a result, each of Leona's four grandchildren inherited approximately four hundred dollars from their father. Thanks grandma!

Leona's tax troubles began when disgruntled associates reported her siphoning untaxed company funds to renovate her Connecticut mansion. She famously told employees: "We don't pay taxes. Only the little people pay taxes." Unable to locate Leona's exemption in the Internal Revenue Code, the judge sentenced her to eighteen months in federal prison.

In her will, misanthrope Leona set aside twelve million dollars for the care of her dog, Trouble. She also directed that Trouble be buried next to her in the family mausoleum in the Sleepy Hollow Cemetery in Westchester County, New York. Her will excluded two of her four grandchildren *"for reasons which are known to them,"* and left a relatively modest amount to the other two on the condition that they visit their father Jay's grave at least annually. The bulk of her estate, estimated to be worth as much as eight billion dollars, was left to the Leona M. and Harry B. Helmsley Charitable Trust for the "care of dogs." Many have speculated that it was not so much her love of dogs that led to her generous pet bequest but her contempt for her family and her fellow man.

Fortunately, Leona's plans to perpetuate a legacy of misery were mitigated by a Manhattan Surrogate Court judge who reduced Trouble's twelve million dollar trust fund to two million. Even considering the cost of a lifetime supply of doggy pedicure toe separators, one wonders how such a figure could be spent in one dog's life. The court also seized on trust language "and such other charitable activities as the trustees shall determine" appended to the pet bequest to allocate trust distributions to the care of the poor and the search for the cure of human disease.

In order to avoid a public fight on the issue of whether Leona lacked testamentary capacity, her executors ultimately settled with the two disinherited grandchildren for a total of six million dollars on the condition that the grandchildren turn over any family documents in their possession and agree not to disclose the details of their family life or inheritance dispute.

Leona died in 2007, survived, aptly, by Trouble. She is interred in the family mausoleum with husband Harry and son Jay at Sleepy Hollow Cemetery. In an ironic twist, cemetery regulations do not permit the burial of pets at Sleepy Hollow. One wry commentator conjectured whether Leona will be exhumed at Trouble's death to be buried in the pet cemetery with Trouble and the other bitches.

SUMNER REDSTONE

Entertainment mogul Sumner Redstone, still alive at the time of publication, is perennially listed as one of America's richest men. Born in 1923, he at one time had voting control of CBS and Viacom and thereby controlled 200 television stations, 144 radio stations, book publisher Simon and Schuster, Paramount and DreamWorks movie studios, the Blockbuster video-store chain, 138 cable networks including MTV and Nickelodeon, along with some 300 Internet sites.

In a 2007 speech to Boston University law students Redstone said, "Money, and I mean it sincerely, has never motivated me. The passion to win has motivated me." *Win at any cost* is more accurate, as Redstone has either sued or been sued by every family member of importance, including his first wife of over fifty years, his second wife, his only brother, only son, only daughter, his only nephew, and his only niece. The issue in virtually every suit was money and control.

By any measure, Redstone is obsessed with control. He is fond of saying that "I'm in control now, and I'll be in control after I die." According to a December 2006 article in Vanity Fair, Redstone, a renowned workaholic, has few friends and is obsessed by the price of his stock, which he views "as a barometer measuring his self-worth."[118]

According to Redstone's brother Edward, they had a difficult childhood. Their parents had an unhappy marriage and tension plagued their home. Edward described their mother as a "crazy tyrant" who favored Sumner, and their father as "mean and tough". Edward directly traces the problems of their family and the conflict between him and his brother to his parents, stating that "I put the problems of today at their doorstep." What follows is a story similar to the family saga described by Shakespeare in *King Lear*.

According to Forbes magazine, "The [Redstone] dysfunction stretches across three generations." The Redstone Empire was begun by Sumner's father, Michael Redstone, from a single drive-in theater on Long Island. In 1959, dad Michael created National Amusements, Inc. ("NAI"), issuing 300 shares to himself and 100 shares to each of his two sons Edward and Sumner. In 1968 dad retired half of his shares and created a trust with the remaining shares for his four grandchildren: Edward's children, Ruth Ann and Michael, and Sumner's offspring, Brent and Shari.

The fighting began in 1971 when Edward sued his brother, Sumner, and his father, alleging that Sumner undermined him when he hired someone else to do his job. Sumner settled the suit by buying out Edward. Later, in 1984, Sumner (through NAI) bought out the beneficiaries of Grandpa Michael's 1968 trust, making him the sole shareholder.

In 2006, Brent sued his father, Sumner, over the terms of the 1984 buyout alleging that his father had cheated him out of his grandfather's inheritance. Sumner and Brent had already been estranged since 2002, when Brent refused to surrender voting control of Sumner's shares placed in trust for him by Sumner in preparation for Sumner's divorce from Brent's mother. In contrast, Brent's sister, Shari, had stayed in her father's good graces by dutifully assigning her voting rights. Brent asserted that after he refused to surrender his voting rights, Sumner retaliated against him by treating him disfavorably, showing extreme favoritism to his sister.

Nephew Michael also sued Sumner in 2006, using information disclosed in Brent's suit. Sumner stated, either as a sign of remorse or for strategic advantage, that "[t]he two days that Brent and Michael sued me are two of the saddest days of my entire life."

Temporarily favored by Sumner, and perhaps Sumner's only ally, daughter

Shari was appointed to important positions in the Redstone empire and was thought to be Sumner's *heir apparent*. Shari, a divorced mother of three and herself a corporate and estate planning attorney, jumped in with both feet, exhibiting many of the same executive skills displayed by her father. Even her father admitted in 2002: "It's like father, like daughter; she has no major weaknesses. She is a great businesswoman." Other executives, however, found her too "assertive and meddlesome," claiming that "she wants power now and doesn't want to wait."

Despite Shari's fast start, it didn't take long for her and her father to clash over who was in charge. Soon they were only speaking through their lawyers. If history is any indication, there is more litigation in store. A fourth generation may now be involved, as it was revealed in Sumner's divorce proceedings that the majority of his shares are owned in trust for his five grandchildren. But handing over the baton won't be easy. When questioned about his age, Sumner retorts that he doesn't plan to die. Metaphorically he may be right, as his toxic legacy is likely to reverberate in the Redstone family for generations to come.

ALFRED NOBEL

Alfred Nobel (1833-1896) was a Swedish scientist who held more than three hundred patents. His greatest scientific achievements related to the invention of dynamite and the application of explosives to wartime use. Despite his scientific achievements, Alfred Nobel is today best known for the annual awards that bear his name.

Alfred donated the majority of his estate for the establishment of the Nobel Prize, to be granted to those who in the previous year have rendered the greatest service to mankind in the fields of physics, chemistry, medicine, literature, and peace. The peace prize is given to the person or society that renders the greatest service to the cause for the brotherhood of nations, in the abolishment or reduction of standing armies, or the spread of peace congresses.

In one of history's great ironies, Alfred Nobel would not be a household name today if it were not for the erroneous reporting of his death. In 1888, when Alfred's brother Ludvig died, a French newspaper erroneously published Alfred's obituary. The newspaper condemned Alfred for his invention of dynamite, calling him "the merchant of death," and asserting that he "became rich by finding ways to kill more people faster than ever before." Much like Ebenezer Scrooge in Charles Dickens' 1843 book, *A Christmas Carol,* Alfred was given a chance to witness his own death, and was pained by what he saw. From that day forward he carefully fashioned his own legacy. In a series of will modifications, Alfred eliminated his relatives, co-workers, and acquaintances, leaving most of his estate (valued at seven million dollars at the time of his death or $250 million in 2008 dollars) to the establishment of the Nobel Prizes.

Nobel did not espouse inherited wealth. He believed that children should inherit only enough to enable them to acquire a fine education and the essentials of life. Having never married and having no children, he found his relatives' interest in his money intrusive and repulsive. In leaving them only items of personal property he said, "[M]y dear people will be awfully disappointed. I am taking great delight in advance in all the widened eyes and curses the absence of money will cause."

Seeing attorneys as *"formality parasites,"* Nobel wrote his will in his own hand and without the assistance of legal counsel. The somewhat unfortunate result was an ambiguous writing that contained a number of irregularities. Unable to be implemented in its original form, and to avoid protracted litigation, settlements and compromises were reached which required the involvement of the King of Sweden and two reconciliation agreements that expanded the interests of Alfred's heirs. Ultimately, however, Alfred Nobel's epiphany allowed him to create a legacy that has enriched the world and perpetuated his family name.

CONCLUSION

Inheritance conflict can occur in spite of a healthy decedent's best laid plans. Conflict, however, is much more likely in dysfunctional families and in families where one or more members suffer from Cluster B personality disorders or significant traits of such disorders.

While children tend to be the focus of most inheritance disputes, they are often mere actors left to play out a script given to them by toxic testators.

Decedents all but receive a pardon when in fact they are likely to be the source of the problem. The point is not to blame parents for being less than perfect, but rather to understand the factors that lead them to perpetuate the difficulties of the past. They were once children and suffered their own hurts and inequities. Without the tools to alter the force of their personal history, they passed their emotional handicaps on to their offspring. Unless interrupted, toxic testators create toxic beneficiaries who in turn become toxic testators. As the Astor family saga in Chapter Five illustrates, victims become predators, who in turn create new victims in a toxic cycle. And so it goes.

A parent's legacy includes his or her genetic and psychological imprint. The pattern of genetic, psychological and financial inheritance continues from generation to generation. However, it is not so dismal or predetermined as it may seem. We all have the power to change. Confronted with his developing reputation, Alfred Nobel changed the course of his life and legacy.

When it comes to family, only understanding and forgiveness can defeat hurt and resentment. Assets, money, and heirlooms come and go, but a toxic legacy of anger, pain, hurt, and resentment can linger for generations.

Chapter Four marks the end of our examination of the seeds of family conflict. We now turn, starting with The Brooke Astor Story in Chapter Five, to the environmental conditions that cause dormant hurts and instinctive behaviors to reawaken and grow into full-blown conflict.

PART II

II

HOW AND WHEN INHERITANCE BATTLES BEGIN

THE BROOKE ASTOR STORY 5

"When you were with her, you felt you were in the presence of a great star. She always wore beautiful dresses and major jewels. Even after she turned 90, she had glamour, and as the first lady of New York society and philanthropy she understood and enjoyed her importance."
  - Dominick Dunne, *Vanity Fair,* October 2006

INTRODUCTION

Many are familiar with the Brooke Astor story that first captivated New Yorkers and the rest of the country in July of 2006. Readers were riveted by the details of the financial abuse of the then-104 year old philanthropist at the hands of her 82 year old son Anthony "Tony" Marshall. The abuse was brought to light when Ms. Astor's grandson Philip Marshall – Tony's son - filed a petition with the New York Supreme Court to have his father removed as his grandmother's fiduciary, claiming that his father had "turned a blind eye to her, intentionally and repeatedly ignoring her health, safety, personal and household needs, while enriching himself with millions of dollars."[119]

The story played in the media as nothing more than a greedy son stealing from his vulnerable mother. Adding to the public interest was the schadenfreude of witnessing a member of high society being treated as a common criminal. The failure of others, especially those perceived to be higher on the social food chain, has long entertained those plagued by their own sense of inadequacy. But to focus only on the drama and wrecked remains of the Astor family is to miss the larger lessons that underlie the story.

Understanding why a son, who already stood to inherit millions, would steal from his mother, risking his entire inheritance and the ruination of his family, requires that we look behind the obvious motive of greed. If it were simply a matter of greed, all children would steal from their vulnerable parents. Some in fact do, but most don't; so why does it happen at all? The answer is complex, but in the Astor family, part of the answer is the cycle of emotional neglect that was the family legacy for generations. At each generation parents preoccupied with their social position demonstrated that money, social standing, and personal pleasures were more important to them than their children.

Neglected children grow to be needy adults looking to resolve the insecurities that come from feeling unimportant in their parents' eyes. In the Astor family, generations of children filled such emotional deficits with the same hollow substitutes chosen by their parents: the trappings of wealth, alcohol, and serial romantic encounters. At each generation, Astor children were the unintended casualty of their parents' pursuit of unmet needs.

The Astor family has been well chronicled. In particular, author Meryl Gordon in her book *Mrs. Astor Regrets: The Hidden Betrayals of a Family Beyond Reproach* has done an excellent job tracing the family dynamic through a number of generations, including the last four which play so prominently. With the benefit of a multigenerational perspective, we see "money substituting for love"[120] as neglected children eventually become economic predators.

If the Brooke Astor story were merely a case of elder abuse or the rich stealing from the rich, it would not be considered one of the most important inheritance cases in modern legal history. What makes the Astor case so significant is *how* son Tony implemented his plan to abscond with his mother's money and social position. Though he may have had his sights on his mother's fortune for years, Tony waited until his mother's memory and cognition began to fail before implementing his plan. The Astor story provides us:

- A detailed account of how an elder's slow decline into dementia creates fertile opportunity for elder financial abuse;
- Insight into the development of the family dynamic over time;
- An illustration of how philanthropy creates social capital;
- An example of how the addition of in-laws can upset a delicate family balance;
- A study of how filial loyalty can be created and maintained with the promise of an inheritance;
- A demonstration of the highly subjective nature of testamentary capacity; and
- An example of the legal protections and remedies available to protect vulnerable elders.

Brooke Astor was considered the *grand dame* of New York's social elite. She had given approximately two hundred million dollars to the City of New York and its charities and had plans to make substantial gifts after her death. Yet, the adoring public knew little about the details of how she became Mrs. Astor, and how her son Tony came to forever live in her shadow. The story of Tony's deceit and criminal trial are well documented, but few are aware that Brooke herself had been sued over the circumstances surrounding the execution of her husband Vincent Astor's will. (Vincent's half-brother, John Jacob Astor VI, accused Brooke of procuring Vincent's estate through undue influence at a time when Vincent allegedly lacked testamentary capacity.) Also, few understood that son Tony, while convicted of stealing from his mother, was himself a pawn in a financial dispute between Brooke and her first husband, and Tony's natural father, John Dryden Kuser, who sued Tony for return of what amounted to child support.[121]

In the spirit of a Shakespearian tragedy, each character in the Astor saga is a combination of villain and hero, thief and philanthropist, both revered and despised. Sorting the characters in the Astor family drama requires the likes of a Broadway *Playbill* of the actors and their roles.

THE ASTOR FAMILY DRAMA

CAST

(In chronological order)

JOHN JACOB ASTOR .... Patriarch, philanthropist, slumlord, and opium trafficker

JOHN JACOB ASTOR IV .... Womanizer who died aboard the Titanic, taking with him his will leaving everything to his pregnant 19-year old wife

JOHN DRYDEN KUSER .... Brooke Astor's abusive first husband and father of Tony Marshall

CHARLES "BUDDY" MARSHALL .... Brooke's second husband and true love who shunned step-son Tony

VINCENT ASTOR .... Brooke's short lived third husband from whom she inherited her name and fortune

BROOKE ASTOR .... The heroine, victim, socialite, philanthropist, and indifferent mother

ANTHONY "TONY" (KUSER) MARSHALL .... Neglected child of Brooke, crooked elder abuser, sugar daddy, thrice married, and indifferent father of twin sons

CHARLENE MARSHALL .... Tony Marshall's third wife, greedy, meddling, despised stepmother and daughter in-law, thief of Tony's affection, and scapegoat

PHILIP MARSHALL .... Neglected son of Tony, meddling grandchild, and dime dropper.

HENRY CHRISTENSEN, III .... Long-time family attorney who exercised questionable ethics when he blurred the interests of his client, Brooke Astor, to favor her son, Tony Marshall.

FRANCIS X. MORRISEY, JR. ...... Successor attorney, convicted of forging Brooke Astor's signature to increase Tony's share.

John Jacob Astor

John Jacob Astor IV

Vincent Astor

Brooke Astor

Anthony Marshall

Charlene Marshall

Philip Marshall

Henry Christensen, III

Francis X. Morrisey, Jr.

ACT I - WHO'S WHO IN THE CAST

A richly detailed history of a family blessed with great wealth and pedigree
and cursed by the social disease of self indulgence.

ACT II - ANATOMY OF ELDER ABUSE

The account of Brooke Astor's slow descent into dementia and her
son's correspondingly bold acts to help himself to a larger portion of her
estate and social positon.

ACT III - BROKEN PIECES

The fallout of a son's deceit, a grandson's tainted intervention,
and a family irrevocably broken.

ACT I: WHO'S WHO IN THE CAST

The original Astor, John Jacob Astor, is considered to be the fourth wealthiest man in United States history, with an estate estimated by Forbes Magazine to be worth $115 billion in 2007 dollars. The son of a butcher, he lived from 1763 to 1848. Astor made his fortune in the fur trade, and parlayed his profits into Manhattan real estate and opium trade with China. The creator of the first trust in America, Astor was a patron of culture and learning, supporting the building of the Astor Library in New York City and subsidizing the scientific and creative works of the likes of ornithologist John James Audubon and poet/writer Edgar Allan Poe.

It is common for subsequent generations to fail to carry the mantel of their prominent founders. This was certainly true of John Jacob Astor's descendants, who seemed more concerned with their social standing, rich living, and romantic dalliances than the personal and social responsibility associated with being left one of the greatest fortunes and honored family names in American history.

There will always be those who blindly aspire to the life of the wealthy. Brooke Astor was no exception. Born Roberta Brooke Russell on March 20, 1902, Brooke's father was a career military man who never attained wealth. Brooke's mother, Mabel, was the daughter of a successful lawyer and a society belle. Mabel's parents were disappointed that she had not married well and cautioned Brooke to not make the same mistake.

On April 27, 1919 at the age of seventeen Brooke married John Dryden Kuser, heir to a vast New Jersey fortune. His mother, Susie Dryden, was the daughter of the founder of the Prudential Insurance Company, and his father Anthony Kuser was the founding stockholder of Fox Films and president of the local power company. Although a man of substantial means, Kuser was a cad; an alcoholic, a womanizer, a gambler, and an abuser. He reportedly beat Brooke, even breaking her jaw while she was pregnant with Anthony Kuser (who later changed his surname to Marshall), who was to be her only child.[122]

Our story's villain, Anthony "Tony" Kuser was born to Brooke Astor and John Dryden Kuser on May 30, 1924. According to Meryl Gordon in *Mrs. Astor Regrets,* there were hints that the birth was the product of "marital rape."[123] Despite being born into great wealth, Tony was not born into great love. John Kuser reportedly "cared nothing for the boy."[124] Meanwhile, Brooke was busy with her social calendar, romantic pursuits, and her career as a writer. Tony was quickly handed off to be raised by nannies. Kuser later left Brooke for another woman, divorcing Brooke in 1929 and ending their ten-year marriage when Tony was only five.

By 1929 Depression era standards the divorce settlement was extremely generous. Kuser paid $680,000 for an apartment and alimony which included a trust fund that brought Brooke $90,000 per year, but contained the condition that if Brooke re-married all future alimony would go into trust for Tony to be held until he attained age twenty-one.

Tony's trust proved toxic for both parents and their relationship with their son. A number of years later, down on his luck from a life of debauchery, Kuser sued Tony in an attempt to reacquire Tony's trust funds. Brooke too repeatedly requested and received portions of the trust from Tony after her 1932 marriage to her second husband Charles "Buddie" Marshall. Instead of rebuffing his parents, Tony tried to win their love by giving them what they wanted - money. According to Gordon, Kuser and Brooke "set an avaricious standard of behavior for their son. They used Tony, sending him the message that all tactics are fair, from emotional blackmail to legal wrangling, in grabbing for a family's fortune."[125] When Tony joined the marines, Kuser took out a $250,000 life insurance policy on Tony's life.[126] With his father handicapping his chances of returning from the war, Tony learned early in life the calloused lesson that profit could be derived from the death of a loved one.

In 1932 Brooke married Buddie Marshall, the man considered to be the love of her life. Tony was eight at the time and from the beginning seemed to be in the way of the newlyweds. He was traumatized when soon after the marriage Buddie fired Tony's longtime nanny, who according to Gordon "had been the one constant in his domestically turbulent life"...[127] "Tony was starved for affection and attention."[128] In the couple's new home, "Tony was exiled to a room built on the roof."[129] Brooke also shipped him off to stay with her parents for months at a time. Two years after Brooke's marriage to Buddie, at the age of ten, Tony was sent to boarding school where he was described by a classmate as "lonely" and "incidental to his parents." Buddie died in 1952, leaving Brooke a widow at age fifty. Brooke received $525,000 at Buddie's death, a handsome sum in the day. However, she believed that she would need more to be able to continue the lifestyle to which she had become accustomed.

On October 8, 1953, less than a year after Buddie's death, Brooke married Vincent Astor, the great-great-grandson of John Jacob Astor. By any standard, Vincent was rich. His holdings included the St. Regis Hotel, Newsweek magazine, and the well known shipping firm, United States Lines. The marriage would make Brooke an extremely wealthy woman and catapult her to the status of American royalty. It was widely speculated that Brooke did not love Vincent. Brooke herself admitted that her primary motive in marrying Vincent was financial security. The marriage was thought to be one of convenience, with Brooke being attracted to the awkward and cantankerous Astor for his money and short life expectancy.

Vincent had inherited more than eighty million dollars when his father John Jacob Astor IV died aboard the Titanic in 1912. The great grandson of the original Astor, John IV built the Astoria Hotel in New York City next to his cousin Waldorf's hotel, forming the famous Waldorf-Astoria. Played by daytime soap star Eric Braeden in the 1997 movie *Titanic,* John IV was returning to the United States with his new wife, nineteen year old Madeleine Force, who was pregnant with Vincent's half-brother John Jacob Astor VI ("Jack"). The new Mrs. Astor survived the sinking, but John IV went down with the ship. Also lost at sea was John IV's will, which would have left his entire estate to his new wife. The fortuitous series of events made Vincent his father's principal beneficiary. Vincent was fond of chortling, "It was a grand ship, the Titanic."[130]

Vincent Astor, "notoriously angry, psychotic"[131] and drunk, was himself the victim of a troubled childhood. He was raised by a tyrannical mother (jilted by her husband John IV in favor of his 19 year old bride), who was known to have locked him in a cedar closet for hours at a time. She was described as "magnificently selfish and spoiled, sharp-tongued, fearless in her pursuit of pleasure, furiously social and permanently dissatisfied."[132] After she and John IV divorced she traveled Europe in search of lovers while Vincent was stored away in boarding schools.

Tony, twenty-nine at the time, was again the odd man out. Vincent did not care for Tony from the beginning. He demanded that Brooke focus her attention on him and limit contact with her needy son. Vincent, however, was extremely fond of Tony's twin sons, Philip and Alec, who were born in 1953, the same year Vincent married Brooke. At one point, Vincent even suggested that he and Brooke adopt the twins at a time when Tony and his first wife were having marital problems. Again passed over in the allocation of affection, Tony faced the real possibility that his mother and stepfather's economic bounty would skip a generation and pass directly to his sons. According to Gordon: "Through their words and deeds, both Brooke and Vincent Astor created a family dynamic that gave Tony good reason to resent his own young sons."[133]

Vincent Astor died on February 3, 1959, five and one-half years after his marriage to Brooke. According to Brooke, "He used to change his will constantly. It was a game with him – almost a social event – and it always put him in a merry mood."[134] Vincent left Brooke two million dollars in cash, a sixty million dollar personal trust fund, valuable real estate on Park Avenue in New York City, Northeast Harbor, Maine, and New York State, and perhaps most importantly, left her in charge of his $60.5 million charitable foundation. It was Brooke's involvement with the foundation that would make her a fixture in New York society.

After Vincent's death, Brooke was sued by Vincent's half brother Jack (born after the sinking of the Titanic) for half of John IV's estate. Jack alleged that Vincent lacked testamentary capacity at the time he drafted his will, and that Brooke had used undue influence over Vincent in part by bringing him alcohol while he lay dying in the hospital. An attorney from the venerable law firm Sullivan & Cromwell successfully defended Brooke in the suit, thus beginning a four-decade relationship between the New York firm and Brooke. Henry "Terry" Christensen III, a key figure in the inheritance drama that would follow, was the third generation of Sullivan & Cromwell lawyers to handle Brooke's legal needs and estate planning.

Vincent was to be Brooke's last husband. With her inheritance of wealth, the Astor name, and her position as head of the Vincent Astor Foundation, Brooke spent the rest of her life dedicated to returning luster to a name tarnished through *"destructive marriages, scandals, and embarrasing peccadilloes."*[135] She also established her position as an important name in philanthropy and the social register. Brooke's inheritance brought her more than just money - it brought social status and the cache of her new family name. According to Philippe de Montebello, the director of the Metropolitan Museum, Brooke "always wanted to be in the limelight."[136] The ability to dispense millions made her popular and powerful. A bit of a narcissist, Brooke reveled in her long-running starring role, and savored the many accolades that her philanthropy brought her. She was fond of saying that "Wealth is like manure – if you collect too much, it stinks. You've got to spread it around."[137]

Even with the death of his mother's last husband, Tony still could not curry his mother's favor. She embarrassed him publicly when in her book *Footprints* she referred to him as a "spoiled"[138] child, and described him as so psychologically wounded in the war that he would "cry out in his sleep."[139] In 1997, she decided to liquidate the Vincent Astor Foundation, depriving Tony of the opportunity of succeeding his mother as head of the foundation that had garnered her celebrity status. Brooke told the *New York Times* that because her son was "not an Astor," "[t]here is no family to leave it to."[140]

Nor could Tony please his mother with his own marital choices. Brooke did not approve of any of Tony's three wives,[141] but she particularly disliked Tony's third wife, Charlene, whom Tony married in 1992. Charlene had been the ambitious wife of the local minister at the church Brooke attended when summering at her Maine retreat, Cove End. Brooke was embarrassed by what she saw as Charlene's gold-digging when Charlene divorced her minister husband and took up with Tony. Perhaps Brooke saw a bit of herself in Charlene.

Like Vincent, Brooke relished changing her will. She signed her first will in 1952, and over the next fifty years executed an astounding thirty-two wills and seven codicils, an average of nearly one new will or will amendment per year.[142] At the time of her death, Brooke had personal assets of one hundred twenty million dollars plus a charitable trust worth more than sixty million dollars. Her whimsy and apparent longevity, coupled with Tony's history of heart disease, placed Tony's inheritance in doubt. Knowing his mother's dislike of Charlene, Tony was concerned that Charlene would not be provided for if he failed to survive his mother.

ACT II: ANATOMY OF ELDER ABUSE

It is with this backdrop that the Astor story of family conflict and elder abuse unfolds. With the reluctant help of Brooke's longtime attorney, Terry Christensen, Tony set out to secure his and Charlene's future. What Tony apparently did not understand or plan for, was the smoldering resentment between him and his son Philip - a resentment that would foil Tony's plan, tarnish the Astor name, and jeopardize his inheritance.

Problems between Tony and Philip surfaced in 2000 following Philip's visit to his grandmother's Maine retreat. After the visit, Brooke, already aged ninety-eight and beginning to fail mentally and physically, decided to give Philip the guest out-cottage. Tony was incensed when he learned of the planned gift, seeing it as a portent of an inheritance pattern that would not favor him. Using what sway he had with his mother, Tony talked Brooke out of the gift. From that point forward, Tony began monitoring Philip's contact with Brooke, not trusting that either of them was acting in Tony's best interests.

Charlene's entry into the family mix upset an already fragile balance. She represented one more emotional mouth to feed in a family suffering from a chronic shortage of love. To Brooke, Charlene's unpolished and avaricious nature made her the least favored of a crop of wives all of whom infringed on Brooke's narcissistic need to be the center of attention. To Philip, Charlene was another obstacle to his father's affections. But to Tony, Charlene's assertiveness and loyalty gave him the courage to step out of his mother's shadow and assert himself as her rightful heir. In the family tragedy that would follow, all parties would point to Charlene as the catalyst for Tony's criminal acts and the destruction of the family.

Philip had reason to resent his father. Fitting a familiar family pattern, Tony had divorced Philip's mother when Philip was only eight. Philip and his twin brother Alec were raised by their mother and stepfather, and the twins only saw Tony sporadically. Viewing Charlene as a greedy interloper who had come between him and his father, Philip's worst fears were realized when he learned that Brooke had gifted Cove End to his father, who in turn gave it to Charlene. Seeing the gift of Cove End as a sign of things to come, Philip mused, "As goes Maine, so goes the estate."[143]

Brooke's longevity, Tony's own fragile health, and his mother's explicit dislike of Charlene, led Tony to conclude that he would have to take matters into his own hands if he were going to provide for Charlene's financial security. Tony sought to inherit not just his mother's wealth, but also her social standing. If he was "not an Astor" through breeding, he sought to be one through the proxy of inheritance.

As the snap of a single twig can start a whole herd running; inheritance "grabs" too are often set in motion by the acute perception that one's fair share has been put in jeopardy. Alarmed by reports of his mother's random gifts of household items to visitors and her attempted gift of the Maine cottage to Philip in late 2000, Tony decided he needed to act quickly to protect his interests. His first business was to have Brooke evaluated medically to see if she still possessed the capacity to manage her affairs. Tony's suspicions were confirmed when Brooke's doctor diagnosed Brooke with Alzheimer's disease. Tony no doubt believed that his mother's diagnosis would prove useful in fending off future encroachments on Brooke's estate. Little did he know that Brooke's deteriorating mental state would later be used to impeach his own actions.

With evidence of his mother's limited and declining capacity in hand, Tony sought to divide the loyalties of his mother's long-term attorney, Terry Christensen. Christensen, a preeminent estate lawyer, allowed himself to be put into a difficult ethical position trying to represent the competing interests of two clients, Brooke and Tony. Perhaps motivated by the wish to keep Tony as a client after Brooke's death, and to garner the multi-million dollar fee that would be earned by settling Brooke's estate, Christensen participated in the fiction that Brooke possessed the capacity to sign numerous will amendments – all of which expanded Tony's share. Ultimately, Christensen was fired after he apparently drew the line indicating that he would no longer cooperate with Tony. He was replaced by a new lawyer, Frances X. Morrissey, Jr., a friend of Tony's who possessed questionable ethics and a history of improper dealings with old and rich clients.

A number of will amendments, known as *codicils,* were signed by Brooke after her 2000 Alzheimer's diagnosis. Some were signed years later, when by all accounts she was suffering from the common manifestations of moderate to advanced dementia, including confusion, loss of cognitive ability, poor memory, and paranoia.

The Brooke Astor case is a classic example of how the slow decline of an elder into dementia provides fertile opportunity for abuse. As is common, the abuse of Brooke accelerated with her increasing loss of capacity, and was accomplished over time in a number of progressively more predatory transactions. This pattern typically starts with modest attempts, and is followed by more aggressive moves as perpetrators become emboldened by the apparent success of earlier attempts. What follows is a brief chronicle of Tony's financial abuse of his mother, beginning in late 2000.

December 26, 2000

It is speculated that Brooke's dementia began in the early 1990s when she reached her own ninetieth year. Staff members reported that Brooke would get lost on her own property and from time to time showed uncharacteristic flashes of temper. But it was not until her attempted gift of the Maine cottage to Philip in 2000 that Tony took Brooke to a neurologist. Tony followed the office visit and the doctor's diagnosis of Alzheimer's with a seven-page letter to the doctor dated December 26, 2000, chronicling Brooke's mental and cognitive decline, citing Brooke's trouble with "simple arithmetic" and confusion about money. Immediately after the diagnosis, Tony shared his view of Brooke's declining competency and the doctor's Alzheimer's diagnosis with Brooke's long time estate planning attorney, Terry Christensen.

January 30, 2002

Shortly after the events of September 11, 2001, Tony began pressing Christensen to arrange "sufficient financial assistance to my wife Charlene upon my death."[144] On January 30, 2002, Christensen prepared a substantial re-write of Brooke's 1997 will, which greatly expanded Tony's share. Under the new will, Tony would receive Brooke's Park Avenue apartment, her Westchester County estate, her Maine property, and five million dollars. In addition, after Brooke's death, Tony would receive an annual income of $4.2 million for life. The will, however, retained the spirit of previous wills, passing Tony's share to charity in the event that he predeceased his mother.

Under the January 30, 2002 will, sixty million dollars of Brooke's estate was still slated to pass to charity. The quality of her January 30, 2002 signature showed decline from her January 8, 1997 and February 2, 2001 signatures:

January 8, 1997

Dated: 8 Jan, 1997

BROOKE RUSSELL ASTOR,

February 2, 2001

Dated: February 2 , 2001

Brooke Russell Astor,
Testatrix

January 30, 2002

Dated: January 30th , 2002

Brooke Russell-Astor,
Testatrix

Early 2002

In early 2002, Tony sold Brooke's cherished painting, Childe Hassam's *Flags, Fifth Avenue* which had long been promised to the Metropolitan Museum of Art, for ten million dollars, taking a two million dollar commission (roughly double the fee charged by established auction houses). When asked why she sold *Flags,* Brooke – whose annual income was estimated to be five to six million dollars - told a friend that Tony said she needed the money. In her diminished state, she wondered if she would have enough money to buy a dress.

April 28, 2003

On April 28, 2003, in a letter believed to be inspired by Tony, Christensen wrote to Tony that "your mother has discussed the possibility of making a gift to you now of all of Cove End." Cove End was Brooke's cherished Maine vacation retreat, a portion of which she nearly gifted to grandson Philip in 2000. The gift tax alone (paid by Brooke) amounted to $3,562,500. Six months later Tony deeded the property to Charlene. Those close to Brooke were suspicious of this gift and the gifts that followed, both because of Brooke's diminished capacity and her active dislike of Charlene. Tony, after the "gift," continued to maintain Cove End out of Brooke's accounts, one of the acts that would lead to his subsequent criminal indictment.

June 24, 2003

With the help of attorney Christensen, Tony accelerated his plan when on June 24, 2003 Brooke was hospitalized with a broken hip. On August 12, 2003, apparently believing that Brooke's death was imminent, Christensen sent Tony another letter under Brooke's signature, informing him of Brooke's wish to make "an additional outright gift to you of $5,000,000. This should provide you with enough money to assure Charlene's comfort assuming that she survives you."

December 17, 2003

Brooke continued to suffer physical, mental, and emotional decline. Her nurses wrote detailed notes about "periods of confusion and illusion. She continues to report being afraid and believes that someone is trying to kill her." The notes further indicate that Brooke was exhibiting "paranoia, undecipherable words, [and] disoriented."

December 18, 2003

Amidst reports of Brooke's paranoia and incoherency, Christensen prepared the "First and Final Codicil" to her substantially revised January 30, 2002 will. Although at trial Christensen had no explanation for the word "final," many believe that it was a message that he would no longer participate in the fiction that Brooke was competent enough to make future changes to her will. The amendment allocated forty-nine percent of the remaining assets of Vincent Astor's non-charitable marital trust for the creation of the "Anthony Marshall Fund." Although the change did not directly benefit Tony, it gave him the social capital he needed to enter the world of philanthropy that had made his mother a New York icon. The Codicil was also a significant departure from Brooke's prior wishes. Only six years earlier, in 1997, Brooke dissolved the Vincent Astor Foundation, stating Tony *was not an Astor* and should not continue her philanthropy. The amendment, the last under Christensen's watch, did however maintain Brooke's basic vision that her favorite charities were to continue as her principal beneficiaries. The Codicil prohibited Tony from profiting from fund assets, and, from naming his successor. Any money remaining in the Anthony Marshall Fund at Tony's death was to pass to the Metropolitan Museum and the New York Public Library. Brooke's signature at the time of the *"Final"* amendment evidenced significant decline.

IN WITNESS WHEREOF, I have hereunto set my hand and seal this 18th day of December , two thousand three.

January 12, 2004

More than three years after Brooke's Alzheimer's diagnosis and less than one month after Christensen's use of the word "Final," Christensen was removed as Brooke's attorney. Hoisted by his own petard, Christensen could not claim that Brooke was incompetent to work with a new lawyer, having prepared legal documents on Brooke's behalf less than a month earlier.

Even before Christensen was informed of his firing, a Second Codicil dramatically expanding Tony's interest was prepared by new attorney Francis X. Morrissey, Jr. The Second Codicil was a complete departure from Brooke's earlier bequests and philosophy. It bequeathed sixty million dollars directly to Tony, disinheriting all charities. The Second Codicil also named Tony as his mother's sole executor and granted him the power to name Charlene and Morrissey as his successors.

IN WITNESS WHEREOF, I have hereunto set my hand and seal

on *January 12* , 2004.

(L.S.)

BROOKE RUSSELL ASTOR

February 10, 2004

Tony arranged for his mother to host a luncheon at the famed Knickerbocker Club where she read from prepared notes praising Tony and Charlene. Brooke's physician later testified that by the time of the luncheon Brooke did not possess the capacity to compose or write her speech. It was thought by many that Tony wrote Brooke's speech to add credence to the recent will amendments that greatly augmented Tony's share. Having Brooke speak publicly about her fondness for Tony and Charlene would serve to confirm her new-found generosity toward them. A good showing would also support the proposition that Brooke was still competent.

March 3, 2004

Morrissey had a Third Codicil prepared at a time when Brooke was extremely weak and confused. Signed under suspicious circumstances, the Third Codicil was the final piece of the puzzle. It directed that Brooke's prized Park Avenue apartment and Hudson Valley county house be sold and added to the estate. Brooke's signature on the Third Codicil appeared stronger than it had been on the previous two codicils, raising suspicions that it was a forgery. The Third Codicil also marked the beginning of Tony's efforts to isolate his mother from the outside world. Tony had already restricted his son Philip's access to Brooke. Tony now began to complete Brooke's isolation by firing her long-time staff and limiting access of all friends and family. With his plan in place Tony could not risk intervention by outsiders.

IN WITNESS WHEREOF, I have hereunto set my hand and seal on *3rd day*

day   , 2004.

Brooke Russell Astor

_____ (L.S.)
BROOKE RUSSELL ASTOR

ACT III: BROKEN PIECES

July 24, 2006

Responding to a number of alarming reports from Brooke's staff of Brooke's decline, Philip petitioned for guardianship of his grandmother. Without a hearing, the court awarded temporary guardianship to long-time friend Annette de la Renta and to J. P. Morgan Chase Bank, and appointed a court evaluator to independently evaluate Brooke's condition. Philip's actions were described by Brooke's neighbor and Tony's friend William F. Buckley, Jr., as "biblical in their betrayal." Referring to Charlene, Philip defended his actions stating that "I don't care about the money, she stole my father."[145] Philip's wife Nan tried to persuade Philip to mediate the dispute "without resorting to lawyers,"[146] but Philip was not to be dissuaded. Without so much as a phone call to his father, Philip set off a chain of events that would forever destroy his father, his grandmother's legacy, and in an ironic twist, his own inheritance.

August 13, 2007

Brooke died August 13, 2007 at the age of 105, leaving an estate worth an estimated one hundred thirty-two million dollars and a charitable trust valued at more than sixty million dollars. Brooke was buried at Sleepy Hollow Cemetery, near another famous New Yorker, Leona Helmsley, who died a week after Brooke.

November 26, 2007

Tony was indicted in a fourteen page, eighteen count indictment that included counts for grand larceny, falsifying business records, conspiracy, and possession of stolen property. Morrissey was also indicted and charged with a number of counts including the forgery of the March 3, 2004 Third Codicil.

October 9, 2009

After a nineteen-week trial, Tony Marshall was convicted of fourteen of the sixteen remaining counts against him. Morrissey was convicted of a series of fraud charges including forging Brooke's Third Codicil. The following is a summary of the verdicts in the Brooke Astor Case:

The New York Times   October 8, 2009

The Verdicts in the Brooke Astor Case

COUNT	CHARGE	DEFENDANT	ALLEGATION	GUILTY
1	Scheme to Defraud	Marshall Morrissey	From 2001 to 2007, schemed to steal money and property by capitalizing on Brooke Astor's diminished capacity	✓
2	Grand Larceny, First Degree	Marshall	Tricked Mrs. Astor into selling a beloved painting by telling her she was broke, and took a $2 Million commission on it	
3	Falsifying Business Records	Marshall	Told Mrs. Astor's accountant that $757,000 she spent was a personal expense, when it was actually a gift to him	
4	Offering a false instrument	Marshall	Filed false information in response to a petition by Mr. Marshall's son Phillip to appoint a guardian for Mrs. Astor	✓
5	Grand Larceny, second degree	Marshall	Used more than $600,000 of Mrs. Astor's money to maintain Cove End, the Maine retreat she gave to me	✓
6	Grand Larceny, Second degree	Marshall	Took a $500,000 drawing of dancing dogs by Giovanni Domenico Tiepolo from the was of Mrs. Astor's apartment	✓
7	Possession of stolen property	Marshall	Same.	✓
8	Grand Larceny, second degree	Marshall	Used Mrs. Astor's money to pay wages to an employee	✓
9	Conspiracy	Marshall Morrissey	Conspired to amend Mrs. Astor's will to leave much of her estate to Mr. Marshall rather than to charity	✓
10	Conspiracy, false instrument	Marshall Morrissey	Same.	✓
11	False Instrument	Marshall	Same.	✓
12	Conspiracy	Marshall Morrissey	Conspired to add a codicil to the Will that would have meant greater executor fees for Mr. Marshall and Mr. Morrissey	✓
13	Forgery	Morrissey	Forged a signature on the amendment	✓
14	Possession of a forged instrument	Morrissey	Same.	
15	Grand larceny, First degree	Marshall	Gave himself salary increases without Mrs. Astor's consent, raising his pay for managing her estate to ver $1 million	✓
16	Grand larceny Second degree	Marshall	Paid the captain of a yacht Mr. Marshall purchased with $55,000 taken from his mother's accounts	✓
17	Grand larceny Second degree	Marshall	Took a painting worth $500,000 by John Frederick Lewis from the Blue Room of his mother's home	✓
18	Possession of stolen property	Marshall	Same.	✓

Much of the trial focused on Brooke's competency. The defense argued that Brooke was not demented, but merely suffering from the ordinary decline associated with advanced age. The defense conceded that at times Brooke suffered from confusion, disorientation, and paranoia, but defended the validity of her gifts and will amendments on the basis that at other times, as reflected in her nurse's notes, she was "alert and oriented." Physicians testifying for both sides were reluctant to make what they believed to be a legal determination as to whether Brooke possessed *testamentary capacity*, stating only that she had diminished capacity and dementia.

In sentencing Tony to a prison term of one-to-three years, Justice A. Kirke Bartley, Jr., himself age eighty-five, lamented "It is a paradox to me that such abundance has led to such incredible sadness."[147] With the criminal convictions and sentencing resolved (absent potential appeals), the Westchester County Surrogate Court will determine the civil portion of the dispute, including the validity of the various gifts and codicils made by Brooke in her waning years. While the criminal convictions of Tony and Morrissey have no direct legal impact on the Surrogate Court proceedings, they are likely to be persuasive on the issue of intent and Brooke's competency. Much of Brooke's estate will no doubt be lost in lawyer's fees and costs. The legal fees associated with Brooke's guardianship alone exceeded two million dollars, and according to one of Tony's lawyers, the legal fees for Tony's defense during the criminal trial exceeded one hundred thousand dollars per week. Money aside, the Marshall family and the Astor name will never be the same.

It is often the case that an inheritance dispute is the death knell of a family. Family bonds are permanently broken as combatants vow never to speak to one another again. Families permanently split into separate camps with children and grandchildren dutifully accepting the directive to disassociate themselves from the members of the other camp.

There will be no reconciliation in the Marshall family. Philip shows no signs of remorse. Asked if he had any regrets in causing his father's indictment, he responded "No, I do not regret my decision. Our goal, and our only goal, was to help my grandmother at the end of her life, and we realized that goal. If I had to, I would do the same again."[148] For his part, Tony said "I was wounded in Iwo Jima and my wounds healed, but the wounds Philip inflicted on me will never heal."[149]

Philip's only comment after his father's conviction was "I hope this brings some consolation and closure for the many people, including my grandmother's loyal staff, caregivers and friends, who helped when she was so vulnerable and so manipulated."[150] With regard to Charlene, Philip stated that his actions were not motivated by money; his motivation was the fact that "she stole my father."[151] Truth be told, Philip was more likely motivated by his deep hurt over his father's lifelong indifference to him and the 2000 veto of Brooke's gift of the Cove End cottage. Philip must have felt that without his swift and dramatic intervention Charlene would have ultimately inherited his grandmother's entire estate.

If Philip's primary concern were really what his grandmother would have wanted, he would not have allowed her name and her pitiful decline to be dragged through the media. According to longtime friend Vartan Gregorian, "She would have been mortified." "She was very private."[152] Philip had to know that a woman who spent her life preoccupied with appearances and social status would not have wanted to be remembered as a demented victim of elder abuse. He also had to know that his 2006 allegations would set off a firestorm of conflict and media coverage. If his wish was truly to protect his grandmother, he would have first gone to his father with his concerns, or have mediated their dispute as his wife had urged him to do. Brooke had fought to protect and promote the Astor name. Now, the Astor name built on fur trading, Manhattan real estate, and philanthropy will forever be associated with elder abuse and fur flying in the courtroom.

After his previous run-ins with his father, Philip believed that his father had disinherited him. With nothing to lose, he was willing to risk bringing down the entire family to prevent Charlene from inheriting his grandmother's estate. In an ironic twist, Philip learned after his father's 2009 criminal conviction that he had not been, and could not have been, disinherited by his father. Apparently, Tony was obligated under his divorce decree with Philip's mother to leave one-third of his estate to Philip and his twin brother, Alec. Now, the cost of a protracted trial and his broken relationship with his father place any potential inheritance in jeopardy. Yet, faced with the likelihood that he has given up at least ten million dollars of inheritance, and knowing that his family has been destroyed, Philip nevertheless claims that he would do it again.

The lessons of Chapter Two help us understand Philip's true, yet most likely entirely subconscious, motivations. Believing that he had been excluded by his father with no possibility of reconciliation, Philip disregulated, acting out his hurt and anger without any thought as to the consequences to all involved, including himself.

CONCLUSION

The Brooke Astor case serves as a platform for the chapters that follow. We now turn to Chapter 6 to learn more about the age-related disease of dementia, and how it makes testators like Brooke Astor vulnerable to the ill intentions of others.

VULNERABILITY IN THE TWILIGHT OF COMPETENCE 6

"[W]ithout memory we are everywhere, or nowhere-no place of birth, no route to work, no Sunday nights with children asleep in the back of the car on the way home. Without memory, all places are equal and alien. We are confined to the eternal "now"- a moment, and then another. We cannot learn, for knowledge is a product of analogy: "just as it was," "better than," "safer," "familiar." Without these, there is no heritage, tradition, ritual, or culture. We have no identity as we stand on this alien ground. How will society treat us so displaced-as refugees and exiles, as the orphans of memory? We have seen the answer in ... institutions that warehouse the elderly as though they were objects to be arranged beside garden paths like potted plants."

- Nora J. Rubinstein[153]

Charles Dickens

Andre Waters

INTRODUCTION

Our focus in this Chapter is on inheritance disputes that begin with the predatory acts of family members. While it is difficult to take advantage of a person whose mental and physical capacities are intact, elder financial abuse is more easily facilitated when the victim begins to fail and must rely increasingly on others.

In contrast to the widely reported abuse perpetrated by strangers, like door-to-door salesmen and internet schemers, studies show that as much as ninety percent of elder financial abuse is perpetrated by family members. The motivations of strangers who prey on the elderly are simple. Common thieves view their victims as mere objects to be manipulated for their own personal gain. They don't have any feeling about it – they just want money.

The motives of family members who abuse their loved ones are much more complex. They may suffer from addiction, financial problems, cluster B personality disorders, or may seek retribution for what they perceive as past wrongs or inequities. They may have pined for years for their chance to enhance their position or to see other family members cut down to size. They have a plan, a devious plan that cannot be implemented while their victim is mentally intact and clear thinking.

The perceived wrongs to be righted vary. Abusers may believe that as children they were never properly recognized or rewarded; that others got more; or that they deserve more because they did more for mom and dad. Perpetrators also tend to project their motives onto others, believing that others are out to steal from their elderly target if they don't get there first.

Abusers may come to these conclusions on their own, or be encouraged by their spouse or others who inject their own hurts, wants, and desires. Whatever their motivation, perpetrators choose self-help believing that there is no forum for their complaints, or that if expressed, their complaints would not be given weight or credence. In any event, they are dissatisfied, they have unfinished family business, and they endeavor to resolve their issues as and when they see fit.

The methods of inheritance self-help are limited only by the imagination of the abuser. Abusers may change beneficiaries on life insurance policies and annuities; re-title real estate; "help" their parents write a new will; or just out-and-out steal their money. Brooke Astor is a quintessential story of elder abuse; more stories are told in Chapter Eight, *Undue Influence*.

Understanding how and when financial elder abuse occurs requires familiarity with the degenerative illness of *dementia*. The mental decline of elders, especially when it rises to the level of dementia, increases their vulnerability. Most of us lose some memory and mental flexibility as we age;[154] but elders are most vulnerable when their decline matures into dementia. The slow progression of the degenerative brain diseases that produce dementia create an extended period of vulnerability in which the elder possesses sufficient testamentary capacity to execute documents and make bank withdrawals, but is really not thinking clearly.

Dementia does not travel alone; it is accompanied by a constellation of other psychiatric conditions that add to the suffering and vulnerability of the afflicted. Up to eighty percent of individuals with moderate to advanced dementia also suffer from one or more of the following conditions: depression, anxiety, paranoia, insomnia, and agitation. A cunning predator will use his victim's failing cognition and growing psychiatric handicaps to his advantage.

Elders have a strong preference to remain in their home. Ironically, the memories, privacy, and control one's home represents can be extremely dangerous to one's health and well being. Studies of prisoners and those subject to voluntary isolation confirm that being alone accelerates psychosis in those with mental issues and causes mental illness where none previously existed.

Early detection of cognitive decline is one of the keys to the prevention of elder abuse. Testing similar to that employed by the National Football League would be useful in obtaining a baseline level of cognitive ability from which deviations could later be measured. Early detection also facilitates early treatment and can alert family members to the need to implement safeguards to protect their declining loved one. Preventive steps of the kind described in Chapter Eleven can be implemented where significant degeneration is detected.

ELDER ABUSE

Each year nearly three million U.S. seniors are the victims of abuse. The problem is even more serious than these figures suggest, as there is evidence that seventy-five to eighty percent of abuse goes unreported. The most likely perpetrators of elder abuse are family members, especially adult children and grandchildren. The rate of abuse increases as seniors begin to lose competence and become more dependent.

Elder abuse awareness increased in the U.S. in the late 1970s along with growing awareness of child and spousal abuse.[155] Between 1973 and 1981, sixteen states enacted legislation to protect elders from abuse. By 1991, the number reached 44. Today, all fifty states have some form of legislation that protects elders from abuse, and all states have created adult protective service (APS) agencies to investigate and prosecute claims. Government initiatives have resulted in a better understanding of elder abuse and have raised the awareness of professionals like attorneys, accountants, and bank personnel, who are in a position to combat it. (See Chapter Nine for further discussion of Adult Protective Services and elder abuse.)

There is a strong correlation between elder abuse and dependence of the victim on the abuser. There is also a high incidence of elder abuse where the abuser is financially dependent on the victim, and where the abuser has a history of mental illness and substance abuse.[156] Caregivers generally have a high potential and opportunity to abuse. Caregiver stress, social isolation, and the economic burdens of care giving all contribute to their potential to abuse. Children with substance abuse or psychological problems who move back home to care for parents create a fertile environment for abuse. Although they are the most able to drop whatever they're doing (usually nothing) and move back home (they're probably being evicted from their apartment anyway) the potential for abuse is so high that families would be smart to decline their "help."

The National Center on Elder Abuse identified the following factors present in physical and financial elder abuse:

- Abuser dependency on elder;
- Elder dependency on abuser;
- Elder frailty, disability, or impairment;
- Social isolation of elders;
- Substance abuse or mental pathology of either the elder or the abuser;
- Persons age 80 or older are abused and neglected at a rate two or three times higher than their percentage in the general population;
- Female elders are abused at a higher rate than males;
- Of older persons about whom reports of abuse or neglect were substantiated by APS, almost half were not physically able to care for themselves;
- In almost nine out of ten incidents of domestic elder abuse and neglect, the perpetrator is a family member; adult children are responsible for almost half of elder abuse and neglect cases;
- Four to five times as many incidences of abuse occur than are reported;
- The likelihood of becoming a victim of financial abuse increases with age;
- The likelihood of financial abuse is relatively constant throughout various economic groups;

• Men are more likely to be the perpetrators of physical abuse and women of psychological abuse.

DEMENTIA

Cognitive ability refers to our ability to think and process information. That ability peaks in our teen years and begins to decline noticeably in our later years.[157] Aging affects mental agility in much the same way as it affects physical agility; just as we cannot run as fast as when we were young, we likewise cannot think as fast. We lose our fluid ability to problem solve and perform new tasks such as learning how to use the computer or the television remote. Older people marvel at how quickly young people learn new technology. They often make light of their own loss of memory and mental flexibility, observing that they are *"getting old"* or offering clichés such as: *"You can't teach an old dog new tricks."*

A slow decline in mental capacity is considered to be part of normal aging. Mental decline becomes abnormal, however, venturing into the realm of dementia, when the loss of memory or cognitive ability begins to affect day-to-day living. Dementia, formerly known as *senility*, literally means *deprived of mind*. It is a chronic and progressive decline of mental capacity characterized by a deterioration of short-term memory and cognition. As a general rule, the impairments that characterize Alzheimer's disease (AD) and associated progressive dementias tend to develop over the course of years, and even decades.[158]

To elevate normal mental decline to a diagnosis of dementia, symptoms must extend beyond memory into other aspects of thinking and problem solving. Typical manifestations include difficulties with speech (losing one's train of thought or problems finding the right word) and the ability to do simple calculations, like making change. Also, the problems must be severe enough to interfere with day-to-day functions like driving, cooking, and taking medications.

Normal human functioning has been characterized as falling into one of two broad categories: instrumental activities of daily living (IADLs), and activities of daily living (ADLs). Instrumental activities of daily living are higher-end functions like using the telephone, shopping, food preparation, housekeeping, laundry, driving, taking medication, and managing finances. IADLs are usually the first elements of function to be affected by memory and cognitive loss. Difficulties with IADLs manifest as much as three years prior to a formal diagnosis of dementia. Family and friends might first notice a decline in their loved one's personal hygiene, failure to properly take medications, and difficulty in managing their finances. A family member who was once fastidious about her finances might start bouncing checks or purchasing items she previously considered frivolous or unnecessary. However, it is when the elder is unable to manage the lower-end self-care ADLs such as dressing, grooming, personal hygiene, and toileting, that a diagnosis of dementia is certain. ADLs are routine "crystallized"[159] skills that are less affected by early stage dementia or MCI, Mild Cognitive Impairment. When such engrained habitual skills fail, a diagnosis of moderate to advanced dementia logically follows.[160]

When it comes to understanding the mechanics of elder abuse, the two most important features of dementia are its onset and progression. As with many degenerative diseases, the likelihood of developing dementia increases with age. Early onset dementia, that is, dementia under the age of sixty, is rare, but does exist. Early onset is usually associated either with a strong genetic predisposition or with serious and repeated head traumas such as those experienced by boxers and professional football players. There is a direct correlation between age and incidence of dementia. The older we get the greater the likelihood of dementia. The incidence of dementia roughly doubles every five years after age sixty-five. It affects five to eight percent of all people between the ages of sixty-five and seventy-four, up to twenty percent of those between ages seventy-five and eighty-four, and as many as half of those eighty-five and older.[161]

Someone with mild dementia has trouble with recent memory; he might ask the same question several times in close succession, or read the morning paper but not remember any details of what he read.[162] Typically, at this stage, the person is beginning to have difficulty with complex functions like using the telephone, managing finances, taking medications or driving. Also, it is common for people with mild dementia to have difficulty controlling their emotions, often appearing irritable and short-tempered. Other early signs include repetitive questioning, unreasonable suspiciousness of other people, mistakes at the bank or with finances, or poor judgment about important issues. Depression is common early in the illness - perhaps reflecting the individual's awareness of subtle changes - and may even be the first sign of a dementia process. As the disorder progresses, sufferers frequently develop significant behavioral disturbances, including agitation, hallucinations, and delusions.

Dementia is the general or umbrella diagnosis used to describe the symptoms of scores of conditions the most common of which is Alzheimer's disease (AD). A common misconception is that Alzheimer's and dementia are two separate diseases. They are not.

Alzheimer's disease is the number one cause of dementia accounting for at least fifty percent of all dementia.[163] AD when combined with vascular dementia ("VaD") - the second most common cause of dementia which results from blockages that impede blood flow to the brain usually from large or small strokes - constitutes as much as seventy-five percent of all dementia cases.[164] Alzheimer's and vascular dementia are the most prominent members of a class of neurodegenerative diseases that gradually destroy brain cells, leading to the loss of function and even death. Whatever its origins, those suffering from dementia end up basically in the same place: diminished memory, compromised cognitive ability, prominent communication problems, and altered personality.

The diagnosis of *mild cognitive impairment* was created to describe the transitional stage between normal aging and the more serious problems caused by dementia. MCI captures the growing number of elderly patients demonstrating cognitive impairment who do not meet the formal criteria for dementia. MCI affects memory, executive function, or a combination of the two, but not everyday cognition which would give rise to a diagnosis of dementia. While those entering MCI may have only memory issues, the same individual at departure (considered early AD) will have significant cognitive problems and noticeable declines in his IADLs.[165]

Executive function refers to higher-end decision making like handling one's finances. It requires the fluid ability to process all available information and formulate an appropriate response. Executive function requires the ability to remember and manipulate all of the relevant bits of information that go into making on-the-spot decisions. Executive function also allows us to formulate appropriate emotional responses in our social interactions.[166]

Although some MCI patients stabilize or even improve, it is now believed that nearly all dementia patients pass through MCI.[167] Individuals with MCI are five to ten times more likely to develop dementia. Although someone with worsening MCI may still appear to function normally, he or she is likely to have increasing difficulty concentrating, completing tasks and making decisions.

Experts now believe that people who develop dementia, especially those suffering from AD, experience brain structure changes years before any signs of memory loss begin. A 2007 report in *Neurology* found that changes in brain structure are present in clinically normal people an average of four years before MCI diagnosis, leading them to believe that AD may be present for many years before symptoms of the disease begin to appear.[168] People with Alzheimer's can live from two to twenty years from onset.

The Alzheimer's Society of Canada has published ten warning signs of Alzheimer's disease:

1. Memory loss particularly of recent events that affects day-to-day function;
2. Difficulty performing familiar tasks like cooking or navigating an automobile;
3. Problems with language;
4. Disorientation of time and space. For example, getting lost going to a familiar place;
5. Poor judgment, like when to seek medical treatment or choosing appropriate clothing;
6. Problems with abstract thinking like balancing one's check book or understanding the value of one's assets;
7. Misplacing things;
8. Changes in behavior or mood, swinging from tears, to anger, or to calm for no apparent reason;
9. Changes in personality, like becoming confused, suspicious, or withdrawn. Changes may also include apathy, fearfulness or acting out of character;
10. Loss of initiative. Persons with AD may become very passive and withdrawn.

There is no definitive medical test for diagnosing neurodegenerative brain disease. Although modern measuring techniques such as MRI and CAT scans allow experts to see the brain, neurodegenerative diseases are still what are called *clinical diagnoses,* meaning that they are more of an art than a science and are derived from all facts and circumstances. Important diagnostic tools include patient self-reporting, input from family and friends, as well as medical and diagnostic testing. Clinical diagnosis of AD can be made with a high degree of accuracy (85% or more),[169] but a final diagnosis of Alzheimer's can only be made after death from an examination of brain tissue.

Once diagnosed, dementia and AD are further categorized according to severity, applying the designations *mild, moderate,* and *severe.* Over time, those affected gradually move from one stage to the next, losing capacity along the way. Sufferers of mild dementia remain functional in most areas of their lives, and likely possess the minimum testamentary capacity necessary to execute a will. However, by the time they reach advanced dementia, sufferers are completely dysfunctional.

The correlation between age and elder abuse is more accurately a correlation between age and decline in cognitive ability: the greater the decline in cognition the higher the potential for abuse. The following graph, based on the author's observations over thirty years of practice, illustrates the relationship between elder abuse and cognitive ability. Note that elder abuse increases exponentially at the very end of competence, especially in the days, weeks, and months immediately preceding the death of the victim.

ELDER ABUSE AS A FUNCTION OF CAPACITY

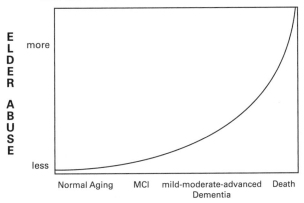

DECLINING CAPACITY

DEPRESSION, ANXIETY, AND AGITATION

Dementia is accompanied by a myriad of psychiatric conditions that include depression, anxiety, and agitation.[170] Depression occurs in thirty to seventy percent of Alzheimer's patients. Many believe that, in part, depression is the result of the loss of function necessary to experience the joy of daily living. The need to be productive and relevant continues to be important for older adults. With retirement from the workforce and cessation of parenting responsibilities, many older adults lose their sense of purpose, which adds to their emotional angst. Depression may manifest itself as unhappiness, withdrawal, fatigue, and general feelings of worthlessness. Depression augments and often masks as dementia. It also compounds the burden of both the afflicted and their caregivers.

Anxiety is the most common psychiatric condition of the elderly. Many consider anxiety to be a natural response to aging. *Agitation* is also a frequent symptom in dementia, eventually occurring in about half of all persons with dementia. Agitation is frequently accompanied by a loss of impulse control and can result in uncharacteristic cursing, insensitivity, tactlessness, or sexually inappropriate behavior. Those with dementia often take their frustration out on those closest to them while appearing gracious and appropriate with strangers. Stories of agitated seniors physically striking loved ones and caretakers are not uncommon.

PARANOIA

A healthy amount of skepticism is an adaptive human trait. Parents teach their children to be wary of strangers, and not to believe everything they hear or read. Certain occupations, such as law enforcement, IRS agents, attorneys, and newspaper reporters, rely on skepticism to ply their trade. Normal skepticism, however, is not to be confused with paranoia.

Paranoia is a psychiatric condition in which sufferers experience intense feelings of suspicion and persecution. No group is more affected by paranoia than the elderly. By some accounts *fifty percent* of those with dementia suffer from some form of paranoia including delusions and/or hallucinations. This type of paranoia is not the same paranoid schizophrenia or paranoid personality disorders that generally develop much earlier in life – the bulk of which occur in the late teens and early twenties. Paranoid elders typically have no history of psychosis.

Although its causes vary, paranoia is a complex symptom of the physical and psychological changes that occur in the elderly. *Physical* factors causing paranoia include mini-strokes, medication intoxication, Parkinson's and Huntington's diseases, and early stage Alzheimer's. *Psychological* factors include severe depression, dementia, and a combination of social isolation and hearing and vision loss. Confused by a decline in their cognitive functioning and perhaps further impaired by hearing or vision loss, sufferers have the feeling of losing control. Unable to comprehend their diminished capacity and the events that are occurring around them, they project the cause of their loss onto others.

Paranoia sufferers have little or no insight into their condition; they are absolutely convinced that they are being victimized. As someone once said: *"I wouldn't be so paranoid if everyone wasn't out to get me."* Lacking insight and in denial of their lost capacity, sufferers believe that external forces are conspiring to control their lives. They often become frightened and anxious, and may even strike out against those they believe are acting against them.

Isolation is an important factor contributing to paranoia in the elderly. Elders – more often women - who live alone lack the normal reality checks provided by social interaction. Left alone with their increasingly distorted thoughts, the isolated paranoiac is free to run amok with his or her mental and emotional distortions.

Paranoid elders suffer from a broad range of delusions, the most common of which are that others are stealing their money; have deserted them despite regular visits; are neglecting them physically; are trying to have them committed; or are improperly switching their medications. In some cases, paranoid elders develop extremely bizarre and complicated delusions and hallucinations. They believe that they are being spied on by telescopes or television cameras, or are being recorded through microphones and tapes.

The object of the paranoid elder's delusion tends to be those with whom they have the most contact. As a result, a favored child who may have been the most involved in their parent's care may find herself accused of stealing. Aside from being hurtful, the false accusations can ignite simmering family conflict. False accusations open the door to a disfavored child who has been waiting for just such an opportunity to discredit their favored sibling. The disfavored child may even support their parent's paranoia by fanning the flames of their delusion. Riding the wave of paranoia, an abuser may take the parent to an attorney to change his estate plan, cobble together asset transfer documents taken off the internet, or employ the help of an unwitting friend to assist in a scheme of self-enrichment.

It can be extremely difficult for someone new on the scene of elder abuse, including professionals, to separate fact from fiction. Certainly, every claim must be examined. Unfortunately, it can be difficult to determine whether the vulnerable adult is really being taken advantage of or is suffering from paranoid delusions.

The input of family members can be extremely helpful in assessing an elder's competence. The shared history and presumed objectivity of family and friends provides valuable insight to the investigator. However, third party testimony may be unreliable when families are in conflict and reporting family members stand to gain from the outcome of the inquiry.

To protect the senior, it is important to identify paranoia early. A radical change in the relationships and long standing estate planning wishes of the elder should be an immediate red flag. Periodic evaluation by a neuropsychologist or other physician specializing in geriatrics will help identify lost capacity and potential confusion. Intervention by the probate court in the manner described in Chapter Nine, *Legal Protections,* may be necessary to prevent the manipulation of the confused senior by competing family members.

HOME ALONE

A growing number of seniors are living alone. Contributing to this trend, which shows no signs of slowing down, are longevity, divorce, mobility of children, and the decline of the multi-generational household. According to a 2005 survey, roughly forty percent of women age sixty-five and older live alone.

Seniors have a strong preference for living in their own home. Geropsychologists believe that physical places such as our home trigger memories of life events that were instrumental in the formation of our concept of self. It is for this reason that seniors, especially as they begin to lose capacity, develop *"attachment to place."*

So strong is the pull to remain in one's home that many seniors continue to live alone long after it is safe to do so. Although home may be where the heart is, studies show that seniors who live alone in advanced age are at risk for health and quality of life issues and are vulnerable to predators. Far from affording the comforts of home, living alone late in life is associated with a great number of physical and emotional maladies, including higher levels of mortality, increased likelihood of dementia, depression, diminished cognitive ability, and even suicide. Seniors living alone are also easy prey for bad characters seeking to take advantage of their diminished capacity. In short, seniors living alone are at risk.

From time to time seniors are discovered living in squalor. It can be a gruesome scene: a senior prone to falling, not bathing, living in filth, not eating properly, and hoarding all sorts of things including old newspapers and garbage. We wonder how such things an happen. Why didn't the senior take advantage of the many available senior housing options that offer safety, security, and human interaction?

How seniors can be allowed to live under such conditions is relatively easy to answer: our system of law, borne from our forefathers' wish to escape the oppression of the Old World, fiercely protects each individual's right to self-determination. Legally, you can't force a competent person to leave her home unless she is a danger to herself or others. To remove an intractable senior from her home may require the involvement of governmental agencies including the courts.

The question of why some seniors refuse to leave their home under virtually any circumstances is more complex. First, they are afraid: afraid of losing control; afraid that they can't afford the cost of new housing, and afraid that their age-related disabilities and perceived loss of physical attractiveness will make them unattractive to their new housing mates. Their home, and the memories it contains, also connects them with their past. Studies show that when given the opportunity to retrieve only one item from their burning home, survey participants overwhelming chose their family photos (even over pets).[171] The reason that we place such a high value on our personal history is that we are our memories.

Food, music, and old movies all trigger memories, but one's home has special meaning. Our home is autobiographical; we decorate and furnish it according to our personal taste, and adorn it with things of personal meaning like pictures of family, gifts received from friends and loved ones, and purchases from our travels near and far. That might explain why we are "appalled" when we see what the new owners "did" to our old house.

Reminiscing of the places and events of our past is more than just daydreaming; it helps ground us to the present, especially as we age. According to Habib Chaudhury, PhD, Canadian expert on aging: Reminiscing about our past allows us to retain our "self-esteem in the face of declining physical and cognitive abilities" and preserves our "self-identity as a foundation of psychological security."[172]

People of all ages reminisce, especially when their self image is threatened. In times of stress and uncertainty, such as divorce, the loss of a job, or death of a spouse, we find comfort remembering better times and past successes. By remembering and re-playing happier times in our life, we are encouraged that we can again experience happiness, competence, and inner security.

Long term memory becomes more important for those with failing short-term memory. Loss of memory, hearing, sight, and cognitive ability all affect one's sense of security and self. Reminiscence provides them with a fertile source of comfort from a time in their life when they were strong and competent. According to Chaudhury, studies have shown that reminiscence increases self-esteem, and reduces agitation, particularly for cognitively impaired and/or institutionalized elderly.[173]

Studies show that attachment to home may be especially important for women who were traditional homemakers. Home is where they cooked, raised their children, and where their late husband held forth. They enjoy the privacy, control, and comfort of their own home, especially if they have a long personal history there. Also, familiarity, routine, and rituals foster a sense of order and security.

SOLITARY CONFINEMENT

Some amount of isolation can be refreshing to a weary soul, but too much isolation, to use an expression, can *"drive you crazy"*. We are social animals by nature and require social interaction to keep us happy, stable, and sane. Our brain relies on social interaction to regulate our thoughts. In the final scene in the movie *A Beautiful Mind,* Professor Nash asks a student to verify whether a man is standing there talking to him. Just as Nash relied on others to help him separate reality from his hallucinations, the brain needs a certain quantity and quality of stimuli to help regulate, direct, and prioritize thought processes. Without it, the random activity of the nervous system goes unchecked. It is as if the brain feeds on itself when no stimuli are available to digest. The brain creates its own reality when none is provided.

Stuart Grassian, M.D., a psychiatrist on the faculty of Harvard Medical School since 1974, and an expert on the effects of solitary confinement, testified in *Madrid v. Gomez* (involving Pelican Bay State Prison, California's "supermax" prison facility) that solitary confinement constitutes cruel and unusual punishment under the Eighth Amendment of the U.S. Constitution. Dr. Grassian testified in support of the proposition that solitary confinement causes severe psychological harm resembling *delirium,* a syndrome characterized by a decreased level of alertness, perceptive and cognitive disturbances, fearfulness, hearing of voices, and paranoid distortions. Dr. Grassian opined that, being confined and isolated results in exacerbation of previously existing mental conditions and creation of mental illness where none before existed.

Although the experience of seniors living alone is qualitatively different from that of involuntary solitary confinement, similar symptoms were observed by Grassian in prisoners of war, hostages, visually and hearing impaired patients, patients confined in ICU, patients undergoing long term immobilization in hospital (e.g. spinal traction patients), Arctic and Antarctic explorers, and pilots during extended solo flights. Despite the differences in the various forms of solitary confinement, some voluntary and some involuntary, the very same syndrome was observed.

Experiments in the early American penal system illustrate the deleterious effects of isolation. Early in American history, no distinction was made between mental illness and criminality. Both were believed to be the product of evil influences and were severely punished. This view of human nature, crime, and punishment began to change by the early 1800s. Superstitions had waned and man had come to be seen as basically good. A more optimistic and humanistic approach began to prevail. It was during this period in the U.S. that large mental hospitals and penitentiaries were born.

Early American penitentiaries practiced strict solitary confinement, with the belief that if those afflicted with mental illness and criminal behavior could only be isolated from the evil influences of the world, they would return to their natural state of goodness. To promote isolation and "healing," prisoners were hooded on arrival and escorted to their cells, where they remained completely isolated.

America's novel approach soon became a model for European prisons. However, it quickly became apparent that the American experiment was a failure, breeding insanity, disease, and death. During a tour of a Philadelphia prison in 1842, a horrified Charles Dickens wrote:

> The system here is rigid, strict and hopeless solitary confinement.... Over the head and face of every prisoner who comes into this melancholy house, a black hood is drawn, and in this dark shroud,... he is led to the cell from which he never again comes forth, until his whole term of imprisonment had expired. He is a man buried alive... dead to everything but torturing anxieties and horrible despair....[174]

Elders often commit themselves to voluntary solitary confinement, jeopardizing their health and exposing themselves to those who would abuse them. Where appropriate, isolated and vulnerable seniors should be persuaded to move to safe and stimulating environments or provided with adequate in-home care.

GRANDMA JOINS THE NFL

The growing appearance of early Alzheimer's disease, dementia, depression, and suicides among former NFL players forced the NFL to address the long-term effects of head trauma on its players.[175] The NFL finally acknowledged the large body of science which had consistently shown that repeated head trauma accelerates the neurodegenerative process normally associated with a much older population.

Measuring memory loss and cognitive function - key symptoms of brain damage – is extremely difficult since each of us starts from a different place educationally, intellectually, and culturally. The key is to establish a baseline or starting point from which changes can be measured.

With a baseline measurement in hand, it is easier to determine whether changes in capacity are normal or are a sign of damage or degeneration. For this reason, the NFL now requires that all players be tested to determine their baseline memory and cognitive abilities. Injured players are periodically re-tested to determine if they have deviated from their baseline measurement.

The American medical establishment should take a page from the NFL playbook and begin baseline testing on seniors. Testing should begin at about age 75 or earlier if there is a family history of AD. Testing should be done by a qualified and trained expert in the fields of psychiatry, neuropsychology, or geropsychology. A baseline for vision, hearing, and speech should also be obtained as they can confound cognitive testing by mistakenly appearing as cognitive or psychological change.

CONCLUSION

Abusers wait to implement their plan until a time when their victim is in a weakened state and dependent on others. Elders are most vulnerable when they begin to suffer symptoms of dementia, including memory issues and diminished cognitive ability. The long pre-clinical period of dementia creates an extended incubation period for predators. Abusers isolate their victims and then engage in increasingly aggressive abuse as their victim's disease progresses and they near death.

To protect elders, professionals and family members must be familiar with the symptoms and progression of dementia. Early detection, perhaps through baseline and periodic testing similar to that employed by the National Football League, increases the opportunity for early treatment and implementation of preventive measures to minimize abuse. Understanding dementia is also critical to understanding testamentary capacity, a concept discussed in Chapter Seven.

We now turn to Part III, *What To Do About It,* to discuss the legal protections and remedies available to prevent inheritance conflict.

PART III

KEY LEGAL THEORIES

TESTAMENTARY CAPACITY 7

"So long as the inner workings of the mind remain beyond our reach, which they clearly now are, behavior must be the basis of assessing capacity."
- Autonomy, Competence, and Informed
  Consent in Long Term Care: Legal and
  Psychological Perspectives[176]

INTRODUCTION

Issues of capacity – the legal ability to understand or to perform a legal act – are critical in the law. Courts must determine whether a defendant has capacity to stand trial, whether a patient is able to give informed consent to medical treatment, whether an individual has capacity to live independently, enter into a contract, or whether a testator has the testamentary capacity to make a will. The capacity to live on one's own and to make personal and financial decisions is discussed in Chapter Nine in the context of guardianship and conservatorship proceedings. The balance of this Chapter addresses the legal capacity necessary to make a will, or *testamentary capacity.*

The right of *testation*, the freedom to choose how one's property is to be disposed of following death, is a fundamental right under Anglo-American law. However, the right is not without limitation. Testamentary capacity is one such limitation dating back at least to the Romans. (The Latin term, *non compos mentis*, denotes someone who lacks the requisite competence to make a will.) The law imposes a capacity requirement to protect testators from making legally binding decisions that they would not have made if they were of sound mind. Looked at this way, the requirement of testamentary capacity, rather than being a limitation on autonomy, instead preserves the testator's true intentions. Testamentary capacity is measured at the precise time of the making of the will.[177] A will executed when the testator lacked testamentary capacity is invalid and legally void.

Although the requirements vary from state to state, four basic elements of testamentary capacity are nearly uniformly required. First, the testator must be able to understand the nature of his testamentary act. In other words, he must comprehend that he is making a decision to distribute his legacy after his death. Second, he must be able to understand the natural objects of his bounty – that is, his blood and marital family. Third, he must be able to understand the nature and extent of his property. Finally, and perhaps the most difficult, he must be able to make a rational plan for disposing of his property while keeping the first three elements in mind. It is not necessary that the testator *actually* understand the four elements; it is only necessary that he have the *capacity* or ability to do so.

Lack of testamentary capacity is the second most common legal basis for setting aside a will, following close behind undue influence,[178] the subject of Chapter Eight. However, despite its wide assertion, attempts to set aside wills solely on the basis of lack of testamentary capacity are rarely successful.[179] There are several reasons why challenging testamentary capacity is a complex and difficult task. They include:

- A strong legal presumption in favor of the competency of testators;
- Logistical and evidentiary difficulties in proving that the testator lacked capacity at the very moment of execution;
- Lack of a definitive and widely accepted medical test to measure testamentary capacity;
- Lack of an equivalent medical model for the legal concept of testamentary capacity; and
- Judicially created fictions of *insane delusion* and *lucid interval.*

The general public and, unfortunately, many attorneys fail to appreciate the difficulty in setting aside a will based on lack of testamentary capacity. Many incorrectly believe that a simple diagnosis of dementia or Alzheimer's disease, or mere evidence of failing health or memory are dispositive proof that a loved one lacks testamentary capacity. Frustrated with this common misunderstanding, the California Court of Appeals in the case *Estate of Mann* observed:

> It has been held over and over…that old age, feebleness, forgetfulness, filthy personal habits, personal eccentricities, failure to recognize old friends or relatives, physical disability, absent-mindedness, and mental confusion, do not furnish grounds for holding that a testator lacked testamentary capacity.[180]

The findings of Eunice Ross and Thomas Reed in their treatise *Will Contests,* provide startling evidence of the low success rate of cases challenging testamentary capacity. In their study of hundreds of appellate cases across the country, they found that *seventy-five* percent of the wills of aged, infirm, and senile testators were upheld; that *eighty* percent of the wills of alcoholics and persons subject to a legal guardianship were upheld; and that *ninety* percent of the wills of drug addicts were upheld. Incredibly, nearly *fifty* percent of the wills of persons adjudicated *insane* were ultimately upheld.[181] These stark findings should be a warning to any contestant seeking to overturn a will solely on the basis that the testator lacked testamentary capacity.

PROPER EXECUTION OF A WILL

Compliance with prevailing legal formalities for executing a will, or *due execution,* is an important factor in proving a will.[182] Recognizing the difficulty in proving the state of mind of the testator at the very moment of execution, courts have come to rely heavily on the integrity of the execution process. Proper execution creates a strong presumption of the testator's capacity and the will's validity. In most states, proper execution requires that the testator be at least eighteen years old and have personally signed his or her will in the presence of at least two disinterested witnesses. If the testator is unable to sign, the majority of states allow someone to sign on the testator's behalf, as long as it is at the direction of the testator and in his conscious presence. Some states require a notary or a third witness to the testator's signature.

Generally, illiteracy does not affect testamentary capacity if the testator knows the contents of the will.

Witnesses, too, must meet minimum requirements. In addition to being the age of majority, witnesses to a will must be *generally competent and credible*. A beneficiary or a spouse of a beneficiary should not act as a witness as they have a vested interest in the outcome and therefore may not be credible. Although most states permit such *interested parties* to serve as witnesses (an interested party is one who takes more under the will than without it), it is good practice not to allow family members and those taking under the will to act as a witness.

Witnesses have historically provided the first line of defense in protecting the integrity of the testamentary process. As testamentary capacity is measured at the exact moment of execution, witnesses are uniquely positioned to attest to the capacity of the testator as well as to the circumstances under which the signing occurred. The Romans required seven witnesses for proper execution.[183] Later, the Anglo-American law required three witnesses.[184] Now, as noted, the majority of states require two witnesses to validate a will.

Modern courts also place heavy weight on the testimony of the attorney who prepared the will.[185] Next in importance are medical witnesses and care providers, followed by expert witnesses. Generally, very little weight is given to the testimony of friends and neighbors.[186]

The drafting attorney is valued as a witness since presumably he or she had direct personal knowledge of the testator's intentions and can describe the testator's general abilities and demeanor at the time of signing. The same can be said of attesting witnesses. Naturally, these assumptions break down when the attorney or witnesses have split loyalties or are working in concert with an influencer or abuser, which may have been the case with Brooke Astor. Brooke's attorneys appear to have been taking their direction from Brooke's son Tony Marshall, turning a blind eye to Brooke's severely diminished state.

Little weight is placed on the testimony of friends and neighbors and others not present at the signing. Friends and neighbors are typically not privy to the testator's most intimate thoughts. It is almost cliché that news reports quote neighbors of heinous criminals like Jeffrey Dahmer or Son of Sam saying things like *"he seemed like such a nice man who kept up his yard and always waved to the neighbors."*

Expert testimony is a recent development in the context of the long history of free testation. The weight accorded to expert witnesses depends on whether the expert knew the testator and whether the expert examined the testator at or near the time of the will execution *(contemporaneous evaluations)*.[187] The testimony of treating physicians and clinicians is given higher weight, as treaters are considered to have had sufficient opportunity to know the testator. With some exceptions discussed below, much less weight is given to the testimony of experts hired after the death of the testator. Courts are skeptical of the "forensic" conclusions of "hired guns" asked to interpret medical records after the fact. Also, with no current medical model for testamentary capacity, courts are not convinced that there is sound medical evidence for their testimony. One commentator stated this point succinctly:

> The value of expert testimony is generally negligible. This reflects a skepticism about the objectivity of experts retained in a partisan battle as well as a sense that the science underlying mental health professionals is insufficiently precise to merit consideration.[188]

The execution requirements for trusts are not as clearly delineated as those for wills. In many states, trusts need not be witnessed. Some states require notarization for trusts only if they own real estate. Trusts that meet the formal execution requirements applicable to wills are easier to defend. It is perhaps for this reason that most trusts are both witnessed and notarized in compliance with state law pertaining to wills. If a trust owns real estate, the best practice is to have the trust executed using the same formalities as required for deeds.

Although we think of trusts in much the same way as we think of wills, they are fundamentally different. While a will takes effect at death, trusts are a lifetime agreement (it is for this reason they are referred to as *living*) between the *grantor* (the maker of a trust) and the *trustee* (which may also be the grantor). Trusts are therefore more in the nature of a *contract* than a testamentary document. As lifetime contracts, courts have historically applied the higher contract standard of competency. This higher standard, however, is beginning to erode as modern trusts have evolved to be more in the nature of testamentary instruments akin to wills.

The higher *contract* standard of competency applies to transactions involving contracts, bank accounts, real estate transfer (deeds), gifts, powers of attorney, and trusts. To legally enter into a contract, the contracting party must understand the legal effect of the instrument and its effect on his property; the more complex the contract, the higher the standard of capacity.

As evidence of the evolving role of trusts, courts routinely apply the much lower testamentary capacity standard to deeds and trusts when executed as part of an estate plan. It is speculated that the reason for this departure is to avoid the incongruous result that would occur if a testator's will were upheld but his deeds, trust, or gifts made as part of the same estate plan were voided.[189] Perhaps in recognition of this practicality, the Uniform Trust Code of 2000 takes the enlightened and emerging view that trusts are more appropriately subject to the lower standard of testamentary capacity applicable to wills rather than the traditionally higher contract standard. Whatever their original purpose, trusts have come to be used as testamentary devices indistinguishable from wills and therefore should require the same standard of capacity.

Other *will substitutes* like beneficiary designations, deeds conferring survivorship rights, pay-on-death (POD) and transfer-on-death (TOD) designations typically do not need to be witnessed or notarized – many may even be submitted on-line. The reason for the lower execution standard is that such will substitutes have historically been viewed not as testamentary dispositions but as contracts executed in the regular course of business. Although it may seem odd that such important instruments need not be witnessed, it is thought that the higher level of capacity required to enter into a contract provides adequate protection to the maker, and the safeguards of proper execution are therefore not necessary.

HISTORY OF TESTAMENTARY CAPACITY

The concept of testamentary capacity has evolved over the centuries and in the last century in particular. Under Roman law, a free person lacked testamentary capacity if he or she was *defectum mentis,* insane (and not experiencing a *lucid moment* at the time of execution), deaf, dumb, or under the age of fourteen. Medieval canonists added the requirement that only one who was legally free could make a will, depriving felons and slaves of such a right.[190]

By the late 1500s, four classes of persons were prohibited from making a will: those who lacked discretion, such as *idiots, minors, drunkards,* and the *senile;* those who lacked legal or social freedom such as prisoners and married women; the physically handicapped such as the *blind, deaf,* and *dumb;* and *criminals.* An *idiot* in the 1500s was defined as a person "who notwithstanding he be of lawful age, yet he is so witless, that he cannot number to twenty, nor can tell what age he is of, nor knoweth who is father or mother, nor is able to answer any such easy question…"[191] A *dull-witted* man could make a will so long as he had the understanding of a 10 or 11 year old.[192]

In the 1800s, the *mentally ill* were feared as evil, possessed of spirits, and a danger to normal, God-fearing people. They were routinely isolated and often abused or killed. The *mentally retarded* were divided into three groups: *idiots, morons, and imbeciles.* An *idiot* was deemed to possess the mental acuity of a two to seven year old. A *moron* had the mental ability of a child between the ages of seven and twelve, and an *imbecile* had the mental capacity of someone more than age twelve but less than someone of their attained age. The civil rights of the mentally ill and developmentally disabled, including the right to make a will, were withheld completely.

MODERN TEST

The pejorative labels once assigned to the mentally ill and the developmentally disabled have been done away with and the standards refined. Today, mental retardation is categorized as *slight, moderate,* and *severe.* The civil rights of all but the most impaired are now protected. The modern conception of testamentary capacity applies one standard to all testators. It is a subjective test that focuses on the understanding of the particular testator in question and requires knowledge that is commensurate with the complexity of the task at hand.

The modern legal standard for testamentary capacity originated in several early English cases, the most important of which is *Greenwood v. Greenwood* (1790). The *Greenwood* standard was intended to apply only to senile testators but has become the yardstick by which all testators are measured. The *Greenwood* court confirmed the principle that the time to measure testamentary capacity is the very moment of execution:

[T]he inquiry and the single inquiry in the case is, whether he was of sound and disposing mind and memory at the time when he made his will; however deranged he might be before, if he had recovered his reason at that time, he was competent to make his will.... If he had a power of summoning up his mind so as to know what his property was, and who those persons were that then were the objects of his bounty, then he was competent to make his will.[193]

As noted above, testamentary capacity has evolved to require that the testator possess four capacities. He must have the ability to understand the nature of the testamentary act, know the natural objects of his bounty, know the nature and extent of his property; and be able to make a rational plan for disposing of his property while keeping the first three elements in mind.

In addition to these four legal elements, many states also require that the testator be free of delusions and hallucinations, sometimes referred to as the *insane delusion* rule. However, in order for a will to be invalidated, the psychotic symptoms of an insane delusion must be shown to have caused the person to devise his or her property in a way that is a departure from what he would have done in the absence of the symptoms. In other words, to be invalidated, the will must be the product of insane delusion. For example, in the *Hargrove* case[194] the will of a decedent who incorrectly believed that the two children born of his marriage were not his was determined to be the product of an insane delusion for the reason that he was not able to know the natural objects of his bounty.

A trained estate planning attorney should ask the testator a series of questions intended to elicit evidence that the requirements for testamentary capacity have been met. Put to the testator in the presence of the attesting witnesses, typical questions include whether the testator has come to the meeting of his or her free will (this question is intended to identify possible undue influence); whether the testator is aware of the specific documents he or she is signing (e.g., will, trust, powers of attorney, deeds, etc.); and whether the testator understands the effect of signing the documents (e.g., which beneficiaries will benefit). It is customary for the attorney to also briefly summarize the testator's assets and ask the testator if his description is a fair depiction of those assets. For evidentiary reasons, it is advisable that the attorney follow the same script and ask the same questions to each testator. Asking the same questions allows the attorney, in deposition or trial, to rely on a description of his or her customary practices rather than be required to recall the verbatim exchange with the testator on the date of execution (a nearly impossible undertaking).

NATURE OF THE TESTAMENTARY ACT

The testator must understand that the will he is signing governs the transfer of his property and that it comes into effect at his death. The general rule is that proper execution creates a presumption that the testator knew the contents of the will. However, simply answering the attorney's question in the affirmative is not sufficient, alone, to support a finding that the testator is competent. Nor is the testator's signature on the document evidence of understanding, as a signature is an autonomic behavior that does not require thought. Reading the will prior to execution is not essential to establish understanding, but can provide strong support for the proposition that the testator knew what he was signing.

NATURAL OBJECTS OF BOUNTY

Knowing the natural object of one's bounty does not require that the testator recall his family by name or the degree of kinship; it only requires that he recall his love for them.[195] On its face the requirement that one know the objects of one's bounty appears straightforward. However, such determination often carries with it societal prejudices, which invite us to look more closely at the concept of what is *natural*. Black's Law Dictionary reflects the prejudice in favor of the traditional modern family when it defines "natural objects of testator's bounty" as those people who would take under the laws of intestacy.[196] The *Kaufman*[197] case illustrates the inherent societal prejudices at play in determining what is "natural." Kaufman was a furniture heir who in the 1950s left his fortune to his male companion of many years who Kaufman acknowledged helped facilitate his "sexual and creative expression." The court set aside Kaufman's will despite his explicit wishes expressed in both his formal estate plan and in a separate writing.

The practice persists of denying the wishes of testators who practice alternate lifestyles. We can only speculate as to the reasons for such predispositions. Perhaps it is adherence to a traditional, even medieval, view of family; the unspoken and perhaps unconscious preference for beneficiaries with the greatest genetic relatedness to the decedent; or the civic responsibility of government-paid judges to not disinherit family members who at some point could become a burden on the state.

The implied moral obligation to leave to one's family dates to a time when wills were procured by the church on the testator's deathbed. Wills were thus influenced by Christian religious views of obligation to one's family. Generally speaking, courts consider one's legal heirs (identified in states' intestate statutes) as the natural objects of a testator's bounty.

Pamela Champine in her study of will contests, concludes that the identity of one's beneficiary is the single most important factor in determining the outcome of a will contest.[198] Wills that benefit socially acceptable beneficiaries, as represented by state intestacy statutes, are likely to be upheld, while those leaving to less socially acceptable beneficiaries are not. Champine identifies this practice as *circular logic:*[199] A testator whose will resembles that of his neighbor is considered to possess capacity but a testator who leaves to "unnatural" beneficiaries does not.

NATURE AND EXTENT OF PROPERTY

The testator need not be able to specifically recall each item he or she owns; he or she only need possess the *capacity* to recall such property.[200] Intact long-term memory would allow the testator to remember his home, his retirement assets, and all but recently acquired assets. The testator need not know the exact value of assets, only their relative value.

RATIONAL PLAN

Of the four elements of testamentary capacity, forming a rational plan requires the highest level of cognitive ability. Utilizing intact *executive function,* the testator must be able to express a basic plan for distributing his assets to his intended heirs. Forming a rational plan integrates all of the elements of testamentary capacity and thus requires that all of the underlying cognitive abilities be present.

PRESUMPTION OF SANITY

The law presumes that adults possess the capacity to undertake any legal task, unless they have been formally adjudicated as incapacitated. A party challenging an adult's capacity must put forward sufficient evidence of incapacity to overcome the presumption. An analogous and perhaps more familiar circumstance exists in the criminal realm where an accused is presumed innocent until proven guilty.[201] Another presumption is that the testator of a properly executed will possessed the capacity to complete the act, and that it was an act of free will. This second presumption places extremely high evidentiary value on the testimony of witnesses to the will and the drafting attorney, and substantially increases the burden on a contestant not present at the signing.

LUCID INTERVAL

Attorney and psychologist Marson states that, "[a] lucid interval is a transient period of apparent mental clarity (or at least capacity) during which an otherwise incompetent adult can validly execute legal documents,"[202] but cautions, "from a clinical standpoint, the lucid interval may be more a legal fiction used by attorneys and judges in difficult cases, than it is an actual clinical reality."[203]

The lucid interval doctrine gives special weight, perhaps undue weight, to the testimony of witnesses present at execution. In a 2009 Michigan Court of Appeals decision,[204] the court placed greater weight on the drafting attorney's opinion as to the testator's capacity than that of the testator's treating psychiatrist. Reflecting an outdated view of the field of psychiatry and the lag between advancements in medicine and changes in the law, the Michigan Court of Appeals reiterated the long-held view of the Michigan Supreme Court that "the opinion of a physician as to mental competency, aside from the question of insanity, is entitled to no greater consideration than that of a layman having equal facilities for observation."[205]

TESTAMENTARY CAPACITY –
THE LOWEST THRESHOLD

Of the legal capacities, testamentary capacity requires the lowest level of cognizance. There are two reasons for the low threshold: First, as a society we place a high value on testamentary freedom; and second, the consequences of getting it wrong are relatively low. A dead testator no longer needs his assets and therefore requires less protection. In contrast, a living testator who mismanages his finances, gives away his assets, or enters into unfavorable contracts jeopardizes his financial independence and places his future at risk. Society has a vested interest in protecting such individuals from their own ill-advised acts both for their own protection and to prevent them from becoming a burden on the state.

Testamentary capacity is a lower standard than that required for the appointment of a guardian and certainly for a conservator. A person who has been adjudged incompetent to make his own personal and financial decisions may nonetheless possess testamentary capacity, as he may nonetheless be aware of whom he loves, the nature of his assets, and be able to formulate a rational plan.

Though similar, the making of a valid *gift* during life requires a higher level of capacity than that required to make a will. As the donor is necessarily deprived of the future use of gifted asset, he could thus be permanently injured by gifting assets necessary for his care and survival. To sustain the validity of lifetime gifts, the *donee* (the recipient of a gift) must show three things: that the *donor* (the gifting party) intended to make a gift; the donor delivered the gift to the donee; and the donee accepted the gift. *Delivery* is proof that the donor intended to give up control of the gifted property.[206] Courts have consistently overturned gifts for failure of delivery where the donor placed stocks or deeds in a drawer or safe deposit box to be removed at death.[207]

MULTIFACETED CAPACITY

In recent years, the medical community has made significant advancements in its understanding of the brain and its ability to measure capacity. With the help of modern imaging devices they are now able to physically see the brain at work. They know that the brain is multi-faceted with different parts controlling various capabilities. Capacity is no longer viewed in a global all-or-nothing proposition.[208] As a result, we no longer speak in the broad parlance of *competence* versus *incompetence*. We now speak in terms of whether the subject has the *capacity* to complete a particular task.

Laypersons find it troublesome and counter-intuitive that a valid will can be created by someone with dementia, Alzheimer's, by an alcoholic or addict, or by someone for whom a guardian or conservator has been appointed. The apparent incongruity can be explained by the fact that the general deficiencies that gave rise to their particular diagnosis or handicap do not address the specific functional ability required to meet the test of testamentary capacity.[209]

Individuals with dementia do not lack testamentary capacity on the basis of their diagnosis alone.[210] Dementia is a progressive degenerative disease affecting different parts of the brain. Whether a dementia affects testamentary capacity depends on a number of factors, including the underlying cause of the dementia as well as the progression of the disease. While a mildly demented Alzheimer's patient (the most common cause of dementia) may possess testamentary capacity, testamentary capacity can be significantly impaired as the disease progresses.

Those with *mild* dementia experience significant impairment of almost all financial functions. Patients at this stage typically recognize family members and can comprehend the value of their assets. They therefore likely possess the testamentary capacity to do a will, create a trust, make gifts and execute other estate planning documents and will substitutes.

In the *moderate* stages of dementia, the individual can no longer perform complex activities (handle medications, drive, prepare meals, or use the telephone without help). Typically they can care for themselves only with prompting (like needing to be reminded to change their clothes and to bathe). Although their distant memory may be largely intact, they may confuse the details or the order in which events occurred. Patients with moderate dementia cannot live by themselves as their judgment is too impaired to leave them unattended. It is extremely unlikely that someone with moderate dementia possesses testamentary capacity. Their dependence also makes them extremely susceptible to undue influence (described in Chapter Eight).

Those with *severe* dementia can no longer control their bowels or bladder.

They often lose weight and cannot speak in full sentences. Sometimes in this stage they become delusional, believing things about other people that are not true. They often believe that people are stealing from them; they want to go "home"; and mistake their spouse for their mother or a child for a spouse. Those with advanced dementia clearly do not possess testamentary capacity.

THE LEGAL-MEDICAL DILEMMA

Determining capacity is a complex and imprecise endeavor involving an unnatural marriage of legal and medical concepts. Capacity is a *legal* question in that it is defined by the courts and legislature. Capacity is *medically* significant because the medical profession treats the diseases that affect capacity, such as schizophrenia, depression, bi-polar disease, and dementia.

Problems arise from the fact that the legal measure of capacity differs substantially from the medical model. Determining legal capacity with medical tools is like trying to use metric wrenches on a 1960 Buick. The law attempts to measure *functional* capacity; that is, the ability to perform a particular task or function like the ability to make one's own medical and financial decisions, or the ability to make a will.[211] The orientation of the medical profession, more particularly neuropsychologists, is to first diagnose and then to treat disease. It categorizes capacity based on its impact on domains such as attention, language, memory, abstract thinking, executive function, mood, and personality.[212]

The legal definition of capacity seeks a black or white, yes or no, conclusion to the question: does (or did) the subject have capacity to perform the task or not? The medical view of capacity is much more nuanced. It looks at the gradations and progression of disease with no bright line delineating capacity from incapacity. There is no medical sign saying you are now leaving New York and entering New Jersey.

The following diagram[213] illustrates the contrast between the legal and medical models of capacity:

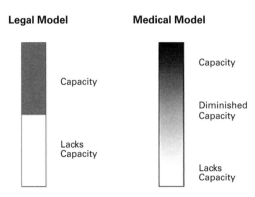

CAPACITY

Contrary to popular belief, most treating physicians (other than mental health professionals) are not trained or qualified to assess legal capacity. They are not paid by insurers to routinely assess capacity, and perhaps for this reason are not proficient at it. Despite their lack of training and difference in orientation, treating physicians are routinely asked by courts to opine on matters of legal capacity. Attorneys are even less qualified. With little or no training or expertise, attorneys are regularly called upon to testify as to their client's capacity. Worse, untrained are unqualified *guardians ad litem* (who are most often attorneys appointed by courts) are asked to assess the capacity of subjects they have only met briefly. Ironically, in apparent deference to their respective professions, attorneys tend to view doctors as the most qualified to assess capacity while doctors properly view capacity as a legal question. With structural deficits in both the legal and medical camps, it can be a case of the blind leading the blind. It is thus not surprising that treating physicians, like those testifying in the Brooke Astor case, are reticent to make determinations of testamentary capacity even when pressed by the courts.

Determining capacity is more an art than a science. Qualified mental health professionals rely on a number of factors in making their clinical determinations. In addition to interviews with the subject and family members, psychologists rely on a number of accepted psychological tests that measure various cognitive abilities including memory, comprehension, communication, mental flexibility, and the ability to calculate.[214] They also test for a variety of behavioral and emotional factors, including anxiety, depression, and dementia.

A medical diagnosis is relevant in determining capacity; however, because a medical diagnosis conveys no specific functional information, it cannot by itself be dispositive of the question of capacity. Decision makers must go further and link their clinical observations and test results to the capacities with which the law is concerned.[215] Contrary to the view of the Michigan Court of Appeals, trained medical professionals familiar with the legal standard of capacity and experienced in applying their clinical knowledge to the legal standard can be valuable and persuasive witnesses.

CONTEMPORANEOUS MENTAL EXAMINATION

The weight attached to the testimony of health professionals varies widely. The most significant factor is the temporal proximity of the professional's examination to the act in question. Contemporary assessments are much more influential than assessments made well before the date of execution, and yet again more significant than a forensic or *neuropsychological autopsy* of an incompetent or deceased testator.[216]

The case of the *Estate of Garrett v. Garrett*[217] is an example of the great weight accorded to contemporaneous mental examinations. In Garrett, the testator's daughter Joni contested her father's will, claiming that her father lacked testamentary capacity and that his will was procured through undue influence. On February 8, 2000, Joe Garrett, gravely ill and in the hospital, directed his second wife, Carolynne, to contact his brother, Larry, to have Larry assist him in procuring a will. Larry had been Joe's CPA and financial advisor for many years. Larry called an attorney with whom Joe had previously consulted and directed the attorney to fax Joe's estate plan revisions directly to the hospital, which the attorney did on February 12, 2000. Joe's treating physician performed a competency evaluation and determined that Joe was competent to sign his will. At the signing, Larry read Joe the contents of the will which was then witnessed by Joe's nurse and a hospital social worker. Wife Carolynne and other relatives were also in the room. At the trial, all of the witnesses to the execution testified that Joe was fully competent and was not subject to any undue influence at the time he signed the will.[218] The treating physician testified that she had performed the standardized mini-mental examination prior to Joe's execution of the will, and that Joe received the maximum score. The court found the contemporaneous mental exam persuasive despite Joe's rapidly declining health and participation of parties who stood to benefit under the will in the procurement and execution process.

CONCLUSION

Challenges to wills solely on the basis that the testator lacked testamentary capacity have an exceedingly low success rate. The great weight placed on the testimony of witnesses present at the execution of the will, and on the testimony of the drafting attorney, places contestants not present at the signing at a distinct disadvantage. They must prove by circumstantial or forensic medical evidence that the testator lacked testamentary capacity at the exact moment of signing. The fact that there is no single definitive medical test to determine capacity only adds to their burden.

Medical experts are a valuable tool in litigation. However, courts generally place less weight on expert medical testimony where the expert did not treat the testator at or near the time of execution. Conversely, high value is accorded to the medical testimony of treating professionals who have a history with the testator or who treated the testator somewhat contemporaneously with the event in question. Contestants who must rely on forensic evidence are advised to seek a mental health professional experienced in applying their clinical observations to the legal definition of capacity. As suggested in Chapter Six, elders should receive regular psychological assessments to both mitigate the effects of disease and build a case against those who would use an elder's declining capacity for their own gain. Chapter Eight, which follows, illustrates why testamentary capacity challenges are almost always combined with a claim that the testator was subject to undue influence.

UNDUE INFLUENCE | 8

"It is impossible to set forth all the various combinations of factors and circumstances that are sufficient to make out a case of undue influence because the possibilities are as limitless as the imagination of the adroit and cunning."
- Matter of Coley's Will [219]

Patty Hearst

INTRODUCTION

Undue influence is the theft of free choice by a person of trust. It is a deliberate act of usurpation. The influencer attempts to replace his victim's thoughts with the influencer's own in furtherance of the influencer's agenda. Undue influence is a form of elder abuse that begins with the trusted influencer gaining the confidence of his vulnerable victim. The influencer then violates that trust by coercing his victim either to gift or bequeath assets to the influencer.

No group is more susceptible to undue influence than elders. When asked why he robbed banks, notorious bank robber Willie Sutton purportedly responded "because that's where the money is." Later he denied ever making that statement, saying that he robbed banks because he "liked to." Willie's quote and misquote are both apropos: people exploit the elderly because they have the money - Americans older than fifty control at least seventy percent of the nation's household net worth – and because it gives them a sense of empowerment.

INFLUENCE

We are all subject to influence by others. Consciously or unconsciously, our thoughts and beliefs are impacted by those around us, including teachers, advertisers, media commentators, friends, and family. In a free society, we evaluate information presented to us and formulate our own conclusions. Choice, however, can only be truly free if the information we receive has not been deliberately manipulated, and we are of sufficiently sound mind to sort fact from fiction. Under normal conditions we use common sense and healthy skepticism to ferret out bad information and to discern the hidden motives of the messenger. We know that a salesman is trying to sell us something so we carefully scrutinize his pitch. A clear thinking consumer may ultimately buy the salesman's product, but only after verifying his claims and doing some comparison shopping.

We adjust our level of skepticism to the level of trust we have in the information or the messenger. We place a higher value on information we receive from family and friends, from whom we expect honesty and loyalty. We drop our guard and suspend suspicion when dealing with people we trust.

Undue influence occurs when someone close to us violates our trust by using his special relationship to further his own interests. The law recognizes the vulnerability of the victims of undue influence and protects them. Undue influence destroys the free will of the victim, thereby making his actions not his own. Undue influence is grounds for invalidating gifts, wills, and trusts procured as the product of the undue influence of another.

THE LAW

What constitutes undue influence varies from state to state, as does the level of proof required of the *contestant.* Most states require that the influencer exert some type of domination or control over the victim aimed at destroying the victim's free will. Rarely do the cases involve physical coercion. Instead, influencers typically employ persistent flattery and suggestion.

Undue influence as a cause of action dates back to the reign of Elizabeth I of England (1533 – 1603). The doctrine was the product of common law and was first invoked to set aside death bed wills prepared by a person importuning the dying man for a legacy. Swinburne, in his 1590 treatise, advocated the setting aside of wills induced "by fear of bodily harm from another through fraud on the testator or by flaterie of someone seeking a legacy."

A claim of undue influence usually depends almost entirely on circumstantial evidence. The victim may have already passed away, or if alive, cannot or will not testify against the influencer. Despite these challenges, undue influence is by far the most commonly asserted ground for invalidating a will, a trust, or deed. The assertion of undue influence is especially valuable where there is not sufficient evidence to challenge the testator's testamentary capacity. When undue influence can be proven, the unfairly procured gift or bequest is exposed for the theft it truly is.

Different as snowflakes, undue influence turns on the facts and circumstances of each case. To set aside a will or other document, the undue influence must be directly connected with the act of execution and must operate at the time of the execution. The relationship of the parties is key. Courts are much more likely to find undue influence where one party is stronger in mind and body than the other and where a fiduciary relationship exists as a matter of law or fact.

Eunice Ross and Thomas Reed, in their legal treatise *Will Contests,* identify five general elements present in a successful claim of undue influence:

1. The testator was *susceptible* to the influence of others;
2. The testator and the alleged influencer had some type of *confidential relationship;*
3. The alleged influencer *used that confidential relationship* in order to secure a change in the testator's post-death distribution of property;
4. The testator *actually changed* the distribution plan as a result of the alleged influencer's actions; and
5. The change *was unconscionable.*

Let's examine the five common elements more closely:

SUSCEPTIBILITY

Courts look at the mental and physical condition of the victim. They will generally not find undue influence over a mentally and physically vigorous individual even if there has been some coercion on the part of the influencer. In contrast, courts are much more likely to find undue influence where the victim is physically ill, has dementia, is an alcoholic, or has some other form of physical or mental impairment.

Susceptibility is not identical to testamentary capacity for two reasons. First, the contestant need not show susceptibility at the actual time of execution of the will. The testator's weakened mental or physical condition over a long period of time prior to will execution is much more legally relevant. Second, the degree of impairment necessary to find the testator susceptible to influence is much less than that required to show that the testator lacked testamentary capacity.[220]

CONFIDENTIAL RELATIONSHIP

Most states define confidential relationship as a relationship in which the victim puts special trust and confidence in the influencer. The confidential relationship may exist as a matter of law as is the case between client and attorney, guardian and ward, trustee and trustor, or principal and agent. A confidential relationship may also be inferred from all facts and circumstances, and can be found to exist with family members, neighbors, attorneys, doctors, clergymen, investment advisors, home health care workers, and nursing home administrators.[221]

USE OF CONFIDENTIAL RELATIONSHIP

Proving that the alleged influencer used his confidential relationship to alter the victim's wishes is the most difficult element of undue influence. Direct evidence is rarely available since acts of undue influence occur over time and most often outside the scrutinizing eyes of witnesses. The best evidence of use of the confidential relationship can usually be found in the circumstances surrounding the procurement of the will. In order to ensure that their influence comes to fruition, and leaving nothing to chance, influencers follow their plan to completion by assisting their victims in preparing their wills, deeds or other transfers. When an attorney is used to prepare legal documents, the influencer will often secure an attorney of his choosing and attend all planning conferences including the execution ceremony.

Some influencers, preferring to maintain complete secrecy, forego the assistance of professionals. Instead, they add their name to the victim's bank accounts, or prepare deeds, wills and other estate planning documents downloaded from the Internet. If witnesses are needed, they co-opt their friends and acquaintances who are frequently unaware of the effect of the acts they are witnessing. Influencers commonly procure and prepare documents that the victim need only sign. Where the victims can no longer sign their name, as was the case with Brooke Astor's third will amendment, influencers may even relieve them of that task by signing for them.

ACTUAL CHANGE

Proof that the influencer altered the victim's wishes can be shown by comparing the newly procured documents to previous versions of wills, deeds, and beneficiary designations. For this reason it is important for families and attorneys to save copies of all of previous estate planning documents.

UNCONSCIONABLE

What is considered unconscionable in the realm of inheritance conduct is naturally quite subjective. Historically, courts have shown a proclivity to set aside wills that disinherit loved ones. As noted in Chapter Seven, greater scrutiny is brought to bear on wills that deviate from the intestate laws of the jurisdiction. The competency of the testator and the level of influence will be more closely scrutinized where the will's disposition is illogical, irrational, or inexplicable.

Determining what is fair and what is unconscionable is well within the ample equitable powers granted to probate courts. There is inherent danger, however, when courts attempt to determine what is morally just. What we as a society consider unjust or unnatural is subject to change over time. While courts in the early 1800s upheld legacies to white mistresses, slave concubines, and their illegitimate offspring, such bequests were presumed to be the product of undue influence during the Civil War and reconstruction. By World War I, courts again returned to the view that transfers to mistresses were not the product of undue influence. While legacies to gay lovers in the 1960s were presumed to be unnatural (as in *In re Estate of Kaufmann*), we might expect a different result today. Allowing probate courts to look behind the stated wishes of testators is a slippery slope and a potential threat to testamentary freedom. However, on balance, we accept the fact that courts must necessarily make the subjective determination of what the testator *"would have wanted"* to prevent testamentary freedom from becoming a virtual Switzerland to which influencers could retreat.

BURDEN OF PROOF AND REBUTTABLE PRESUMPTIONS

Burden of proof is the minimum amount of evidence a contestant must proffer in order to prevail. In criminal matters, the state must prove its case *beyond a reasonable doubt.* In civil matters, *clear and convincing evidence* or *preponderance of the evidence* is required depending on the case and the jurisdiction. Unfortunately, there is no uniformity among the states as to a contestant's burden of proof in an undue influence contest.

Evidentiary *presumptions* are available in undue influence cases to aid contestants who must meet their burden of proof. To invoke the presumption of undue influence, contestants must first establish that: 1. A confidential or fiduciary relationship existed between the testator and the alleged influencer; 2. A will was prepared or procured with the participation of the influencer; and 3. That the influencer unduly benefited from the will thus procured. If the minimum proofs are offered, the law will *presume* that undue influence did in fact occur. The burden to show that the testator was not unduly influenced then shifts to the proponent (the party defending the validity of a will). If the proponent produces sufficient evidence to rebut the presumption (in the form of credible witnesses, medical testimony, etc.) then the presumption is defeated. Although the overall burden of proof remains with contestant/plaintiff, the proponent/defendant must produce substantial evidence on its own behalf in order to avoid losing its case on the presumption alone.

THE VICTIM

Statistically, the typical victim of undue influence is over the age of seventy-five, female, and unmarried. She also has some form of cognitive impairment and usually suffers from physical, mental, or emotional dysfunction (especially depression) which makes her dependent on others.

Victims tend to live alone, or with the influencer, and are isolated from the outside world. They are physically or psychologically dependent on the influencer. Those with children are most often estranged from some or all of them. Victims tend to be financially independent with no designated financial caretakers or natural beneficiaries; are taking multiple medications; are frail; and are afraid of being sent to a nursing home.

A surviving spouse who relied on his or her deceased spouse for companionship and decision-making will likely be vulnerable to an influencer who positions him or her self as confidant and provider. Individuals of advanced age who are alone are prone to feelings of loneliness and depression. Depression leads to problems with attention, concentration, memory, and other cognitive functions. Depressed individuals may suffer from sleep disturbances, lack of energy, apathy, and social withdrawal. Depressed victims are also more likely to give up hope and abandon efforts to free themselves from the grasp of their influencers.

STOCKHOLM SYNDROME

A number of factors conspire to keep elder abuse and undue influence a dirty little secret. According to the 1996 National Elder Abuse Incidence Study (NEAIS), as much as seventy-five to eighty percent of elder abuse cases go unreported. Embarrassment, brainwashing, and fear of abandonment all contribute to the non-reporting by the victim.

Other factors further deter the reporting of abuse. Victims who realize that they have been duped are embarrassed to report the abuse, especially if the perpetrator is a family member or trusted friend. They are often overwhelmed by the thought of using the legal system, and are afraid they will be put into a nursing home if others learn of their vulnerability. They also lose confidence in their own judgment.

Victims frequently develop strong emotional bonds with their abusers, much like the Swedish bank hostages in 1973 who fought off police sent to rescue them in what has come to be known as the *Stockholm Syndrome*.[222] Famed newspaper heiress Patti Hearst is another example of the hostage/captor connection. After being kidnapped and held for ransom in 1974 she later joined the militant cause of her captors. Brainwashed victims initially deny that any abuse has taken place and may even defend their influencer. Victims believe that they are at great risk if their valued relationship with their abuser ends. Similar identification is also found in cases of incest victims, physically abused children, and prisoners of war.

For a number of reasons, relatives may not intervene even when they perceive that a vulnerable loved one is being manipulated. They may be suspicious but feel they are unable to prove their suspicions; they may feel that it is not their place to intervene; or they may have already severed ties with their loved one as a result of the relationship poisoning initiated by the influencer. Regardless of the reason, the exploitation is likely to continue if there is no intervention.

THE INFLUENCER

Influencers, whether due to resentment, repressed anger, or other rationalization, come to believe that they are entitled to the victim's assets. The most pernicious predators are those with long-term controlling relationships with their elderly victims. Abusers suffer a comparatively high incidence of mental illness. In a 1989 U.S. study, forty eight percent of abusers had a history of mental illness. They tend to possess antisocial and narcissistic traits, and have a history of multiple unstable relationships.[223] They do not feel remorse for their actions, and when confronted, frequently respond with more aggression and anger toward the victim.

Children whose lives have not gone well tend to be the most available to care for an ailing parent. Without steady employment or stable housing they volunteer to move in with mom to "take care of her." Statistically, this is the child that is most likely to steal from mom and to influence her to disinherit more successful beneficiaries.

MODUS OPERANDI

The arsenal of tools used to unduly influence another is limited only by the creativity of the influencer. However, studies of undue influence show a fairly consistent pattern of deceit. Most influencers rely on a combination of timing, isolation, and brainwashing to implement their plan. Undue influence begins when the victim is physically dependent or mentally impaired. Over-medication is an extremely effective way of making the victim increasingly dysfunctional and increasingly dependent. The next step is to isolate the declining senior. Once isolated, the influencer can begin to poison the elder's relationships through misinformation, manipulation and lies. The influencer simply tells friends and family that *"mom isn't feeling well"* or *"now isn't a good time to visit,"* at the same time telling mom that nobody has called. Relationship poisoning is accompanied by self-promotion. The influencer's manipulations are intended to brainwash the victim into believing that the influencer is the only one who will protect and care for them; that others don't care about them; or that they are plotting against them either to steal their money or to put them in the nursing home. All the while the influencer paints himself as the savior.

TIMING

Undue influence occurs when motivation meets opportunity. A child, for example, may be unhappy with his role in his family, but powerless to change his lot while his parent has full capacity. That can all change when a parent, the keeper of the status quo, begins to lose capacity. The window of opportunity opens when the parent has lost enough cognitive ability to be easily influenced but not so much so as to be unable to sign documents or to mimic the script provided to him. Such was the case with Brooke Astor's speech at the Knickerbocker Club on February 10, 2004, where she lauded her son and daughter-in-law, a speech which her doctor later testified she did not have the capacity to compose.

ISOLATION

Undue influence is most effective when the victim is isolated. As discussed in Chapters Three and Four, isolation is associated with a host of physical and emotional maladies. Isolating the victim accelerates the victim's decline and susceptibility to influence. Once isolated, the influencer can more easily ply the tools of undue influence, including self-promotion and relationship poisoning. In the biblical story of Jacob and Esau, Jacob waited until his blinded father Isaac was alone before he deceived his father into giving him the birthright intended for Esau.

RELATIONSHIP POISONING

Damaging the relationship between the victim and the natural object of his or her bounty facilitates the influencer's drive for control. The influencer may conjure up lies about his perceived competitors. He may accuse them of being greedy, of having financial troubles, only wanting money, or the most combustible lie: *"they want to put you in a nursing home."* Not satisfied only to poison the well of the victim, the influencer may also lie to friends and family about the victim, claiming that mom is mad at them, doesn't want them to visit, or doesn't approve of the person they married. Poisoning both sides of the equation rather quickly ruins lifelong relationships.

SELF-PROMOTION AND CLUSTER B

Although anyone can engage in self-promotion, influencers with personality disorders do it best. They have a long history of manipulating others. Plagued by the inability or unwillingness to see themselves as the problem, they blame others. They are also good at seeking allies, convincing them to buy into their distortions. They have a sense of entitlement, are exploitive, and will do anything to get their fix of power and attention. Narcissists in particular make excellent influencers: they want what they want, they don't care whom they hurt to get it, and they experience nearly as much pleasure depriving others of their rightful share as they do from their stolen share.

IDENTIFYING THE SIGNS

The following are common elements and signs of undue influence:
- The elder lives alone and has no children;
- The elder begins to fail physically, emotionally, or mentally and loses cognitive function;

- A previously disfavored child or family member suddenly arrives on the scene and assumes a caretaker role;
- A non-family caretaker takes over management of the elder's finances;
- Long-time advisors such as the elder's attorney, accountant, and financial advisor are replaced summarily and for no apparent reason;
- The caretaker is named as agent under a power of attorney or owner of accounts ostensibly to assist the elder in the payment of bills;
- Large checks drawn on the elder's accounts are written to cash, to the caretaker, or to the caretaker's family;
- The elder is never "well enough" to see visitors or to come to the phone;
- The caretaker accompanies the elder at all times and speaks for the elder;
- The elder speaks of the caretaker in terms of "what would I do without her," and speaks of family and long-time beneficiaries as only wanting her money;
- Gifts or bequests by the elder that treat people unequally, cruelly, or are designed to punish;
- With regard to preparation and execution of the elder's will:
  1. The will is a do-it-yourself job created by the influencer;
  2. Where an attorney is involved, the influencer chooses the attorney and attends all meetings;
  3. Witnesses to the will are acquaintances of the influencer and have little or no history with the testator;
  4. The will is a radical departure from previous wills, naming entirely new beneficiaries and fiduciaries;
  5. There is secrecy surrounding the execution and existence of the will; and
  6. The will is created a short time before death.

THE PROTOTYPICAL CASE

In their survey of undue influence cases, the authors of *Will Contests* identify characteristics of the five most common influencers and the likely outcome of will challenges in which they are involved:

1. By far the most common influencer is the child who influences the disinheritance of one or more children: the "Esau and Jacob" case;

2. The second spouse who facilitates the disinheritance of children of an earlier marriage: the "David and Bathsheba" case;

3. A brother, sister, niece, nephew, or cousin of the victim who receives the lion's share of the estate to the detriment of the other family members;

4. The helping professional; and

5. The neighbor or acquaintance.

Ross and Reed observe that courts are most hostile to professionals, acquaintances, and greedy family members, making such cases the most likely to be overturned on the basis of undue influence. Esau and Jacob cases constitute the largest number of will contests and depending on the facts and circumstances can be overturned in court, but David and Bathsheba cases are almost unwinnable by contestants.[224]

The following two contemporary cases further illustrate the application of the undue influence doctrine.

In re Estate of Alice G. Clark, Deceased. Supreme Court of Pennsylvania (1975)
Alice G. Clark was a childless widow who lived alone since the 1951 death of her husband. She executed her will approximately four months prior to her death in 1971. In the last five years of her life, Alice had been hospitalized nine times for anxiety, depression, and chronic psoriasis. Ten months before execution of her will, Alice was diagnosed with cerebral arteriosclerosis, arteriosclerotic heart disease, and dementia characterized by decline of short-term memory. Two months prior to her death (and two months after the execution of her will), Alice was hospitalized for nearly two months and was in a constant state of confusion and disorientation. Witnesses testified that for the last two years of her life Alice showed dependence, confusion, forgetfulness, repetition and disorientation.

John H. Smith befriended Alice a few years prior to her death and gradually assumed more and more of Alice's business duties. John originally met Alice after her husband's death when he assisted her in the auction of some of her husband's personal property. Alice was put off by her original encounters with John, sometimes calling him a "crook."

On the date of the execution of her will, John and his wife accompanied Alice to the bank, where John informed the manager that Alice wished to designate John as her agent in order to sign checks. With regard to Alice's will, John testified that when he and Alice were alone she dictated and he wrote her exact wishes on a piece of paper. He then took the paper to a typist who typed it in legal form. Only John witnessed Alice's signature. He then took the writing to two of his acquaintances who neither saw Alice sign the writing nor were aware that they were witnessing a will. John then took the will to his home for safekeeping along with all of her stock certificates, bonds, and deeds. Approximately three weeks after the signing of the will, Alice gave John her savings passbook along with a withdrawal slip for the entire account, allegedly telling John that she wanted $1,500 in cash for Christmas presents and wanted him to have the remaining $21,500 as a gift.

In his defense, John produced several witnesses at trial that stated that Alice's mind was clear and unfettered during the period immediately surrounding the execution. A bank secretary who saw Alice on the day she signed her will and executed the power of attorney stated that Alice was lucid, assured, and handled her affairs in a businesslike manner. Alice's own doctor testified that he had seen her the week before she signed her will and that he believed she was capable of executing a legal document if it was explained to her. Despite Alice's numerous physical and mental maladies, the court did not find that Alice lacked testamentary capacity. The court did, however, set aside Alice's will on the basis that John had unduly influenced her to his gain. The court stated that it placed heavy weight on the secrecy surrounding the execution of the will and the fact that John was the scrivener. The court distinguished testamentary capacity from the susceptibility required to support a claim of undue influence, stating:

> Undue influence is generally a gradual, progressive inculcation of a receptive mind. The 'fruits' of the undue influence may not appear until long after the weakened intellect has been played upon... the particular mental condition of the testatrix on the date she executed the will is not as significant when reflecting on undue influence....[225]

Kathleen Jones and Jeneva Newton v. Robert C. Walker, Court of Appeals of Missouri, Western District 774 S.W.2d 532 (1989)

After his wife died in 1971, Orville Woods left California and moved in with his sister Kathleen Jones in Boise, Idaho. After three months Orville left Kathleen's home and moved in with his other sister Jeneva Newton in Ashland, Oregon, where he stayed a short time. Both sisters testified that Orville had a drinking problem. While living with Jeneva, he also had a propensity for urinating in wine bottles or out the window even though he had a bathroom available.

After leaving Oregon, Orville returned to his birth state of Missouri where at the age of 57, he married his second wife, Elizabeth. The marriage did not last long. Elizabeth testified that Orville drank all the time: "He had a can of beer in his hand all the time, cigarettes, can of beer, not eating."[226] Also, Elizabeth testified that numerous people came to the house to borrow money from Orville that she never saw repaid.

Orville met Robert Walker, a Red Cross volunteer, about the time of his divorce from Elizabeth. The two met as "Bob" was assigned to bring Orville to the hospital for prostate surgery. The day after his surgery, Bob brought Orville to attorney Mr. Jayne. At the meeting, at which Bob was present, Orville indicated that he would like to leave everything to his two sisters (Kathleen and Jeneva) and his brother, equally. Jayne drew up the will as directed by Orville, but a few days later received a call from Bob stating that Orville had changed his mind and wanted to leave everything to Bob and Bob's wife.

Suspicious of Bob's representations, Jayne queried Orville on Orville's next visit outside the presence of Bob. He asked Orville a number of questions intended to assess his capacity. Orville failed miserably. He didn't know where he lived, his doctor's name, or Bob's wife's name. When Jayne refused to prepare the proposed amendment, and suggested that a guardian be appointed for Orville, Bob fired Jayne. He took Orville to his own attorney, Mr. Atherton, who prepared a will leaving everything to Bob and his wife, which Orville signed.

On the same day that Bob brought Orville to Jayne, Bob also went to the bank with Orville and had his name added to Orville's safe deposit box. Around the same time, and on Bob's suggestion, Orville sold two properties and placed the proceeds in a joint account with Bob. Orville also changed his life insurance policy to name Bob as the beneficiary and began referring to Bob as his "business manager."

Orville moved in with Bob and his wife three months after the will was signed, where Orville resided until his death approximately four years later.

Orville's sisters brought suit to set aside Orville's will. The court agreed with the contestants, denying Orville's will on the basis that it had been procured through Bob's undue influence. The court found that all of the elements of undue influence were met: Bob had a confidential or fiduciary relationship with Orville; Bob benefited from Orville's revised will, and Bob was active in procuring the will which benefited him.

Despite the various maladies of both Alice G. Clark and Orville Woods, neither case was winnable solely on the basis of lack of testamentary capacity. Both cases instead depended on the doctrine of undue influence to undo the acts of predators.

Timing and isolation were key factors as both Alice G. Clark and Orville Woods suffered significant physical and emotional impairments and were completely dependent on their influencers. Both were susceptible to undue influence, both had a confidential relationship with their caretakers, and both caretakers used that confidential relationship to change their victim's dispositive wishes (both by gift and bequest) to favor themselves. In Orville's case, the fact that he disinherited family members in favor of relatively new acquaintances was another factor considered by the court.

BROOKE ASTOR

The Brooke Astor story is a classic case of undue influence. Addled with dementia, Brooke was susceptible to the undue influence of her son, Tony, who isolated her with the intent to make her more vulnerable and to hide his deceit. As her son and agent under her power of attorney, Tony had a confidential relationship with Brooke which he used, with the help of Brooke's long-time attorney Christensen and later with attorney Morrissey, to obtain substantial gifts and bequests. The result was unconscionable as Brooke's long-term commitment to charity was undermined in favor of Tony who was already well provided for in her will.

The Brooke Astor case would have been difficult to contest solely on the basis of testamentary capacity. At Tony's criminal trial, the prosecution and defense presented conflicting expert medical testimony as to her competence. Further complicating matters was the fact that both of Brooke's attorneys had compromised their position as disinterested witnesses, one criminally. While courts normally rely heavily on the testimony of the drafting attorney and witnesses to the execution, in Brooke's case that evidence was tainted.

CONCLUSION

Undue influence is the most commonly employed and successful basis for overturning gifts and bequests made by vulnerable testators. Its value in defeating predators makes it an important doctrine to understand and employ.

The cost of litigation and the difficulty in proving abuse after the fact dictates early intervention. Chapter Nine discusses the legal protections available either to prevent elder abuse or to stop it after it has been discovered. The legal protections discussed in Chapter Nine must be implemented during the life of the elder, while the legal remedies discussed in Chapter Ten may be employed either while the elder is alive or after his or her death.

PART IV

THE COURTHOUSE STEPS

LEGAL PROTECTIONS 9

"[T]he law…is the firm and solid basis of civil society, the guardian of liberty, the protection of the innocent, the terror of the guilty, and the scourge of the wicked."
- Charles Lawrence, British military officer
and Governor of Nova Scotia, Oct. 14, 1754

INTRODUCTION

A loved one's failing health, especially failing memory and cognition, should prompt consideration of available protective measures. It is during the time of uncertain capacity that abuse of the elderly is borne. Increasingly vulnerable to suggestion and manipulation yet arguably in possession of donative and testamentary capacity, declining elders are easy prey for wrongdoers. The first signs of trouble are usually missing money, an aura of secrecy, a rekindled relationship with a troubled child with whom the elder was traditionally conflicted, and behavior that is out of character, including travel, large gifts, or new living arrangements.

Elder abuse is like a malignant tumor; the earlier the intervention the greater the chance of a favorable outcome. Early implementation of the legal protections discussed in this chapter can minimize emotional trauma, and preserve the elder's assets for his or her future use. Early intervention also preserves evidence of wrongdoing in the form of witnesses, financial records, and the opportunity to evaluate the victim medically. Conversely, proving elder abuse years after it has occurred, especially after the victim has passed, causes a number of evidentiary problems, including lost financial records, unavailable or deceased witnesses, wasted assets, and reliance on forensic psychological evidence, which as noted in Chapter Seven lacks the weight of more contemporaneous evaluations.

Before involving the courts or outside agencies, a family meeting - not including the elder or the alleged perpetrator - should be called to determine whether informal resolution is possible. Every effort should be made to allow the elder the greatest autonomy possible without compromising his or her safety. If the consensus is to pursue an informal intervention with the alleged abuser, the family should meet with the problem family member to discuss the perceived issues and possible resolutions. Outside professional help in the form of a family counselor or mediator (discussed further in Chapter Eleven) should be considered. However, if the consensus is that approaching the problem family member would be futile, or would accelerate or exacerbate the abuse, then the next step is to seek legal counsel. At all times, care should be taken to avoid putting the elder family member in the middle of a family tug of war.

Legal help comes in many forms. Generally, the local police and the county prosecutor are not the place to start. They are not likely to get involved unless they believe that the elder is in immediate physical danger. Law enforcement tends to be more concerned with crimes perpetrated by strangers, and is reluctant to involve themselves in murky family disputes which they perceive to be a civil rather than criminal matter. Instead, help should first be sought either from the local Adult Protective Services (APS) office or by contacting an elder law attorney to discuss various legal options including the creation of powers of attorney or commencement of guardianship or conservatorship proceedings.

ADULT PROTECTIVE SERVICES/ELDER ABUSE

All fifty states have enacted legislation authorizing adult protective services (APS). APS laws establish a system for reporting and investigating elder abuse. APS are typically organized under the Department of Human Services either at the state or county level. APS will investigate all complaints and involve law enforcement or the court system as appropriate. A number of states have adopted specific criminal statutes that punish those who engage in elder financial abuse. Additionally, all states and territories have laws authorizing the Long Term Care Ombudsman Program (LTCOP), which is responsible for advocating on behalf of long term care facility residents who experience abuse.

Elder abuse is broadly defined to include physical abuse, psychological abuse, financial exploitation, and neglect of the elder. In most states, APS laws apply only to older persons who are unable to protect or care for themselves due to physical or mental disability or who are unable to make or communicate decisions about their needs. The states vary widely as to the age and circumstances under which a victim is eligible to receive protective services.

A complaint to APS generates an investigation. An agency worker will visit the alleged abuse victim, usually within twenty-four hours of the reported abuse. APS may apply for guardianship/conservatorship and may facilitate health, social, psychological, medical and legal services. In an emergency, the APS may file a petition, and a police officer or other agency may take the elder into protective custody. Emergency services are continued until the imminent danger is averted or a preliminary hearing takes place to establish probable cause. Services are provided only with the protected individual's consent unless he is deemed incompetent.

Unfortunately, APS offices are notoriously underfunded. Their high case loads and lack of financial training are a source of continuing frustration for those who report elder financial abuse. APS agencies rarely have the resources to properly investigate financial exploitation, and routinely refer such complaints to law enforcement who in turn decline the referral on the basis that it is a matter for the civil courts.

Adult protective services will likely not get involved if the abuse is more subtle, like misuse of the elder's funds by a family caretaker, questionable gifts, or where a will or trust is believed to have been procured through undue influence or while the elder was of questionable capacity. In such cases, the best recourse may be to petition the probate court (sometimes called *surrogate court*) for the appointment of a guardian or conservator.

GUARDIANSHIP

The law of guardianship evolved from English roots, and originally reflected a crude understanding of mental health. It required a finding that the allegedly incapacitated person be an "idiot," "lunatic," a "person of unsound mind," or "spendthrift." As noted in Chapter Seven, present day notions of incapacity employ much more finely tuned medical and functional criteria. The test has evolved to be less label driven, more specific, and more focused on how the individual functions in society.

Today, guardianship proceedings focus on the individual's ability to provide for his or her essential needs for medical care, nutrition, clothing, shelter, or safety. The 1997 Uniform Guardianship and Protective Proceeding Act defines an incapacitated person as "an individual who, for reasons other than being a minor, is unable to receive and evaluate information or make or communicate decisions to such an extent that the individual lacks the ability to meet essential requirements for physical health, safety, self-care, even with appropriate technological assistance."

Current theory is that an individual should never be considered incapacitated merely because of his or her physical or mental status. Just because someone is very old, frail and chronically ill does not mean that she is incapacitated or in need of a guardian. Capacity is no longer an all-or-nothing proposition; states restrict guardianship to only those tasks the individual is incapable of exercising, allowing her the greatest possible autonomy over the remaining activities of her life.

Guardianships are generally one of three types: *guardianship of the estate* (more commonly known as a conservatorship), limited to property matters; *guardianship of the person,* involving personal and medical decisions; and *plenary guardianship,* granting power over both property and personal matters. In some cases courts prefer to appoint different individuals or entities to act as guardian of the property and the person. They will appoint a bank as guardian of the property and a family member as guardian of the person. (Remember that in the Brooke Astor case, Annette de la Renta was appointed as guardian of Brooke's person and J. P. Morgan Chase Bank guardian of her finances.)

Appointment of a guardian or conservator puts an end to misuse of the vulnerable individual's funds and endless will and trust revisions, as gifts and bequests become subject to court review. A guardian/conservator may also hire legal counsel to recover assets that have been wrongfully obtained. As noted in Chapter Seven, the appointment of a guardian is not conclusive proof that the individual lacks the capacity to execute a will or medical directive, or enter into a valid contract, general power of attorney, or a trust.

The probate court has jurisdiction in guardianship matters. (The term probate derives from the Latin word *probatum,* meaning to try, test, or prove.) Proceedings are commenced by petition (by the *petitioner*) – who can be anyone interested in the *protected individual's* (sometimes called *respondent* or *ward*) welfare. Petitions are often accompanied by a treating physician's written statement as to the ward's medical condition. Social service agencies and hospitals may petition for guardianship if no family member is available or willing to act on a vulnerable individual's behalf.

For a guardian to be appointed, it must be shown by *clear and convincing evidence* that the *respondent* lacks sufficient understanding or capacity to make or communicate informed decisions *and* that serious injury is likely to result to the respondent or others in the near future by reason of the incapacity. Additionally, it must be shown that the guardianship is necessary to provide for the respondent's continuing care and supervision. This second requirement is intended to uphold the individual's right to self-determination. If an alternative to the guardianship is available – such as an existing power of attorney or a do-not-resuscitate declaration – it is generally the view of courts that the guardianship should not be granted.

When granting guardianship, priority is given to family members in the following order: spouse, adult children, and parents. As further protection, all interested parties (basically immediate family) receive notice of the proceedings, and are offered an opportunity to object to the appointment. The respondent must also receive notice of the petition. State law usually permits, but does not compel, the presence of the alleged incapacitated person at the guardianship hearing. Whether the respondent is required to attend the hearing depends on the health of the respondent and local court practices.

Before granting the guardianship, the court will independently verify that the respondent's physical and mental condition are accurately represented in the petition. As part of its investigation, the court will appoint a *guardian ad litem* (GAL),[227] typically a practicing attorney, to interview the respondent, the petitioner, and other family members, and to file a report with the court summarizing his or her findings. If the GAL's report supports the appointment of a guardian, and there are no objections from other family members, the court will issue *letters of authority* granting the guardianship and outlining the powers granted.

If no family member is available, the court may appoint a guardian paid by the state. Often such guardians are lawyers whom the judge knows and respects. In recent years, state laws have been liberalized to also permit nonprofit entities to act as guardian. Several states have created public guardians to act as the guardian of last resort when no private individual or entity is available. Banks and other corporate trust entities frequently serve as guardians of the estate (conservator), but not of the person.

Once appointed, the guardian must procure medical and custodial care for the ward and attempt to restore him or her "to the best possible state of mental and physical well-being" so that he or she can return to self-reliance as soon as possible. In making these decisions, the guardian must consult with the ward if the ward is lucid and able to communicate. The guardian has the power to consent to or refuse medical treatment. Where no conservator has been appointed, the guardian must conserve the ward's assets and apply them toward the ward's support and care. The guardian must file detailed annual financial reports outlining the ward's annual income and expenditures made on his or her behalf. A nursing home may not compel an individual to obtain guardianship as a condition of providing care.

Challenging a loved one's capacity can be painful and risky. The moving party must allege that the loved one is incapable of handling his or her own affairs. Entitled to his day in court, the respondent is questioned, examined, pulled and prodded, and in some cases must appear in court. It can be hurtful and damaging for all involved. The stakes are high. An unsuccessful petition will irrevocably damage the petitioner's relationship with the respondent, and ratify the respondent's capacity. An unsuccessful petition may also cast the petitioner as the wrongdoer.

If a loved one retains even a modicum of capacity, there may be no recourse to either APS or the courts as the law places a high value on the individual's right to self determination. The probate court and APS will not intervene if they determine that the elder has knowingly consented to the actions that the family finds so objectionable.

A good example is the case of a long-term widow in her eighties who fell in love with her shady, late-fifties handyman with a criminal past. Soon after their romance began, the family noticed that the widow's assets were being systematically depleted. The lonely widow was like a love-struck teenager, truly believing that her handyman loved her. She was not concerned that her money was being depleted. In fact, she was more concerned that her meddling daughter would break up the romantic relationship that gave her so much pleasure. The frantic and exasperated daughter had absolutely no recourse while mom, although vulnerable to the romantic maneuvers of a skilled con man, was still in possession of her faculties.

GUARDIAN OF THE ESTATE OR CONSERVATOR

The probate court may appoint a conservator to manage a vulnerable individual's financial affairs. The procedure for establishing a conservatorship is much the same as that for establishing guardianship, except that a conservator must procure a bond to protect the assets over which he or she has authority.

For the court to appoint a conservator it must be shown by a *preponderance of the evidence* (a lower standard than that required for guardianship) that the respondent is unable to manage his property and business affairs effectively, and that the respondent's assets will be wasted or dissipated unless proper management is provided. A lower standard of capacity is required in conservatorships because management of one's financial matters requires a higher level of cognitive skill. Although the same person may act as guardian and conservator, the duties are usually separated when the respondent has substantial assets.

Soon after appointment, the conservator must *inventory* the incapacitated person's assets. Thereafter, financial accountings must be prepared at least annually, and a final accounting prepared at the end of the conservatorship. Accountings are filed with the probate court and made available to interested parties upon request. Conservators must have their annual accounting approved by the court and typically are required to obtain prior court approval for major transactions such as the sale of real estate.

The economic cost of appointing a guardian or conservator can be substantial. Attorney fees, court costs, and expert medical testimony (if needed) can add up. Fees for court visitors and *guardians ad litem* must also be paid. A guardian may request a fee, and most conservators, especially banks, are paid a fee for their services. If the guardianship petition is successful, most courts will order that all costs be borne by the estate of the incapacitated person.

PROTECTIVE ORDER

A protective order (obtained by petition to the probate court) is appropriate when protection is needed for a particular transaction - as opposed to the ongoing protection of a conservatorship. A protective order might be appropriate, for example, where the respondent is to receive a personal injury settlement that would disqualify him or her from Supplemental Security Income (SSI). In that case, a protective order might be granted to allow the petitioner to establish a *special needs trust* granting the respondent access to the settlement without disqualifying him or her from SSI.

LIMITED GUARDIANSHIP

Courts are sensitive to the delicate balance between protecting vulnerable adults and depriving them of their civil rights. For the most part, courts have addressed this balance by granting only those powers absolutely necessary to protect the elder from imminent danger while reserving to the elder the greatest possible autonomy. Probate courts have the option of appointing a limited guardian whenever the loss of capacity is less than complete. Limited guardianships often take the form of a guardian appointed solely for the purpose of making the ward's medical decisions.

TEMPORARY/EMERGENCY GUARDIANSHIP

A court may appoint temporary (emergency) guardians where the respondent's property is at risk. Temporary guardians are granted only those powers necessary to address the emergency. If the incapacity and the need for a guardian persists, the court may subsequently appoint a permanent guardian.

A preliminary injunction or temporary restraining order may be granted where the vulnerable adult's financial well-being is in imminent danger. A *personal protection order* (PPO), most commonly used in the context of domestic violence, may be available to protect a vulnerable adult from physical or emotional harm.

CONCLUSION

A petition for guardianship can be a humanitarian act even though it is frequently experienced by the respondent as an unnecessary encroachment on his personal rights. When unwarranted, a guardianship proceeding is an offense to the elder and can itself be a form of elder abuse. Although the legal system is geared to protect the rights of respondents, from time to time dishonest petitioners use the court system to wrest control of an elder's affairs. On the whole, however, the legal system works effectively to ferret out bad actors, and does an excellent job protecting vulnerable individuals.

The appointment of a guardian or conservator creates a formal *fiduciary* relationship, which imposes extensive fiduciary duties on the appointee which are more fully described in the next chapter. Legal remedies like those described in Chapter Ten may be in order to address abuse that occurred prior to the guardian's appointment, where a fiduciary has breached his duty, or where the victim has passed away.

LEGAL REMEDIES | 10

*"Justice is the constant and perpetual will
to allot to every man his due."*
- Ulpian (170-223)

Thomas Moore

Robert Morganthau

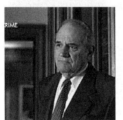

Adam Schiff

*Anna Nicole Smith and
J. Howard Marshall II*

INTRODUCTION

There may come a time when all due preventive measures have failed to
avert abuse. When wrongdoers have taken improper actions that cannot be
undone, recourse is to the courts[228] to pursue remedies against the wrongdoer,
rescind his bad deals, or to set aside wills or trusts wrongfully procured.

The probate courts of the United States have jurisdiction over matters
involving the vulnerable and the deceased. The history of American probate
courts make them uniquely qualified to dispense equity, restore wronged
parties to their rightful position, and to censure wrongdoers.

As noted in earlier chapters, bad actors seeking to gain access to their
target's bounty start by placing themselves in a position of trust and influence.

They become exceedingly helpful, taking their target to medical appointments, managing their finances, and perhaps even moving in with them. Their helping role may be informal in the sense that they "did everything for mom," or they may have been formally appointed under a power of attorney, will, or trust. Although their position of influence may give them a short-term strategic advantage, it carries with it a host of fiduciary responsibilities that obligate them to act in the best interest of the principal (the person who has placed trust in them).

Criminal courts may become involved where wrongdoers have engaged in larceny, extortion, fraud, forgery, or embezzlement. Such was the case with Brooke Astor, whose elderly son stood accused of at least eighteen counts of criminal misconduct in a grueling five-month highly publicized trial.

PROBATE COURT: COURT OF EQUITY

In addition to having exclusive legal and equitable jurisdiction over matters involving estates, wills, and trusts, modern day probate courts also have jurisdiction over the affairs of minors and the vulnerable. The historical roots of probate jurisdiction can be directly traced to the English Court of Chancery which evolved in the 15th Century to provide equitable relief to those for whom a common law award of damages was inadequate.

English *common law* courts enforced the king's law through a complex system of writs. Courts of law could hear a case only after a breach had occurred and the only remedy available was an award of money for the loss caused by the breach. The rigid nature of these common law remedies was inadequate to address the needs of estates, trusts, minors, the vulnerable, and women. In time, the aggrieved came to complain to the king directly, who in turn referred them to his right-hand-man, his Chancellor.

Until the appointment of layman St. Thomas Moore in 1530, all of the king's chancellors were officers of the Roman Catholic Church. They were literate men trained in Roman Catholic Canon law. Their literacy, training in Roman Catholic Canon law, and role as the king's personal confessor made them well suited to address the problems of a vulnerable population. Sometimes referred to as the *Keepers of the King's Conscience,* chancellors applied the principles of good conscience and reason derived from church Canon law.

Eventually, petitions were addressed to the Chancellor directly, and by the 15th century the court received its official title of *Court of Chancery.*

The need for equity in the legal system was recognized long before the English Court of Chancery. Aristotle (384 – 321 BC) in his fifth book of the *Nicomachean Ethics* viewed a judge's equitable powers as a necessary supplement to the black letter of the law:

> When, therefore, the law lays down a general rule, and thereafter a case arises falling somewhat outside the general model, it is then right, where the lawgiver's words have turned out to be too simple to meet the case without doing wrong, to rectify the deficiency by deciding as the lawgiver would himself decide if he were present on the occasion, and would have enacted if he were aware of the case in question.

The Court of Chancery introduced new remedies previously unknown in the rigid writ system of the common law courts. The Court of Chancery could grant new equitable remedies including:

- *Specific performance* (to force a defaulting party to make good on his promise);
- *Constructive trusts* (to place wrongfully taken property under the control of the court);
- *Reformation* (to change the terms of a document to more properly reflect the intent of the drafter); and
- *Rescission* (the reversing of a voidable contract or agreement).

The Court of Chancery also proved essential to the law of trusts, as the law courts only recognized the rights of trustees, the *legal* owners of trust property. Trustees could simply ignore the rights of trust beneficiaries, who merely held a *beneficial* interest in trust property. Using equitable principles, the Court of Chancery looked beyond the legal ownership of trustees to protect the rights of beneficiaries. Another distinction between law and equity was the unavailability of a jury in equity. As equity courts dispensed fairness, input from an impartial jury was deemed unnecessary.

With the limitation that equity could not overturn the law courts (following the maxim, "equity follows the law"), equity was not otherwise bound by the limits of common law. Instead, equity operated under general principles of fairness and honor known as *maxims of equity*. One such maxim was that to gain entry to the court of equity one must enter with *clean hands*. In a related maxim, "one who seeks equity must do equity". In other words, one seeking equity must have himself acted fairly and honorably.

The Chancery Court became the third English court of competent jurisdiction in inheritance matters. The English courts had long divided inheritance matters between the king's law courts and the ecclesiastical courts. Inheritance of land was assigned to the law courts while the inheritance of personal property fell within the jurisdiction of the ecclesiastical courts. Religious courts also had jurisdiction over matrimonial disputes, probate, wills, and the disenfranchised. However, since the ecclesiastic courts were notoriously weak, the Chancery Court increasingly took over matters relating to estate administration. Though a will would be initially admitted to the ecclesiastical court (which would supervise the appointment of the personal representative), the Chancery Court would assume jurisdiction over administration, especially in contested estates. Although the concurrent jurisdiction of the Chancery and Ecclesiastical courts continued for a time, the superiority of the Court of Chancery ultimately led to its becoming the preferred court.

In time, the Court of Chancery came to develop its own dizzying set of complexities, procedures, and inefficiencies, comically detailed by Charles Dickens in his 1852-1853 novel, *Bleak House*. To solve the problems caused by the overlap of common law and equity courts, the English legislature enacted the Judicature Acts of 1873 and 1875, effectively fusing common law and equity. The Acts abolished the separate courts and replaced them with the High Court of Justice, with jurisdiction over both common law and equity. The former English Chancellor became today's Speaker of the House of Lords and a member of the Cabinet. Despite being merged out of existence, the Court of Chancery was to leave a permanent imprint on probate procedure, infusing it with fairness and equity.

Today, in the U.S., most law courts have equitable powers.[229] However, several states, notably Delaware, still have separate courts for law and equity. Other states have separate divisions for legal and equitable matters within a single court.

AMERICAN PROBATE COURTS

Although heavily influenced by the English experience, American colonists never recognized ecclesiastic courts. Nonetheless, the distinction between law and equity persisted in the United States through the 19th Century. A vestige of that separation continues as the right to a jury trial, guaranteed in civil cases by the Seventh Amendment of the Constitution, does not apply to probate courts.

The structure, authority, and even the name of probate courts vary across the United States. Only ten states have separate and distinct probate courts;[230] eleven states conduct probate business in District Courts;[231] ten states administer probate in a combination of courts;[232] nine states administer probate matters in their circuit courts;[233] six in Superior Courts;[234] two have Courts of Chancery;[235] and one state, Idaho, has adopted a Magistrate Division to administer probate matters.

Probate courts preside over the settlement of estates, whether the decedent died with a will (*testate*) or without (*intestate*). In cases where the decedent died testate, a petitioner may proceed either formally or informally. In a *formal* petition, the court will determine whether the formal execution requirements of the will were followed, whether the testator possessed testamentary capacity, and whether the will was procured by fraud or undue influence. In an *informal* probate proceeding, the court is not asked to rule on the validity of the will (all parties essentially acknowledge its validity) and thus makes no such determination.

Probate courts determine heirs, supervise estate administration, supervise settlement and distribution, and have the final word in matters of will interpretation. Probate courts also have exclusive jurisdiction over the validity, administration and settlement of *trusts*. Upon request, probate courts also supervise the appointment or removal of trustees, review trustee fees, review interim and final accountings, and ascertain trust beneficiaries.

The probate court in most states has concurrent jurisdiction to determine the partition of property, impose constructive trusts, and hear and decide claims by or against a trustee for the return of property. In a carryover from the Court of Chancery, probate courts have jurisdiction over minors, incompetents, probate administration, and will contests. The Seventh Amendment right to a jury trial is suspended in most probate matters as the court makes its decisions based on the maxims of equity. State statutes define what matters may and may not be brought before the probate court. Typically, however, unless a matter involves an estate of a decedent, a ward, or a trust, it may not be brought before the probate court.

FIDUCIARY RELATIONSHIPS

According to Black's Law Dictionary, a fiduciary is "a person having a duty, created by his undertaking, to act primarily for the benefit of another in matters connected with his undertaking," or "in the nature of a position of trust or holding confidence."[236] The Russian expression for a fiduciary, most often referring to an executor, is *dusje-prikasstjik,* which literally means *agent of the soul.* A *fiduciary relationship* is a relationship of trust. It can arise by agreement, such as in the case of a trustee or agent under a power of attorney; by court order such as in the case of a guardian, conservator, or personal representative; or informally through a *confidential relationship* in which the principal reasonably places his trust in another to look after his interests.

According to one commentator: "Fiduciary obligation is the highest order of duty imposed by law. In the relationship with the principal, the *beneficiary* of the relationship, the fiduciary must exercise utmost good faith and candor, must disclose all relevant information, and must not profit from the relationship without the knowledge and permission of the principal. The fiduciary must make every effort to avoid having his own interests conflict with those of the principal, and, when conflict is unavoidable, the fiduciary must place the interests of the principal above his own."[237]

Personal representatives, trustees, guardians, conservators, and agents under powers of attorney are all fiduciaries. Although their individual mission may vary, there are more similarities than differences in the standards by which their conduct is judged.

Trustees and personal representatives owe a fiduciary duty to those possessing the equitable or beneficial interests in trust and estate property. A *trustee* must consider the changing needs of each beneficiary in accordance with the terms of the governing instrument and controlling law. A *personal representative* generally winds up the decedent's affairs by collecting assets, paying creditors, and distributing property to estate beneficiaries in accordance with the terms of the decedent's will and the law of the governing jurisdiction. Like trustees, personal representatives have the same power and title to property that an absolute owner would have, which he must administer not for himself but for the benefit of beneficiaries and creditors of the estate. A *conservator* or *guardian* must act in the best interest of the ward. An agent under a power of attorney stands in the shoes of the principal, and must make decisions that the agent himself would have made if he were present and able.

CONFIDENTIAL RELATIONSHIP

In addition to the formal fiduciary relationships described above, a fiduciary relationship can arise *informally* from a *confidential relationship* (sometimes called an *implied fiduciary* or *fiduciary in fact*). Unlike formal fiduciary relationships, confidential relationships are not based on formal appointment; they are instead a question of fact to be ascertained from the circumstances of the relationship. The onerous nature of fiduciary obligations necessitates that an informal fiduciary relationship not be lightly imposed.

The most common confidential relationship scenario is where one family member assumes the responsibility for the care of another. In the course of such care, the caretaker may place his or her name on accounts, real estate, and other assets of the needy family member in order to facilitate the management of assets, payment of bills, and avoidance of probate.

Little evidence is needed to establish a fiduciary relationship in family or family-like situations. There is a virtual presumption in favor of a fiduciary relationship where one family member undertakes the care of another. It is quite natural to presume that a family member is looking out for another family member's best interest, and it is thus fair to presume a fiduciary relationship unless rebutted by evidence to the contrary. The touchstone of an informal fiduciary relationship is justifiable and verifiable reliance on the part of the person receiving care. That kind of reliance is common in families. We lower our guard and trust that family will act in our best interest. But informal relationships, even between family members, are not automatically presumed. As, I. Mark Cohen notes: "[A]lthough the Bible may make us our brother's keeper, the law does not so presume."[238] A number of conditions must be met for an informal relationship to create fiduciary duty. First, the relationship must be a pre-existing relationship. Second, the *"two-way street"* rule must be met: the principal must reasonably trust the would-be fiduciary to look after his interests, and the would-be fiduciary must be aware of that expectation.

In some states, an informal fiduciary relationship is imposed upon each party to a joint bank account. In those states, each account holder is considered an agent of the other with a duty to account for his withdrawals.

FIDUCIARY DUTIES

Fiduciaries are held to the highest standard of behavior under the law. They must comply with the duties imposed on them by statute, court rule, case law, as well as the instrument or order granting their fiduciary status. Various fiduciary duties overlap, but the basic duties required of all fiduciaries are as follows.

Duty of loyalty: The foundation of any fiduciary relationship is the fiduciary's absolute duty of allegiance. Fiduciaries owe an undivided duty of loyalty to carry out their duties for the sole benefit of the person or persons on whose behalf they act. A fiduciary may not profit personally (earning a fee for fiduciary services rendered is *not* considered a profit), share a benefit, or direct a benefit to a third party. A fiduciary may be found to violate the duty of loyalty by taking excessive compensation for fiduciary services.

Duty to inventory: A fiduciary is required to prepare an inventory of the assets over which the fiduciary has control. Depending on the nature of the fiduciary relationship, the fiduciary may be required to file the inventory with the court and supply copies to all beneficiaries or interested parties.

Duty to properly account: Fiduciaries must properly and periodically account for income and expenses. Within a relatively short time after accepting their appointment, fiduciaries must typically create and make available an opening inventory. Thereafter, fiduciaries must account to beneficiaries annually and upon termination of the fiduciary relationship. Jurisdictions vary as to the form of accounts, but in all cases there should be a clear showing of seven fundamental items: income received, income disbursed, balance of income on hand, additions to principal, deductions from principal, principal on hand, and changes in investments. All disputes are resolved against the fiduciary who does not keep accurate accounts.

Duty to preserve assets: This requirement principally refers to the duty to maintain real estate. For example, a fiduciary upon appointment should immediately change the locks on real estate and maintain all utilities, insurance, and taxes. Title to non-real estate assets should be changed into the name of the fiduciary.

Duty to act impartially: A fiduciary must treat all heirs and beneficiaries impartially. Impartiality most often arises in the relationship between income and remainder beneficiaries. For example, where a trust provides income to a surviving spouse for life with remainder to children, the trustee must balance the needs of the current income beneficiary (surviving spouse) against the rights of the remainder beneficiaries (children). The trustee's investment in non-income generating assets would favor remainder beneficiaries while excessive income distributions would be to the detriment of remaindermen. The duty to act impartially requires the fiduciary to balance the rights of these economically adverse interests.

Prohibition against self-dealing: The most blatant example of prohibited fiduciary conduct occurs when a fiduciary enters into a transaction which includes him, her, or itself. Self-dealing is an obvious conflict of interest, and is directly at odds with the duty to administer the trust or estate for the sole benefit of beneficiaries or protected individuals. Examples of self-dealing include the fiduciary's buying, selling, leasing, borrowing, or lending assets to or from the trust or estate. Confronted with self-dealing, a court will not inquire into the fairness of the transaction or the good faith of the fiduciary. Rather, the fiduciary will be liable for any losses incurred by the estate or trust, and must remit any profits, regardless of fairness or even good faith. A fiduciary may avoid liability for self-dealing only by receiving some combination of the following: advanced court approval; the full consent of all beneficiaries after full disclosure of the transaction; or exculpation under a statute or the governing instrument. To sustain an action for breach of fiduciary responsibility, a moving party need only prove that there was self-dealing; he or she need not prove that the transaction was unfair or imprudent.

Conflict of interest: The rule against conflicts of interest is similar to the prohibition against self-dealing, except that conflicts do not necessarily involve a direct transaction between the fiduciary and the trust or estate. Unlike self-dealing, which adopts a *no further inquiry* rule, a fiduciary has not breached his duty to avoid conflicts of interest if the transaction was fair to the trust or estate and entered into by the fiduciary in good faith.

Duty to invest: Fiduciaries must properly invest assets under their control. The *prudent investor rule* established by the Restatement (Third) of Trusts and the Uniform Prudent Investor Act govern proper investment. The underlying theoretical basis of the prudent investor rule is the *modern portfolio theory,* which focuses not on the prudent or speculative nature of individual investments but on the management of the portfolio as a whole. No investment is imprudent *per se* under the modern portfolio theory. Rather, each investment is evaluated in the context of the entire portfolio. Modern portfolio theory requires diversification of assets, proper risk and return trade-offs in relation to the distribution requirements of the trust, reasonable expenses, impartiality between income and principal, and a duty to delegate to obtain sound investment advice. A trustee or other fiduciary who breaches the investment duty will be personally liable for the loss.

Fiduciaries are held to a number of additional duties including the duty to collect assets; the duty to distribute assets; the duty to pursue debts owed to the estate; the duty to pay debts and taxes; and the duty not to commingle assets with the fiduciary's personal assets.

BREACH OF FIDUCIARY RESPONSIBILITY: LEGAL AND EQUITABLE REMEDIES

Fiduciaries are *personally* liable for breaches of their fiduciary responsibility. A breach can occur through a fiduciary's *misfeasance, malfeasance,* and *nonfeasance.* Misfeasance is the improper and unlawful execution of an act that in itself is lawful and proper; malfeasance is the commission of a improper or unlawful act involving or affecting the performance of one's duties; nonfeasance is the failure or omission to do something that should be done or especially something that one is under a duty or obligation to do.

Where a fiduciary has breached his responsibility, the law seeks to place those to whom the duty was owed in at least the same position that they would have occupied had there been no breach. The court may employ both legal (that is, money damages) and equitable remedies to make the affected parties whole, and may do one or more of the following:

- Compel the fiduciary to perform its fiduciary duty;
- Enjoin the fiduciary from committing a breach of fiduciary duty;
- Compel the trustee to redress a breach of fiduciary duty by paying money, restoring property, or other means;
- Order the fiduciary to account;
- Appoint a special fiduciary or receiver to take possession of and administer the property of the trust or estate;
- Suspend the fiduciary;
- Remove the fiduciary. Courts will not remove a fiduciary without a strong showing of wrongdoing. A fiduciary, however, can be removed for a variety of reasons, including but not limited to: lack of capacity, unfitness, the presence of a conflicting interest, repeated or flagrant failure or delay in providing accountings or information to the beneficiaries, commission of a crime, gross or continued underperformance of investments, or unreasonable or corrupt failure to cooperate with a co-fiduciary;
- Reduce or deny compensation to the fiduciary. In deciding whether to reduce or deny compensation, the court may consider whether the fiduciary acted in good faith, whether the breach was intentional, the nature of the breach and the extent of the loss, whether the fiduciary has restored the loss, and the value of the fiduciary's services;
- Void any act of the fiduciary (sometimes called *rescission*); and
- Hold the fiduciary personally liable for attorney's fees and other costs incurred to redress the breach. A fiduciary is not personally liable on a contract entered into on behalf of the ward, trust, or estate unless the fiduciary fails to reveal his or her representative capacity and to identify the ward, trust, or estate.

In addition to the power to proscribe the actions of a wayward fiduciary, probate courts may employ the following additional equitable remedies to reach beyond the fiduciary to third parties and transactions the fiduciary effected while acting as fiduciary:

Rescission is a remedy that undoes an improper action like an ill-conceived or improper contract. It is sought when money damages would be inadequate. Rescission arises when fraud, mistake, duress, disability, unconscionability, illegality, or undue influence produce an inappropriate wealth transfer or otherwise improper obligation on those the fiduciary represents.

A *constructive trust* arises under the doctrine that equity treats as done that which under good conscience ought to be done. A trust may be imposed by the court over the fiduciary and third parties when the circumstances under which the property was acquired (fraud, misrepresentation, concealment, mistake, undue influence, duress, breach of fiduciary relations, or similar equitable considerations) make it inequitable for the holder to retain it. When property is obtained by a third party under such circumstances, the holder may be charged as a constructive trustee and be required to hold the property for the defrauded person, or, according to venerable jurist Benjamin Cardozo: "When property has been acquired in such circumstances that the holder of legal title may not in good conscience retain the beneficial interest, equity converts him into a trustee."[239]

Legal damages against the fiduciary in the form of an award of money may be appropriate when property cannot be recovered (perhaps because it was sold to a *bona fide* purchaser, spent, or gambled away), and where no other equitable remedy is available to return the beneficiary to the position he or she enjoyed prior to the breach.

DEFENSES TO ALLEGATION OF BREACH OF FIDUCIARY DUTY

One or more of the following defenses may be available to a fiduciary depending on the facts and circumstances surrounding his or her actions:

- The transaction was authorized by the terms of the trust or will;
- The transaction was approved by the court;
- An action was not brought against the fiduciary within the time allowed

(statute of limitations);

- Those with the equitable interests (e.g. will and trust beneficiaries) consented to the fiduciary's actions;
- Those with equitable interests ratified the transaction;
- Those with an equitable interest released the fiduciary from liability; or
- The transaction involves a contract entered into or claim acquired by the fiduciary before the person became a fiduciary.

"STANDING" TO SEEK JUDICIAL RELIEF FOR BREACH OF FIDUCIARY DUTY

Legal historian Henry Summer Maine celebrated the fact that law and society in the twentieth century had evolved to a point where one's social position no longer affects her legal rights. Status, however, has not entirely disappeared from the law; one such area is probate,where only heirs and beneficiaries have standing to come before the court.

In order to bring suit against a fiduciary, one must have legal standing. To have standing, the litigant must demonstrate a sufficient connection to and harm from the challenged action. Anyone who has a present or future beneficial interest in an estate or trust, whether vested or contingent, has standing to bring a petition to remedy a fiduciary's breach of duty. A trustee has standing to bring a petition to remedy a co-trustee's breach of trust. A successor trustee would have standing to sue a predecessor for breach of trust.[240]

While the ward or individual holding an equitable interest is living, a civil action may be brought against a fiduciary either by the ward personally, by an agent acting under a power of attorney (if the power of attorney authorizes the agent to commence litigation), or by a conservator. If the victim is deceased, the action can be brought by the personal representative for the estate or by an heir or interested party. Interested persons include heirs of the decedent (as determined by state intestate statutes), legatees (those taking personal property under a will), devisees (those taking real property under a will), children, the spouse, creditors of the decedent, a co-personal representative and a successor personal representative.

TORTIOUS INTERFERENCE WITH AN INHERITANCE OR GIFT

There are times when an aggrieved party has no recourse in probate court. Non-heirs frequently fall into this category as they would not share in an intestate estate if successful in preventing admission of the will or trust. Examples include cases where the testator was prevented from signing a will, or where a will was executed but later destroyed by an heir. In such cases, the non-heir lacks standing because he or she would not share under intestate statutes (which leave to spouses and members of the blood line), and cannot prove that she would have taken under the lost or destroyed will. In other words, for non-heirs, without a will there may be no way to the courthouse steps.

Jointly owned assets, beneficiary designations, and transfers-on-death (TOD) present a similar problem. Not being included in the decedent's probate estate, non-heirs have no standing to object. The need for a legal forum for wronged non-heirs has grown along with the popularity of these *will substitutes*.

To give voice to non-heirs, a growing number of states recognize a legal action known as *Tortious Interference with an Inheritance or Gift. Tortious interference,* for short, is a non-probate tort action which allows aggrieved contestants, including non-heirs, to sue the wrongdoer directly in a separate cause of action outside probate court.

One author analogizes tortious interference to pass interference in football.[241] She sees the testator (or *donor* when a gift is at issue) as a quarterback intending to throw a pass to the plaintiff, the "intended receiver," who is prevented from catching the pass as a result of the defendant's pass interference. Although there is no guarantee that the intended receiver would have caught the pass (that is, ultimately would have been named beneficiary), the defendant is nevertheless penalized for depriving the plaintiff of that opportunity.

Perhaps the most famous tortious interference case involved 1993 Playboy Playmate of the Year, Anna Nicole Smith. In 2002, Anna (born Vickie Lynn Marshall) was awarded nearly ninety million dollars in a tortious interference action against her stepson E. Pierce Marshall (ironically, E. Pierce was 28 years her senior).

Not much of Anna's life was noteworthy prior to meeting Texas billionaire J. Howard Marshall II. She quit school in the eighth grade to work at Jim's Krispy Fried Chicken Shack, where she met and at age seventeen married deep fryer, Billy Smith. Anna worked as an exotic dancer under the stage names of "Miss Nikki," "Robin," and ultimately "Anna Nicole" because it sounded classier.

Anna's difficulties with step-son Pierce began in the early 1990s soon after she started dating his father. The senior Marshall, who had an estimated net worth of $1.6 billion dollars, met Anna in 1991 while she was performing in Houston, Texas. In June of 1994 at the age of 26, Anna married Howard, who at age 89 was sixty-three years her senior.

Anna claimed, and witnesses corroborated, that she married Marshall only after he verbally promised to gift her half of his estate. Mr. Marshall died in August of 1996, a mere fourteen months after the nuptials were completed. Much to her surprise, the late Mr. Marshall made no provision for her in his will or numerous trusts.

Anna first attempted to overturn Marshall's will and trusts in the Texas probate court. However, she abandoned her claim when she discovered that (through the use of a number of trust arrangements) J. Howard's estate actually had no assets. Instead, she opted to pursue a claim directly against her stepson, who she believed had tortiously interfered with his father's promised gift.

Nicole's suit against her stepson ultimately bore fruit, after passing through the labyrinth of state and federal courts, including the United States Supreme Court in *Marshall v. Marshall.* Anna was awarded forty-four million dollars in compensatory damages and forty-four million dollars in punitive damages for a total award of approximately ninety million dollars. The federal District Court found that E. Pierce, acting in concert with his father's attorney, had backdated, altered, and destroyed documents, misrepresented facts to J. Howard, and had committed perjury, all in an effort to block J. Howard's promised gift to Nicole.

Although *Marshall v Marshall* brought wide attention to the claim of tortious interference, the cause of action dates to the early 1800s. Today, twenty-five of the forty-two states that have considered it, now recognize it. The elements of tortious interference are as follows:

1. The plaintiff had an expectancy;
2. Conduct by the defendant interfered with it;
3. The defendant intended to interfere with it;
4. The defendant's conduct was tortious, such as by fraud, duress, or undue influence;
5. But for the defendant's interference, the plaintiff would have received the inheritance;
6. Damages.

Where available, a tortious interference claim may be favored over a probate procedure because a plaintiff in a tort claim may receive *compensatory damages* (the loss of what the plaintiff would have received but for the actions of the defendant); *consequential damages* (indirect losses due to the defendant's actions including pre-judgment interest, litigation costs and attorney's fees); and in some states (like the state of California in Anna's case) even *punitive damages* (damages over and above economic damages intended to punish the defendant for malicious, anti-social, or fraudulent acts).

Another advantage of tortious interference claims is the source of funds available for the defendant's defense. In probate, a defendant acting as personal representative may be able to use the assets of the estate to defend claims. Well-positioned wrongdoers who are also heirs often have little to lose. They can defend their bad acts out of the assets of the estate. If they prevail, they enjoy the full benefit of the estate. If the will or trust is determined to be invalid, their heir status guarantees that they nonetheless inherit under the laws of intestacy. By contrast, in a tortious interference action, defendants may not use the funds of the estate to defend claims, thus preserving the estate's assets while the challenge is litigated.

WILL AND TRUST CONTESTS

Will contests generally involve one or more of four basic issues:

1. The *testator's mental state* (e.g., testamentary capacity, undue influence, or mistake);
2. The *testator's failure to properly execute or the scrivener's failure to properly draft the will or a provision thereof* (e. g., lack of proper witnesses to the

will, failure to observe statutory execution requirements, alterations after execution, or forgery);

3. The *conduct or status of a third party* (e.g., a beneficiary's fraud or undue influence on the testator or a beneficiary's murder of the testator). For *fraud* to exist there must be a misrepresentation of a material fact, and the testator must have relied on the representation. Fraud comes in two flavors: *fraud in the execution* and *fraud in the inducement.* An example of fraud in the execution is where a testator with poor eyesight is told that the document he is signing leaves equally to his children when in fact it leaves everything to the one making the fraudulent misrepresentation. A bad actor that convinces a testator to disinherit one of his children with untrue statements about the child's financial or personal life is an example of fraud in the inducement. *Duress* exists when an unlawful act of one person induces another person to make a contract or perform some act under circumstances that deprive the person of his or her exercise of free will. Duress requires compulsion or coercion by which one is illegally forced to act due to fear of serious injury to person, reputation, or fortune. For example, a will procured while a gun was being held to the head of the testator would be the product of duress. *Mistake* occurs where the testator signed the wrong will; and

4. Whether *another will* should be admitted to probate instead of (or in addition to) the originally executed will.

If a will is invalid, it has no effect. All or part of the will may be adjudged as void. When a will is voided the clause that revokes all prior wills is also ineffective, and thus the prior will may be admitted to probate. If only a part of the will is voided, then only that part is void and the balance may be valid.

CRIMINAL COMPLAINT

Famed New York District Attorney, Robert Morgenthau (the model for the original district attorney Adam Schiff in the television show *Law & Order*) stated that Anthony Marshall and attorney Francis X. Morrissey, Jr. had been indicted for "swindling Mrs. Astor out of millions of dollars and valuable property" and that they "took advantage of Mrs. Astor's diminished mental capacity." Mr. Morgenthau, 90 years old himself at the time of these statements, sent the message that, "It happens fairly frequently that a son or daughter or grandson will steal from their parent or grandparent. That's why these cases are important, because we want the public to know that if you take advantage of an elderly person with diminished capacity, you're going to get prosecuted."[242]

Criminal charges that may be asserted against those who prey on the elderly include larceny, extortion, fraud, forgery, embezzlement, obtaining money by false pretenses, larceny by conversion, unlawful possession or use of a credit card, and identity theft. An increasing number of states have passed laws that provide explicit criminal penalties for various forms of elder abuse.

Larceny is the actual or constructive taking of property belonging to another person without the consent of the owner and with the intent to unlawfully deprive the owner of his or her property. A person can become the victim of larceny when, for example, a stranger gains access to her home on some pretext and upon entry steals jewelry or cash. Even if the elder has unwittingly consented to an individual's entering the elder's home, the individual may nonetheless be prosecuted for larceny if he or she commits a theft.

Extortion occurs when an individual maliciously threatens to accuse another of a crime or offense or maliciously threatens injury to the other person, his or her property, or an immediate family member for the purpose of extorting money or gaining pecuniary advantage.

Fraud is a general heading under which a number of different types of criminal acts are classified. It is generally unlawful for a person in a *relationship of trust* with a *vulnerable adult,* through fraud, deceit, misrepresentation, or unjust enrichment, to obtain, use, or attempt to obtain or use, the vulnerable adult's money or property to directly or indirectly benefit that person. A vulnerable adult is defined as an elderly or disabled adult who lacks cognitive skills required to manage his or her property. A person in a relationship of trust is defined as a person who is a caregiver; a relative by blood, marriage, or adoption; a household member; a court-appointed fiduciary; or another person who was entrusted with or had assumed responsibility for the management of the vulnerable adult's money or property.

Forgery is the uttering (attempt to pass the forged instrument) or publishing (actually passing) of a forged instrument. Examples of forgery include the writing of another's name on a check, increasing the amount of the check, or altering the payee.

Embezzlement is another fraud-related crime that is frequently committed against the elderly. Embezzlement is committed when an individual who is an agent, trustee, or another person of trust, who by virtue of his position, fraudulently disposes of or converts property to his own use without the owner's consent. Embezzlement under a particular figure, often $100, is a misdemeanor, while embezzlement over another figure, often $1000, is a felony.

Embezzlement can also occur when one party takes more than his fair share of a jointly owned bank or investment account. Even though joint accounts permit either party to legally transact on the account without the consent of the other owner, embezzlement can occur when one withdraws from the account without the consent of the co-owner. Refusal to return the wrongfully obtained money upon request is evidence of the intent to embezzle.

A criminal complaint can also be filed on the basis of physical or emotional abuse or neglect of a vulnerable adult. The law imposes a duty on certain individuals (like health care workers and law enforcement) to report cases of suspected abuse, neglect, or exploitation of vulnerable adults.

BROOKE ASTOR

The Brooke Astor case illustrates both the extensive duties imposed on fiduciaries and the civil and criminal consequences for their breach. Son Tony was both his mother's formal and informal fiduciary. As agent under her power of attorney and informal caretaker of her finances, he was fully subject to the fiduciary duties described in this chapter which required him to place his mother's interests above his own. Tony breached his numerous fiduciary duties when he procured lifetime and testamentary gifts from his failing mother and conspired to change the provisions of her will. The fact that his actions were discovered while his mother was still alive allowed for his removal and preservation of her estate.

Tony's son, Philip, initiated the legal intervention when he petitioned for his father's removal as fiduciary. That petition was immediately granted by the court, which appointed Annette de la Renta and the J.P. Morgan Stanley Bank as Brooke's new guardians. The case against Tony became a criminal case when the court evaluator (or what is sometimes called a *guardian ad litem* or GAL) referred the case to the New York District Attorney.

New York District Attorney Morgenthau's statement that elder abuse will be prosecuted was well articulated, but by no means should his statements be interpreted to mean that all financial elder abuse will be prosecuted. In reality, the manpower available to pursue criminal actions is limited, both at the police and prosecutorial level. Brooke Astor's case was likely chosen for prosecution because the abuse was flagrant, she was a revered public figure, and the anticipated media attention would prove useful in deterring others from abusing vulnerable adults.

CONCLUSION

Pursuing legal remedies of the type discussed in this Chapter Ten is a matter of last resort. It is rarely an experience from which winners emerge. Legal proceedings are public and often humiliating displays of family dysfunction which seal the fate of families and family cohesion. It is with this thought that we turn to Chapter Eleven: *An Ounce of Prevention.*

AN OUNCE OF PREVENTION 11

We shall not cease from exploration
And the end of all our exploring
Will be to arrive where we started
And know the place for the first time.
  - T.S. Eliot

If we could read the secret history of our
enemies, we would find in each man's life
sorrow and suffering enough to disarm all
hostility.
  - Henry Wadsworth Longfellow

OVERVIEW

Many of the problems of inheritance are themselves inherited. They are both genetic and acquired, but they are not inevitable. Inheritance disputes can be explained and predicted, and are to a large degree preventable.

Understanding is the first and usually the most difficult step. It requires one to put oneself in the shoes of stepparents, siblings, and step-siblings, the most frequent inheritance combatants. Avoiding conflict also requires that we critically examine our own contribution to the conflict. Easier said than done, as we humans are challenged when it comes to seeing ourselves objectively. We also rarely put ourselves in the shoes of those with whom we conflict, preferring instead to react to the reactions of others. Unfortunately, these undeveloped and little used skills are required as each participant must examine his or her unique role in family disputes: the villain, pacifist, mediator, pugilist, appeaser, victim, etc. Each must suspend his or her personal feelings and try to understand the perspective of other combatants who are acting out long held roles, feelings, and emotions. The recommendations that follow apply to a greater or lesser extent to all inheritance participants including will makers themselves.

Ideally, parents should lead in the prevention effort. They are in the best position to create family peace and minimize future fighting. Even in the most dysfunctional families parents hold at least a modicum of respect and authority. They can use that power, perhaps as they never have, to build bridges and mend fences. They may not ultimately be able to undo the old hurts that brought the family to its current state, but they must never stop trying.

Parents can best lead by having their affairs in order. Similar to succession planning in business, parents need a transition plan and a transition team after they die. Unfortunately, parents fail to plan for a number of reasons:

- They are paralyzed by their terror of death;
- They procrastinate;
- They do not want to invest in the cost of getting professional help;
- They believe that their estate is not large enough to warrant professional assistance;
- They are extremely private, distrusting, or too embarrassed to disclose their personal and financial matters;
- They are superstitious, believing that by planning for death they will accelerate its arrival;
- They have good intentions but become too ill to attend to their business;
- In the case of toxic testators, they fail to plan in order to leave a swirl of conflict and thus remain the center of attention after their death.

It is especially important for parents who anticipate conflict to plan ahead. Whether the issue is a family business, a history of sibling rivalry, or conflicted relationships between children and stepparents, greater care is required when handling combustible ingredients.

Children too must plan for the death of a parent. Children who see trouble brewing should take preemptive steps. They can agree to set aside old rivalries and learn to get along, or band together against a toxic parent. The best defense against a toxic testator is for family members to refuse to be pitted against one another. They can simply agree verbally or in writing not to be pawns in their parent's toxic plan. For example, they may agree that they will equally divide their inheritance no matter what their parent's will or trust provides. They may also agree to confer in all decision making no matter whom the parent appoints as fiduciary. Siblings should commit to keeping family business private and to exclude their spouses from discussions. Whether or not such agreements are legally binding is moot, since they are simply agreements to agree.

Brothers and sisters have a deep and long-term influence on us, and we on them. We must acknowledge this profound influence in our lives. If we want to improve our relationships with siblings, we must recognize that they, like us, are a product of upbringing. We must learn to accept them as human beings with strengths and flaws, just like us.

We need to see our brothers and sisters not as enemies or sources of pain or frustration, but as people who have been programmed by their own personal experiences. Even though they may have grown up in the same house, their experiences are unique to them. As Greek philospher Heraclitus of Ephesus once observed, "Upon those who step into the same rivers, different and again different waters flow."[243] They, too, are fragile human beings fighting their inner terrors and doing their best not to be pushed out of the proverbial nest.

We don't have to love one another just because we are brothers and sisters, but for our own inner peace, we must step back and empathetically examine our sibling relationships. Even if there is little chance that new insight will create peace, it is still likely to reduce the acrimony a notch or two. At a minimum, we will be better able to anticipate their motives and moves.

The stepparent–stepchild relationship is particularly fraught with problems, as both vie for the love and affection of the natural parent. Children must understand that their natural parent is, or was, a person with real needs that the stepparent fulfills or at one time fulfilled. Children must also understand that the stepparent has legitimate concerns about her economic well being after the death of her spouse. Stepparents, in turn, must understand that children see their inheritance as the final statement of their parent's love, and that the stepparent is perceived as interfering with that connection. Finally, the natural parent in a second marriage must be sensitive to the personal dynamic between his children and new spouse and take every step possible to keep the peace between both camps during life and after death.

Personality disorders, addictions, and mental illness are often difficult to address. With little or no insight into their problems, family members who suffer from such personal issues tend to be in denial of their problems and are extremely resistant to change. Despite these challenges, the only humane course is to persist in encouraging them to seek treatment. They are not bad people even though their actions can be extremely disruptive to family harmony.

There is no single silver bullet that will prevent inheritance disputes. Instead, prevention requires a multi-faceted approach that combines psychology, good lawyering, a lot of self-awareness, and a good dose of common sense.

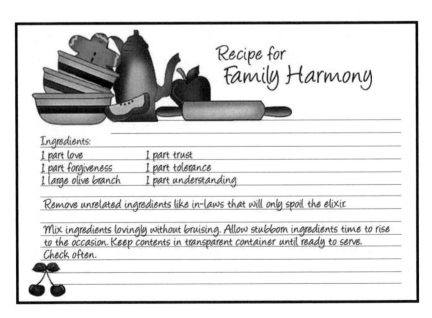

Recipe for
Family Harmony

Ingredients:
1 part love   1 part trust
1 part forgiveness   1 part tolerance
1 large olive branch   1 part understanding

Remove unrelated ingredients like in-laws that will only spoil the elixir.

Mix ingredients lovingly without bruising. Allow stubborn ingredients time to rise to the occasion. Keep contents in transparent container until ready to serve. Check often.

The following sixty-one recommendations are aimed at avoiding, minimizing, and resolving inheritance conflict. The recommendations are organized according to the stage of the conflict or potential conflict. The proper party to implement each recommendation varies, and in some cases the recommendation applies to more than one participant. For instance, although estate planning would seem to only apply to testators, spouses and children of elderly testators can encourage or facilitate them to plan. Children sensitive to family issues can assist parents in anticipating future problems. Testators may also look to family members for help in making estate planning decisions.

At the first sign of trouble, the proper course of action depends on the nature of the trouble, the competency of the victim, and how far the conflict has progressed. The final recommendation is for the parties to seek *facilitative mediation*. Mediation involves the use of a trained mediator who tries to bring the disputing parties together to resolve their differences. Facilitative mediation is voluntary, nonbinding, and relatively inexpensive. One wonders in retrospect whether Philip Marshall wishes he had heeded the advice of his wife and sought to mediate the dispute with his father.

ISOLATION, ASSISTANCE, AND LIVING ARRANGEMENTS

1. *Avoid isolation.* Elders should not be exposed to the dangers of isolation. Seniors living alone and who are experiencing cognitive decline are easy prey for influencers and abusers. Declining seniors should either receive ample family assistance, in-home care, or move to a setting where they can be around people as much as possible.

2. *Begin paring down possessions.* It is difficult to persuade seniors to leave their home no matter how bad their living conditions. Legally, you cannot force competent persons to leave their homes unless they are a danger to themselves or others. Seniors will often negotiate and stall for time claiming that they can't move until they have sorted through their mountain of accumulated stuff. Remove that barrier by assisting them in paring down, donating unused items to charity, gifting other items to family members, and throwing out the junk. You are going to have to do this job eventually; you might as well begin the process while your family member is alive and able to participate in the process. Be prepared for a fight. Each item you consider junk, they will view as a treasure. Seniors

frequently resist change of any kind, and their belongings anchor them in place. They may also intuitively know that cleaning out is the first step to moving to the next phase of their life.

3. *Hire it out.* Seek outside help from the growing number of companies that help seniors do everything from moving to organizing to scrapping. You can solicit help from local senior housing and assisted living communities. They are experts at overcoming the real and imagined obstacles to leaving one's home, and know how to address the red herrings presented by resistant seniors.

4. *Explore senior housing options.* The senior housing industry has exploded in recent years. Today, there are many options which offer progressive assistance, starting with independent living, assisted living, and finally, nursing home care. Continuing care retirement communities offer all of the options under one roof. Senior communities offer social contact and a protective environment. Meals, laundry, medical reminders, and other services can be purchased on an as-needed *a la carte* basis. Unfortunately, many seniors still associate senior living with nursing homes. Take your loved one for a tour so she can see for herself how much the industry has changed. Senior communities have community outreach programs, seminars, and open houses to introduce potential residents to their facilities.

5. *Professional home care agencies.* If the elder remains in his or her own home, consider outside help. It is best to retain licensed, insured, and bonded home health care or private duty agencies. They will do the necessary background checks on employees and backfill for sick workers and no-shows. Perhaps most importantly, undue influence can be minimized as most agencies prohibit employees from accepting gifts or bequests from their clientele.

6. *Everyone chips in.* If the decision is to share the care of an elder remaining at home, all family members should keep a log of their time, travel, and costs. Ideally, everyone should be paid for their efforts on an ongoing basis, perhaps monthly. However, if that is impractical – if for no other reason than that the elder is financially conservative and thinks that everyone should help for free – then costs and time spent can be sorted

out after the parent has passed. Getting paid may be difficult; studies show that approximately eighty-seven percent of those providing long-term care are unpaid.[244]

7. *Direct negotiation of home care.* If you decide to hire outside help directly and bypass professional home care agencies (which is not recommend but would cut the cost roughly in half), you should do background checks, sign a written agreement documenting the arrangement (including a no-gift, no bequest provision), and arrange payroll through a professional payroll company to prevent violation of state and federal tax and employment laws.

8. *Moving in with mom or vice versa.* Still the most widely practiced method of caring for the elderly, moving in with a parent is often a recipe for disaster. It creates tensions within the caretaker's household, and activates old jealousies and sibling rivalries. However, if it is determined that the senior should live with a caretaker family member or vice versa, the arrangement should be preceded by a family meeting and documented with a written lease or care agreement. A care agreement written by an elder law attorney will avoid having payments for services later characterized as gifts for purposes of Medicaid or other government benefits. It is only fair that a family member who is willing to care for an aging parent be compensated for his services. Other family members should be willing to pay for the luxury of being relieved of such day-to-day responsibilities. A fair wage can avoid the jealousies and suspicions that fester when one family member is doing the bulk of the work. It also minimizes a caretaker's temptation to simply take what they think they deserve.

Payment of fifty percent of the going commercial rate for family-provided services is fair. Consider hiring a payroll service to assure that all employment forms and taxes are filed and paid. Also consider an arrangement with a home health care agency whereby the family caretaker is employed by the agency which in turn handles payroll, training, and backup.

A family member with a history of substance abuse or who is financially dependent on the elder should never be allowed to be the principal caretaker of an elder. Studies show that this population is the most likely to abuse.

9. *Assemble your team.* Engage a team to perform legal, accounting, bill-paying, and investment services. Team members may be family members possessing the requisite skills, or professionals if the elder's budget permits. Regular and periodic review of all transactions helps keep everybody honest and in compliance with various state and federal laws. The team should meet regularly to assess the elder's personal and financial condition.

10. *Meet regularly.* Family members should meet regularly to review the income, assets, tax, investment, and medical status of their aging loved one. Transparency, full disclosure, and accountability help keep everyone honest. Family members should be encouraged to report suspicious behavior.

ESTATE PLANNING GENERALLY

11. *Employ experts.* Use a qualified elder law attorney to prepare the elder's estate plan. The complicated mass of laws relating to elders (local, state, and federal income, estate and gift tax, property taxes, Social Security, Medicare, Medicaid, Veterans benefits, etc.) requires that you hire an expert. Kids, don't try this at home!

12. *Estate planning.* Do estate planning early and make changes as necessary to remain current with the elder's changing needs and circumstances. A basic estate plan varies somewhat from state to state but typically includes powers of attorney (health and financial), a will, and a revocable trust. The estate plan should appoint fiduciaries and make bequests that are fair and reasonable. Assets should be re-titled to give full effect to the testator's dispositive wishes.

13. *Save old wills and trusts.* Save all old wills and trusts in order to establish a pattern of behavior. A documented history will help identify eleventh-hour changes procured by fraud or undue influence.

14. *Use two agents for financial powers of attorney.* Powers of attorney are useful tools in managing the affairs of declining elders. An agent stands in the shoes of the principal and may exercise all of the powers of the

principal as if the principal were himself present. Officially appointing an agent creates a fiduciary relationship that provides better recourse in the event of any wrongdoing. To avoid abuse by a wayward agent, consider appointing co-agents who must act together.

15. *Use a single health care advocate.* Health care powers of attorney involve time-sensitive emotional issues that are potentially a matter of life or death. In this respect they are fundamentally different from financial powers, which govern mundane day-to-day financial and administrative matters. A single health care advocate who shares the principal's views on life and death is able to make urgent health care decisions without the potential for conflict that may arise with co-advocates. A disagreement between co-health care surrogates would result in paralysis at a potentially critical juncture. The principal is protected from ill-advised decisions of a single health care agent by the strict ethical code under which health care professionals operate.

16. *Address personal property separately.* Leave a separate list of cherished personal property with instructions as to who should inherit each item. Personal property is often a source of conflict among family members. Most states admit a separate personal property list (sometimes called a *Personal Property Memorandum*) as part of the will. A separate list can be handwritten or typed but must be signed and dated. The list should be of sufficient detail to effectively describe each item being gifted.

17. *Update plan regularly.* Make estate planning changes when there has been a change of circumstances, especially divorce. Although most states' matrimonial laws nullify beneficiary designations and will provisions that favor former spouses, it is unclear whether a former spouse continues to be empowered under medical or financial powers of attorney. To avoid unwanted and bizarre results, former spouses should be immediately disinherited and stripped of all powers. Additionally, estate planning should be reviewed after other life changes, like the death or divorce of a child, or the illness, addiction or incapacity of any beneficiary.

18. *Keep the detials of your estate plan private.* Some parents have a history of including their adult children in their decisions, including those related to financial matters. Others are more private, operating on a need-to-

know basis. Yet others treat their personal matters like the recipe for Coca Cola or McDonald's secret sauce. Each family has a system that works for them. That said, estate planning is essentially autobiographical and un-democratic. Testators need not seek approval or consensus for their plan. Although they should speak with potential fiduciaries to inquire hypothetically whether they would be willing to act, testators need not definitively commit to a particular choice. By not committing, testators minimize future hurt feelings if they later change their mind. All potential fiduciaries should be on call to act if and when needed.

19. *Special assets may require open discussion.* There are situations where family input is advisable. Issues like care for a handicapped child, succession of a family business, or continued enjoyment of a vacation home require parents and children to be on the same page.

20. *Prenuptial agreement.* Second marriages are one of the most significant indicators of inheritance conflict. A prenuptial or a post-nuptial agreement will minimize conflict at death by clearly stating the relative entitlements of spouses and other beneficiaries such as children not of the marriage.

21. *Clearly identify gifts and loans.* Parents often help adult children who are experiencing financial distress. It is the parent's prerogative to structure such advances as either loans or gifts. Unpaid loans from mom and dad can be a source of conflict, activating jealousies about who got more. Parents should resolve uncertainty regarding lifetime advances by addressing them in their estate plan. Parents can forgive such advances with a statement in their will or trust to the effect that: "transfers made during my life to my children, if any, were gifts and need not be repaid." Conversely, where transfers were intended as loans, proper loan documentation should be procured and repayment required at the parent's death perhaps as a setoff against the borrower's inheritance.

22. *Properly fund trusts.* All assets should be funded or appropriately re-titled into trust to avoid probate and confusion as to the testator's intent. If, for example, the will or trust leaves equally among the testator's children, life insurance policies and annuities should name the trust as beneficiary. If for tax or other purposes it is appropriate to name beneficiaries directly, then include a statement in the trust that all beneficiaries are to receive an

equal share taking into consideration assets that pass outside the trust.

23. *Avoid joint ownership.* Joint ownership (i.e., placing a child's name as a joint owner of a parent's asset) is an inefficient method of passing assets at death and can produce unintended results. Adding a beneficiary as an owner of assets like real estate confers significant and sometimes irrevocable lifetime rights, exposes the donor to the co-owner's liabilities, and limits the donor's ability to change his or her mind in the future. The most efficient and predictable plan is to fund all assets into trust.

24. *Pre-arrange funeral.* Making funeral arrangements and choosing the form of interment in advance can avoid conflict and the strong emotions that such decisions sometimes elicit. For example, re-married widows and widowers should determine in advance who is to be buried with whom. Pre-planned and detailed written funeral instructions avoid controversy and angst.

25. *Include an "in terrorem" clause to prevent will contests.* Latin for in order to frighten, an *in terrorem* clause (also known as a *no contest,* or *forfeiture* clause) penalizes will contestants with disinheritance.

Although disinheritance clauses may appear to be a simple solution to prevent fighting, they have a number of limitations, including the fact that courts are reluctant to enforce them. Even states that uphold such clauses strictly construe them in order to prevent an outcome that is unconscionable or against public policy. Such was the case in *Girard Trust Co. v. Schmitz,* where the court refused to uphold an *in terrorem* clause that required family members to sever their ties with one another in order to inherit.

States vary in their treatment of no-contest clauses. A minority of states recognize them unconditionally under the view that testators should have the same absolute right to dispose of their property at death as they had during life. Such states support use of no contest clauses to deter frivolous or unfounded will contests, and protect testators from having the details of their life dragged through the public court system. States upholding no contest clauses only penalize unsuccessful contestants; successful contestants are not punished.

A minority of states including Florida, Indiana, Louisiana, and South Carolina consider forfeiture clauses invalid, reasoning that their citizens should have full access to the judicial system. These states take the view of the South Carolina justice who stated that: "no citizen should be obstructed by risk of forfeiture from ascertaining his rights by the law of the land."[245]

The vast majority of states adopt a third approach: they enforce no contest clauses only if the contestant acted in *bad faith* and without *probable cause*. Proponents of this majority position believe that beneficiaries should be allowed to challenge a will as long as they do so in good faith and with reasonable cause to support their claim. A contestant with probable cause who brings his claim in good faith will not be penalized with forfeiture even if he loses in court.

Courts are mixed as to what constitutes a *contest*. Some hold that the mere filing of a suit, without more, is sufficient to cause a forfeiture, while others require that the case move well beyond the initial filing. Some states permit a *safe-harbor* filing wherein contestants apply to the court for a determination as to whether a certain act constitutes a contest, and whether a provision in a will or trust violates public policy. The court's decision allows the potential contestant to better assess the risks of moving forward with a full petition.

Testators should consider adding a no contest clause where a will contest is anticipated. It may give a contestant without hard evidence of wrongdoing second thoughts before bringing a claim. However, testators should be aware of the legal maxim that *"equity abhors a forfeiture."* Courts are reluctant to enforce provisions that unfairly punish those who are merely exercising their legal rights.

Many estate planning attorneys view no contest clauses as unnecessary and even dangerous. They believe that the cost of bringing frivolous suits is a sufficient deterrent against challenges that lack probable cause. They also fear that *in terrorem* clauses can be misused by bad actors to prevent rightful heirs from challenging their actions.

NAMING FIDUCIARIES

26. *Name spouse as primary fiduciary.* Absent special circumstances, one's spouse in a first marriage should be named as primary and sole fiduciary. As recently as the 1970s, well-heeled husbands even in first marriages commonly named a bank and trust company as trustee of trusts established for their wives and children. Today, such arrangements would be unacceptable to most wives, as women have become full participants in the family economic unit.

In second marriages where there are children not of the marriage, each spouse should consider establishing his or her own separate revocable trust. While each spouse may act as the other's fiduciary, it may be preferable to appoint a neutral third-party or professional (corporate) trustee to mediate the disparate interests of the surviving spouse and natural children. It is not advisable to name a spouse as co-fiduciary with children not of the marriage. Stepparents and stepchildren are natural competitors and in most cases should not be forced to work together.

27. *Make logically defensible choices.* Determining who is "in charge" is an emotionally loaded issue. It is perceived as the testator's statement as to who is the most competent and trustworthy. Such decisions are reminiscent of the day when mom went to the store and put one of the children, usually the oldest, in charge. Mom hadn't left the driveway before younger children would protest: *"you're not the boss of me,"* or more prophetically, *"who died and left you in charge."* Appointing fiduciaries can be seen as an act of favoritism and should be thoughtfully considered. Naturally the testator wants the best person for the job to ensure that his wishes are properly carried out. However, parents must still be sensitive to their children's emotional reactions. Children can rationalize an older sibling being appointed simply on the basis of seniority. They can also accept the naming of in-towners over out-of-towners on the basis of convenience and geographic desirability. Children, however, cannot accept appointments that disturb the traditional family hierarchy and

pecking order. Where children are equally situated, appoint them as co-fiduciaries. Don't leave anybody out; name a younger or less able child as successor to a successor if for no other reason than that he sees that you remembered him.

28. *Be aware of long-established sibling roles.* In addition to age, name children on the basis of traditional family leadership roles. It is an insult in the order of disinheritance to take a leadership role away from a deserving child who has traditionally held that role and served it well.

29. *Appoint a committee.* Naming a committee of fiduciaries has a number of benefits: Two heads are better than one; a committee keeps each member honest; communication with non-fiduciary beneficiaries is facilitated by having more than one spokesperson; and multiple fiduciaries can share the workload and minimize burnout and resentment. Misunderstandings can quickly escalate when a single overburdened fiduciary fails to respond timely to beneficiary inquiries. In turn, a single fiduciary may resent repeated inquiries from what he perceives as greedy or overly-eager beneficiaries. The failure of an overburdened fiduciary to timely respond to inquiries raises suspicions that the fiduciary is trying to hide something. A committee solves many of these problems and should be considered *as long as all of the members of the committee get along.*

NAMING BENEFICIARIES

30. *First marriages.* Except where extenuating circumstances dictate, in first marriages one's surviving spouse should be named primary and sole beneficiary. A testator's first obligation is to his or her surviving spouse. As children can no longer be expected to care for ill or aging parents, spouses must leave each other in the best possible position to provide for their own needs. The risk that children will be disinherited is minimal as they are the logical beneficiary of both spouses.

31. *Balance the needs of second spouses and children.* Second marriages are one of the leading causes of family inheritance conflict. Care should be taken to accommodate the financial and emotional needs of both the surviving spouse and children. Consider an outright transfer to natural children at the death of the first spouse in an amount that will not jeopardize the

well-being of the surviving spouse. Parents who completely withhold all distributions to their children until after the death of a stepparent create a potential deathwatch. There is no impatience like that of stepchildren waiting for a stepparent to die in order that they may receive what they believe to be rightfully theirs.

32. *Leave to children equally.* Treat children equally. An unequal allocation is a blatant and unforgivable showing of favoritism that will re-activate old sibling rivalries and hurt feelings. Children have unequal needs growing up. Some will naturally receive more based on special skills (travel sports, private schools, piano lessons), or special needs (braces, glasses, special shoes, or furlough from physical labor). The past is the past; don't be tempted to leave unequally at death to account for early inequities. Don't penalize successful children by leaving more to their needy siblings, or conversely, reward successful children because they are favored. Exceptions to this general rule are the truly handicapped and those who would use their inheritance to further an unhealthy lifestyle of addiction or sloth.

33. *Make lifetime gifts.* Attempt to accommodate special needs through lifetime gifts. Lifetime gifts, like a dowry for a daughter or a stake for a son, have been used throughout history to accomplish inheritance objectives. Be aware, however, that children have extremely sensitive antennae for detecting favoritism and are likely to become aware of such gifts.

34. *Family businesses.* A family business should pass to those family members who have been active in the business and who are instrumental to its future success. The fragile nature of businesses requires that there be a smooth transition from one generation to the next. A seamless transition requires the gradual passing of the torch while parents are alive. Parents should groom their successors by gradually transferring responsibility and authority to their successors over time. Non-business assets can be used to equalize the share of children not active in the business. Life insurance can be used to augment the value of the estate to ensure that sufficient assets are available to achieve an equal distribution to all children.

35. *Disinherit only as a last resort.* Be certain before you disinherit, as it leaves a lasting legacy of hurt and rejection. If your final decision is to disinherit, you are best advised not to explain your reason for disinheriting. From a

legal standpoint, presenting a reason only invites a challenge on the basis that the precondition was erroneous. Contrary to its portrayal in movies, the law does not require the disinherited to receive "one dollar." Modern estate planning documents simply state that "For reasons best known to me, I make no provision hereunder for …."

36. *Ethical wills.* Create an ethical will that supplements the formal legal estate plan. Not a legal document or a matter of public record, an ethical will expresses the decedent's thoughts and feelings on such important issues as family unity, education, spirituality, child rearing, and love. Ethical wills take the guesswork out of the question of what the decedent "would have wanted."

ESTATE PLAN EXECUTION

37. *Hire a qualified attorney.* Avoid the use of estate planning documents downloaded from the Internet or the Suze Orman package. In addition to knowing the law, a qualified attorney has experience working with families and can counsel clients on the pitfalls associated with various courses of action. An attorney has an ethical duty to the testator, must represent him or her zealously and loyally, serves as the most important and objective witness of the testator's intentions, and ensures compliance with execution formalities.

38. *Be alert for undue influence.* Special attention is required if the testator is susceptible to undue influence. If the testator was brought to the attorney's office by someone, the attorney must speak to the testator outside the presence of that person as to the testator's understanding and intent.

39. *Choose credible impartial witnesses.* Procure thoughtful and impartial witnesses who are neither family members nor a beneficiary. Although beneficiaries may witness a will, it may be used as evidence of undue influence. To avoid any appearance of impropriety, beneficiaries should not participate in the execution ceremony.

40. *Formal and informal discussion.* For the most part, attorneys and witnesses are not formally trained in assessing capacity. Nonetheless, courts have historically relied on the common sense perceptions of lay witnesses on the belief that the average man should be able to identify

cases where capacity is lacking. Without formal psychological measuring tools, attorneys and witnesses rely on the testator's appearance, actions, and interactions at the time of execution. Experienced estate planning attorneys should engage the testator in a series of formal questions designed to satisfy the elements of testamentary capacity and the absence of undue influence. For evidentiary purposes, attorneys typically ask the same series of questions at each and every execution, including:

- "Have you come here of your own free will?"
- "Do you realize that you are signing your will, trust, and powers of attorney?"
- "Do you realize that by signing these documents you will be leaving your entire estate to your three children equally?"

It is also prudent to summarize the financial assets of the testator to be sure that the testator appreciates the size and nature of his or her estate. Apart from this formal line of questioning, time should be taken to engage in the normal chit chat that accompanies any social interaction, as such intercourse offers valuable clues as to the testator's capacity.

41. *Review and summarize documents before signing.* The attorney should review and summarize all estate planning documents with the testator before execution. Execution should proceed only after the attorney is satisfied that the testator understands what he or she is signing and that the terms of the documents are consistent with the testator's intent.

42. *Use a self-proved will.* A self-proved will (or a subsequently executed self-proving affidavit) may be admitted to probate without the testimony of witnesses. To qualify, the testator and the witnesses must declare before a notary public (in a separate special written statement appended to the will) that the testator, in the presence of witnesses, signed the instrument as his or her last will and that each of the witnesses, in the presence of the testator and in the presence of each other, signed the will as witnesses. A self-proved will is presumed to satisfy the requirements of execution.

43. *Videotaping.* The legal community is split on whether will signings should

be videotaped. Proponents believe that videotape doesn't lie, and that the tape will show the circumstances surrounding the signing. Opponents believe that videotape unfairly highlights the deficits of a feeble testator who may have hearing problems or be nervous in front of the camera. In practice, will executions are rarely videotaped. Most attorneys believe that videotape only detracts from the strong presumption of capacity accorded to a properly witnessed and executed will.

44. *Make a contemporaneous gift.* To preempt a foreseeable will contest, some attorneys recommended that the testator write a check to the potential contestant contemporaneous with the execution of the will. Acceptance of the gift serves as evidence that the contestant believed the testator had testamentary capacity on the date of execution. The greater the gift the more likely it will prevent (the legal term is *estop*) the donee from contesting the will. The author is not aware of any decided cases that uphold this strategy.

45. *Keep executed estate planning documents in a safe place.* Wills and other estate planning documents should be kept in a safe place away from those who could be tempted to alter or destroy them. Historically, drafting attorneys retained an executed copy of the client's entire estate plan, and the only original copy of the will. In recent years, a number of law firms have gone paperless and thus no longer retain original printed documents. Paperless firms, however, retain "PDF" copies of executed documents which may be admitted to probate in the event the original cannot be located.

46. *Keep estate planning content private.* Clients often ask whether they should give a copy of their estate plan to their children. With the exception of health care powers of attorney (living wills), the answer for most families is "no." As in the movie *Back To The Future,* you don't want knowledge of the future to affect the course of history. As its author, you reserve the right to change the ending of your personal history. Giving documents during life creates the expectation that no changes will be made. Later changes will be viewed as taking away something previously given. We don't know the future; keep open the possibility that things may change.

ADMINISTERING THE ESTATE
AFTER THE DEATH OF THE TESTATOR

47. *Fiduciaries must be transparent.* In addition to their numerous legal duties, fiduciaries must also manage the expectations and anxieties of beneficiaries. Fiduciaries can make their job much easier if they keep all interested parties informed. Nothing fuels anxieties like the unknown. Trust and estate administration can take months or even years. The length and formality of the process sometimes raises suspicions. The best way to prevent unrest is to make the process as transparent as possible. Fiduciaries should reach out to beneficiaries as soon as possible after appointment and regularly communicate thereafter. Unless there are special circumstances, the initial communication should contain a copy of all relevant estate planning documents, and a brief explanation of the administration process. Beneficiaries will naturally want to know how much they're going to receive. Fiduciaries should explain that they are gathering information and will give beneficiaries an initial inventory as quickly as possible.

48. *Get professional help.* Fiduciaries should not try to administer estates and trusts without professional help. Engaging the services of an accountant, financial advisor, realtor, and a qualified attorney insulates the fiduciary from liability, eases the burden of administration, and assures compliance with all applicable laws and regulations. Funneling communications through the attorney also insulates fiduciaries from information-hungry beneficiaries who can torment a busy fiduciary.

49. *Keep in-laws out of the process.* Except in rare cases, in-laws only complicate matters. In-laws bring their own agenda, upset established family roles, and can quickly throw an already difficult process into disarray. In-laws do not have a direct interest in family affairs and should not be part of this particular family dynamic. One can only speculate whether Tony Marshall would have had the same compulsion to grab for his mother's estate had it not been for his wife, Charlene, who lived most of her life as poor as a "church mouse."

50. *Have a family meeting.* Unless you think it will only result in chaos, bring all family members together (without in-laws) in the attorney's office for

a classic reading of the will. After seeing such scenes depicted in movies, the American public has come to expect a formal reading of the will. Give them what they want. A formal reading may quell anxieties, give credibility to the process, and set the tone for a smooth administration.

51. *Make interim distributions.* The longer beneficiaries go without receiving a distribution the more anxious they become. Make an early distribution of a small portion of the estate or trust. Interim distributions not only allay anxieties but may also estop beneficiaries who accept the distribution (evidenced by cashing the distribution check) from challenging the administration of the will.

SIGNS OF TROUBLE

52. *Stay involved.* Be proactive to prevent abuse before it occurs. Stay regularly involved with elders and do not allow them to be isolated by a family member or caretaker. Be alarmed if you can never see your loved one outside the presence of the caretaker, or if he or she is never well enough for visitors or to come to the phone.

53. *Regularly test for cognitive ability.* Loss of executive function significantly impacts vulnerability. Unfortunately, internists and family physicians are neither trained nor reimbursed for routine cognitive screening. Cognitive function should therefore be regularly assessed by a trained psychiatrist, neuropsychologist, or geriatrician. Obtaining a cognitive baseline prior to signs of decline allows for the accurate assessment of change and decline.

54. *Alert financial advisors and institutions.* Report irregularities to financial advisors, banks, and other financial institutions. Doing so locks up the money before it is hijacked by wrongdoers.

55. *Call authorities.* Contact Adult Protective Services and law enforcement if there are signs of financial or physical elder abuse.

56. *Revise estate plan.* If the elder target has sufficient capacity, create or amend powers of attorney, wills, and trusts as necessary to remove wrongdoers from positions of authority and replace them with fiduciaries who have the elder's best interests in mind.

57. *Create an irrevocable trust.* The testator may create an irrevocable trust to protect at-risk assets. Being irrevocable, the testator permanently forgoes the right to alter the trust or take back funded assets. Safely within the castle walls of the trust, funded assets are outside the reach of bad actors. An independent trustee - a corporate professional trustee should be considered for this purpose – or committee of family members should be appointed to administer the trust on behalf of the testator. The trustee would be required to produce and disseminate periodic accountings to safeguard against irregular or suspicious activities. There are a number of income tax consequences associated with irrevocable trusts that must be discussed with the drafting attorney or a certified public accountant when exploring this option.

58. *Install a trust protector.* Add an independent trust protector to the irrevocable trust described above. Trust protectors are usually attorneys who can react to changes in circumstance, consent to extraordinary disbursements, and address assaults on the trust by would-be abusers and influencers. Naturally, the trust protector must be beyond reproach in character and reputation.

59. *Commence protective legal action.* Commence guardianship or conservatorship proceedings where the measures described above are ineffective, impractical, or impossible.

RESOLVING CONFLICT
AFTER PROBLEMS ERUPT

60. *Family settlement agreements (after testator's death).* In what amounts to a contract, heirs may agree on a reasonable interpretation of a decedent's will or trust. Courts generally favor the use of family settlement agreements unless they substantially alter or undermine the testator's intent. To be binding, all beneficiaries must consent. Some states require the consent of the acting trustee or personal representative. A stricter standard applies to trusts. Some states require that such agreements be used only to resolve a contest, controversy, or question of construction or interpretation. A more liberal standard applies to wills, where the beneficiaries may simply agree on an interpretation whether or not there exists a controversy or

question of interpretation. Court approval is advised, especially when minor or incompetent beneficiaries or heirs are involved. The court may require the appointment of a *guardian ad litem* to interview interested parties and protect the interests of minor or unborn beneficiaries.

"Discourage litigation. Persuade your neighbors to compromise whenever you can....As a peacemaker a lawyer has a superior opportunity of being a good man. There will still be business enough."
   - Abraham Lincoln: Address On Legal Ethics 1850

61. *Facilitative mediation.* Facilitative mediation is a relatively inexpensive and effective way of resolving family disputes. Families can avoid the cost and emotional trauma of litigation by enlisting the services of a third party, neutral mediator trained in such matters. Referral to mediation is usually by the court, but the parties can voluntarily agree to mediate their dispute without court involvement.

Once communication has broken down, family members become emotionally frozen in their positions. Aggrieved family members naturally seek legal counsel to understand their rights and how the law will resolve their conflict. What happens next, including whether the family will permanently fracture depends, in part, on the training and experience of the lawyers involved.

Lawyers are trained to think in "war" mode, as our ethical code requires that we zealously advocate on behalf of our clients. Nothing in our Canons of Ethics addresses the emotional fallout of our advocacy. Once the parties "lawyer up," communication generally takes place only through lawyers, and a permanent wedge is driven between the disputing parties. Litigation only furthers the divide. The long-term effect of playing the lawsuit card is that the parties may never speak to one another again.

Some families are irrevocably broken by the time they seek legal counsel. For them all that remains are legal remedies. Other families, though strained to the breaking point, are salvageable and every attempt should be made to craft a resolution that preserves their life-long relationships.

Many in the legal community recognize the limitations of traditional legal remedies. One judge observed: "The bottom line of every case I've ever settled is one or both participants' perception that they have been dishonored or disrespected."[246] Another jurist stated that, "In many cases it isn't about the money or how many feet of property they are going to get or who caused the accident; it is about the apology and the recognition of fault and error in a society where we are not allowed to say, 'It is my fault and I am sorry.'"[247] With such a disconnect between what combatants desire (vindication, exoneration, to be heard) and what is awarded (money), it is not surprising that both sides in traditional litigation are dissatisfied with the end result.

The parties in facilitative mediation retain their voice. A neutral mediator, who may be an attorney, retired judge, or a layperson trained in mediation, promotes communication in the hope that the parties can work to resolve their differences. Although frequently accompanied by their attorneys, participants in facilitative mediation are allowed to speak their mind in a structured environment. Facilitative mediation is said to be focused on the future, with the goal of preserving family relationships.

Mediators do not render a decision; they simply promote resolution of the dispute. They do not give legal advice; do not opine as to the relative value or merits of either party's case; and do not predict the possible outcome of the dispute should the parties fail to reach a mediated settlement and proceed to litigation or arbitration.

Mediation can be a useful tool in will contests, trust disputes, guardianship and conservator cases, appointment of personal representative, visitation or care giving issues, health and medical care decisions, financial and accounting issues, living arrangements, sale of real estate, and personal property title disputes. Mediation may not be appropriate where there is suspected abuse, possible criminal activity, severe power imbalances, or capacity issues of key parties.

Mediation is one of the *alternate dispute resolution* or "ADR" tools employed by modern courts to ameliorate court backlogs and to minimize the uncertainty and the emotional burdens of litigation. The relatively high satisfaction of those who participate in ADR makes for happy judges, clients, and attorneys.

Facilitative mediation should not be confused with evaluative mediation or arbitration, both of which are designed to expedite resolution of cases without trial. Both look to a third-party mediator or arbitrator to assess the relative strength of their assigned case, and suggest a settlement "price" that, if rejected, can result in sanctions to the losing party.

Facilitative mediation is entirely voluntary and non-binding. The parties pay the mediator a pre-agreed and often pre-paid fee. They are typically required to sign an agreement (sometimes called "consent to mediate") which addresses the general ground rules of the mediation including the fact that the proceedings are confidential. Statements made during mediation may not be used in later legal proceedings. Ethically, mediators may not disclose information learned in private sessions with one side to the other side without the disclosing party's consent.

If the parties come to an agreement the mediator typically documents their agreement in a *memorandum of understanding,* which becomes the basis of a formal legal settlement.

FINAL THOUGHTS | 12

FINAL THOUGHTS

We spend our life competing for love and acceptance. As infants we attach to our parents, and later with siblings, friends, love interests, our spouse, children, and family. These relationships are critical to our concept of self, safety, and belonging. We never lose our need for human contact, and quickly lose our bearings when deprived of it.

Despite the importance of our relationships we are innately and fundamentally challenged. Our innate fears pit us against one another for what should be an abundant, if not unlimited, resource: love. Man has evolved to be an anxious being, afraid of lions and tigers and the prospect of being separated from the pack. Ironically, these anxieties interfere with the very relationships we so desperately seek. Our deepest yearnings and most profound fears compete with each other; the greater our yearnings the greater our fear that what we seek will be taken away. Our human propensity to conflict with others is a reflection of this internal conflict.

The short answer to Rodney King's question *"Why can't we all just get along?"* is that our insecurities compete with our desire for real intimacy. We act preemptively against perceived competitors that we fear will steal our sources of love. It is for this reason that the most important relationships in our life —our parents, siblings, and marriage partners – are often characterized by ambivalence. And this phenomenon is not limited to individual relationships; world history is dominated by conflict over resources and ideology. Countries and religions trample one another in their desperate attempt to secure resources, borders, and to assert their ideology.

Our innate fears also make us myopic. We are prone to struggle for day to day survival even as technology allows us the freedom and opportunity to connect with others. We are driven in our temporal pursuits to avoid looking at death. We spend precious hours each day watching television, surfing the internet, chasing greater wealth, appearing successful, and fighting with those we fear will steal our stuff. If we can muster the courage to rise above the clatter of every day living we can more clearly define our purpose and legacy.

Building family harmony and avoiding family conflict is a much harder task than may appear on the surface. It begins by looking at our contribution to the conflict. As many of the grievances of our early life are played out in inheritance disputes, understanding family conflict also requires that we step into the shoes of those with whom we conflict. To do so requires that we put aside our personal baggage and realize that our rivals are just as much the product of their past and fears as we. Our quirks, deficiencies, and ulterior motives are just as transparent to them as theirs are to us. Rival family members are the product, perhaps even prisoners, of their past just as we are. They too are handicapped when it comes to seeing their contribution to the problem.

Personal change is extremely difficult; changing others, especially those with whom we compete for valuable resources, is nearly impossible. Resolving inheritance conflict thus requires that we look at our own desires, motives, needs, and terrors. We need to stop and wonder *"Why is this thing (inheritance,*

role of authority, dinner setting for twelve) so important?", "Why am I so upset?" ...
"Why is it that every little thing about my parent, stepparent, sibling, or sister-in-law annoy me so much?" and ultimately, "What difference does it make anyway?"

"When I was young, I set out to change the world. When I grew a little older, I perceived that this was too ambitious, so I set out to change my state. This too, I realized as I grew older, was too ambitious, so I set out to change my town. When I realized I could not even do this, I tried to change my family. Now as an old man, I know that I should have started changing myself. If I had started with myself, maybe then I would have succeeded in changing my family, the town, or even the state – and who knows, maybe even the world."

A story told by an old Hasidic Rabbi

It is hoped that *Blood & Money* has left you, the reader, with a new commitment to contemplate your life and legacy; and that if you are on a toxic path, you change course as did Alfred Nobel. While few of us will leave a financial or philanthropic legacy akin to those left by the famous altruistic testators in Chapter Four, we can all aspire to the legacy of John Estrada, as told by his son Fred Estrada way back on page xv: to live on in the hearts and minds of those we leave behind, to make them feel loved and proud to be our child, brother, sister or loved one.

We now turn to the Appendix, *How We Got Here: History of Inheritance,* to examine how we arrived at this place in modern inheritance law.

HOW WE GOT HERE
- A HISTORY OF INHERITANCE

"Learn the laws of inheritance, and teach them to the people; for they are one half of useful knowledge."
- Prophet Muhammed

"Every major legal tradition struggles to link its formal structures and processes with the beliefs and ideals of its people."
- John Witte, Jr.[248]

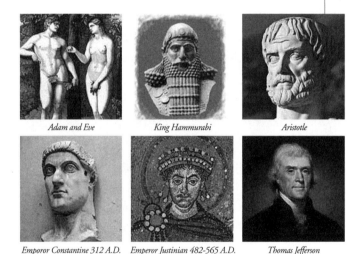

Adam and Eve   *King Hammurabi*   *Aristotle*

Emporor Constantine 312 A.D.   *Emperor Justinian 482-565 A.D.*   *Thomas Jefferson*

INTRODUCTION

The stability of a people demands that there be a system of inheritance in place to govern the orderly transfer of property from one generation to the next. The potential for conflict in inheritance is high, and the need for a system to avoid it is manifest. "As humans die and institutions remain,"[249] inheritance customs and laws bridge the gap between the living and the departed. Historically, both religion and government have claimed jurisdiction over inheritance. Whether it concerned the passage of one's possessions or one's soul, both played a role: government with its focus on maintaining social order and religion's focus on the moral, ethical, and spiritual elements of passage.

Historically, the stakes were much higher than determining who would inherit dad's Ford pickup; they involved who would eat and who would not. The death of an individual, apart from being emotionally upsetting to the decedent's loved ones, also had the potential to upset the natural balance of power within a family and without. In early societies, it was of utmost importance for the clan or tribe to maintain control of the resources necessary for survival and maintenance of power. If inherited property were allowed to leave the survival unit, it could disturb the balance of power, resulting in chaos and disruption of the economic system.

Inheritance laws therefore serve a number of purposes:
1. Maintenance of social and economic order;
2. Minimization of conflict;
3. Facilitation of commerce by providing continuity from one generation to the next;
4. Promotion of individual industry (allowing people to direct their assets at death motivates them to work hard during life); and
5. Prevention of dependents from becoming a burden on the state.

For individuals and cultures alike, death gives meaning to life. The Prophet Muhammed addressed this issue in his words that began this chapter, as he instructs his followers to use the lessons of inheritance laws to understand the laws of life. And there is plenty to learn as the laws of inheritance are as old as civilization itself, with formal and informal codes and customs existing for millennia. It is with this perspective that we now trace the history of inheritance from pre-historic man to the modern U.S. laws of intestacy.

EVOLUTION OF INHERITANCE LAWS AND WOMEN'S RIGHTS

Together with agriculture, industrialization, and medicine, our system of law is responsible for the explosion in human population. Laws regulate man's instinctive behaviors toward survival, and allow humans to live harmoniously in close proximity.

If evolutionary psychologists are correct, we would expect that virtually all human behavior is explainable in terms of how it is adaptive to survival and reproduction. Consistent with evolutionary principles, inheritance laws have evolved over time to adapt to man's changing needs and family structure. Inheritance laws have evolved to place the resources of survival in the hands of those dependent on the decedent. Family size has consistently decreased over the course of history, as it has taken the cooperation of fewer and fewer people to obtain food, stay warm, and defend against predators. Inheritance laws have evolved to meet the changing needs of the survival unit as man has moved from nomadic hunter to tribal clan member to nuclear family member, and now to a system where children remain dependent on parents for much longer only to disperse geographically, leaving parents to rely principally on themselves in their advanced age. As we will see later in this Appendix, inheritance laws have changed to meet the changing structure and needs of the family survival unit.

The family structure of early societies was the clan or tribe, as opposed to today's conjugal family consisting of a father, mother, and children. Property passed along patrilineal lines from fathers to sons. The ability of women, especially married women, to own property and to direct its passage at death was limited for fear that it would pass outside the family. For much of history, women could not own property. Whatever modest personal possessions they acquired during life passed to her husband, his family, or children on death. Women were thought to be vulnerable to scheming men of other tribes who would trick them out of property valuable to the tribe.

Scholar Kate Millet speculates that the origins of the view of woman as both the tempted and the temptress derives from what she calls "the two leading myths of Western culture...the classical tale of Pandora's box and the Biblical story of The Fall."[250] In Hesiod's tale, Pandora is the first woman created by Zeus. She is a "beautiful evil" sent to earth to torment men as punishment for man's theft of the secret of fire. Pandora is given a box which she opens in a weak moment, only to release on mankind the evils of poverty, sickness, and old age.

The story of Adam and Eve in the Book of Genesis contains a similar view of women. According to Genesis, Eve succumbed to the temptation of the serpent by eating the forbidden fruit, and then persuaded Adam to do the same. God thus cast Adam and Eve out of Paradise into a world of toil: "In sorrow shalt thou bring forth children, and thou shalt be under thy husband's power, and he shall have dominion over thee."[251] The view of women as weak, untrustworthy, and requiring supervision and subservience to men thus ensued.

Social psychologist Roy F. Baumeister rejects the view that the limited role of women in history is the result of the sinister acts of men or the religious and mythological depiction of women as the weaker and more vulnerable sex. Instead he attributes women's limited role in history, culture, and ownership to evolutionary forces. Specifically, Baumeister points to the evolutionary impact of reproduction on the behavior of the sexes. Historically, twice as many women as men produced offspring. As one man could impregnate many women, the genes of men who did not beat out their male competitors "were destined to reproductive oblivion." Like the male lions in Chapter One, men had to compete for the right to mate. Men battled, took risks, and formed alliances with other men to band together against competing groups of men. By contrast, women developed intimate relationships, avoided risks, and stayed by the hearth. Thus began the differing roles of men and women. In their role as risk-takers, men became the hunters, warriors, pioneers, inventors, and creators of culture. Men went on to form cultural institutions like government, armies, and churches, becoming the coincidental beneficiaries of the institutions of their creation. As land was the principal source of power and authority, men became its logical title holder.

From the Middle Ages and continuing through most of the nineteenth century, married women of England were governed by the doctrine of *coverture*. While an unmarried woman had the right to own property and to make contracts in her own name, married women did not have such rights. Instead, through the act of marriage a woman underwent a *civil death* whereby her legal existence was incorporated into that of her husband. According to Millet, "her husband became something of a legal keeper, as by marrying she succumbed to a mortifying process which placed her in the same class with lunatics or idiots, who were also 'dead to the law.'"[252] A wife's adoption of her husband's name, signifying the transfer of legal responsibility and authority over her from her father to her husband, is a remnant of the coverture system.

Legal historian Sir William Blackstone described the rights of married women in his influential eighteenth century treatise *Commentaries on the Laws of England:*

> By marriage, the husband and wife are one person in the law; that is, the very being or legal existence of the woman is suspended during marriage, or at least is incorporated and consolidated into that of the husband.... But though our law in general considers man and wife one person, yet there are some instances in which she is separately considered; as inferior to him, and acting by his compulsion.[253]

The practice of coverture and the medieval view of women as weak and untrustworthy began to erode in the mid-nineteenth century, due in large part to the efforts of the Women's Movement. Beginning in the mid-1800s, a series of Married Women's Property Acts were passed both in England and in the United States, which gradually granted women equal or nearly equal legal and inheritance rights.

The advancements in women's inheritance rights in modern Western law were presaged centuries earlier by the laws of Judaism and Islam. Long before women were given the right to inherit property in Western culture, the laws of these two religions had established a limited form of inheritance and support rights for the surviving wife and female relatives of a decedent.

Despite the delay, the inheritance rights of women in the Western world have evolved from a system where women had no rights at all to the modern system in which women enjoy the same rights to inherit and own property as their male counterparts.

Inheritance laws will continue to evolve to adapt to the changing family. The high incidence of divorce, extended human life expectancy, the growing unmarried single population, same-sex unions, and the changing needs of stepchildren all portend the continued evolution of inheritance laws.

FAIRNESS AND EXPECTATION

The customs, mores, and laws of the day define societal and individual inheritance expectation and provide a standard from which fairness can be measured. A daughter living in a culture where the prevailing rule is that the eldest son inherits (primogeniture) will likely believe that she has been treated fairly when her brother inherits the family farm and she receives only house wares or items of jewelry. Her hope, like that of Cinderella discussed in Chapter One, is that she will marry an eldest son who has inherited his family farm. Although she may not fully accept the custom, she knows that all daughters in her community are subject to the same rules. Unless she is a radical who challenges – and perhaps is instrumental in changing – prevailing thinking on the fairness and efficacy of the law, she accepts her treatment on the basis that she is being treated like everyone else in her position and thus fairly.

Fairness, of course, is subjective. Rules, no matter how generous or restrictive, are measured by whether they are applied evenly. A baseball player making five million dollars per year is hurt and angered when another player with his same earned run or batting average is earning ten million dollars. It doesn't matter that his five million dollar salary is more than the lifetime earnings of the average worker. He will be seen as greedy by many sports fans but in his mind it's not the money, "it's the principle," the principle that he be treated the same as others in his position.

Today, in the United States, the expectation is that natural children will be treated equally. Children are hurt and angered to learn that a sibling has received one dollar or one heirloom more. As with the ballplayer, outsiders will view them as greedy or petty, but the child will not be dissuaded, saying that "it's the principle" or "what's fair is fair."

Achieving fairness in inheritance is further complicated by the fact that a financial inheritance is seen as a representation of a parent's love. Here too, fairness is governed by expectation. During life, a son may expect his father to teach him how to hunt, play catch, fix a fence, or engage in the other father-son activities that his brothers or friends enjoy. The daughter of that same father may expect only a pat on the head, a kind word, or a moment of conversation. If favoritism is shown or a child's expectations are not met, the child will experience lingering hurt that may last a lifetime. The slight of the father may be so small that he may not be aware of it, and may not even recall the incident or behavior when confronted many years later. The feeling of not having received sufficient love from a parent clouds the child's inheritance expectations. To be "even," the slighted child feels that he must receive more at death to make up for the love he believes he didn't receive during life.

PRIMITIVE MAN

Inheritance was of little importance to primitive man, who possessed only a few tools, utensils, and weapons. Early hunters and gatherers owned no lands or herds, and currency was yet to be invented. What few implements the decedent owned were distributed to the surviving members of the clan to allow them to continue to scratch out an existence. In these early days, there was no title to land; one's land or territory extended as far as rivals knew not to tread. As no single person could muster the authority to ward off challengers, land was "owned" by the kinship or clan through their collective exercise of dominion and control.

The inheritance practices of early man were dominated by superstition. Some early peoples buried the decedent's possessions with the decedent in the belief that physical life continued in a different realm. Providing for the needs of the dead in the afterlife led to the widespread custom of burying food, utensils, treasure, slaves, and even wives with the decedent. On this belief, the Herero of southwest Africa would slaughter the dead man's goats in order that the spirit of his herd would pass with him. The practice of providing for the needs of the dead was common in the Stone and Bronze Ages and of course in Egypt and pre-Columbian Mexico, whose great burial tomb treasures are scattered in museums around the world.

Another primitive custom was to destroy the decedent's possessions to prevent his spirit or magic from haunting his survivors. The Papua of New Guinea, for example, burned the hut of the decedent on this belief. Needless to say, estate sales would not have fared well during this period!

EARLY CIVILIZATIONS

Early secular and religious codes contained mandatory inheritance schemes that allowed limited freedom of choice. These early prescriptions shared a number of common characteristics: sons were favored over daughters; the inheritance rights of wives were severely limited or nonexistent; and the larger patrilineal family unit was favored over the nuclear family.

The Code of Hammurabi survives as the only substantially complete pre-Hebrew legal code.[254] Hammurabi (1810 B.C. – 1750 B.C.) was the sixth King of Babylon, the world's first major city-state located about fifty-five miles south of modern day Baghdad, Iraq. Written on a large stone monument and predating the Old Testament by three centuries, Hammurabi's Code was rediscovered in 1901 and now sits in the Louvre Museum in Paris. The Code contains 284 written laws received from the God Shamash. The following is a summary of the Code's most pertinent inheritance laws:

- Only sons inherit the father's estate. All sons share equally, with the exception of a portion of the inheritance reserved for a bride-price for an unmarried son, a dowry for an unmarried daughter, or property specially allocated or gifted during life to a favored child;
- Women had extremely limited property rights which included only a life interest in gifts received from their husband or contained in their dowry;
- No special birthright attached to an eldest son, but an eldest son usually acted as the executor;
- Land necessary for the sustenance of the family like a "field, garden, and house" were allocated to sons;
- A field or garden left to a minor son would be held by the child's mother until the child was old enough to take possession;
- A father could disinherit a son who exhibited un-filial conduct;
- If a wife died after she bore sons, then her father could make no claim for a return of his daughter's dowry;
- Illegitimate sons acknowledged by the father shared equally with the father's other sons;
- Gifts could be made by the father/husband to his wife during life. But if no such gifts were made then she would receive the same share of a son. Further, the wife could stay in the father/husband's house without interference from her sons, but if she decided to leave the house then she would have to give back any gift made to her by her husband during life, but could take her dowry with her.

THE JEWS

The law of the ancient Israelites is found in the Pentateuch (Greek word meaning the five rolls), the first five books of the Old Testament (Genesis, Exodus, Leviticus, Numbers, and Deuteronomy). The Jews call these five books the Torah, meaning the law or literally, direction or guidance. The Torah is the "constitution" of the Jewish law. All other sources of Jewish law are based upon or dependent on it. The Talmud, a remarkable compound of poetry, mysticism, and traces of Greek philosophy, contains a complete compilation of additional law which bears somewhat the same relation to the Torah as English common law bears to constitutional and statutory law.

Said to have been revealed to Moses on Mt. Sinai, the Old Testament reflects the influences of earlier cultures and codes such as the Code of Hammurabi. The most important contribution of the Jews to our legal system is the existence of the Torah, which was adopted by Christianity as part of its basic law. The Quran also was heavily influenced by Old Testament moral reasoning. The impact of the law of the Jews on all Western laws, including the law of Continental Europe and English law, thus cannot be overstated. The inheritance laws of the Old Testament are discussed below on page 226 under Biblical Law.

THE GREEKS

Ironically, despite their advanced thinking, the ancient Greeks never developed a unified Greek state (they were organized into separate city-states). Some experts argue that they did not have a unified system of law;[255] that there is no evidence of a single Greek legal treatise, teacher, or school of law;[256] and that the Greeks did not even have a word to describe the abstract concept of law.[257] Despite their apparent lack of formal laws, Greek philosophy would fundamentally influence Western law through its rediscovery by the West in the 1100s and use in interpreting Jewish law, Roman Law, the Quran, and most importantly for us in the West, Roman Catholic Canon law.

Greek religion was polytheistic, with each tribe having its own gods. In addition, each family had its own personal gods, with the father of the house as its chief priest. Typical of early inheritance patterns, priesthood passed within families from fathers to sons.

It was believed that the gods disliked moving, preferring instead to be attached to a particular piece of ground. The Greek family therefore found its roots and connection to their personal gods in their family home and lands. Consequently, private ownership of land was a concept that developed very early in Greek civilization. Greeks received their authority from the land; a landless Greek had little standing in the community, and foreigners could not own land in a Greek state.

Primogeniture had little appeal to the Greeks, as each son was to have his own personal connection to god through his lands. Property tended to be inherited equally among sons while daughters were disinherited except for a dowry and the right to be maintained while she was single. Sons had to assume the family debts and obligations when they took over the property. If there were no sons, the father's inheritance passed to his brother, and if there was no brother, then to the brother's son. Wills were not permitted in Athens until Solon (c. 638-558 B.C.), who allowed them only if there were no male descendants.[258]

When a girl married she left her own clan and its gods and joined her husband's family to worship his gods at his altar. The marriage of a bride had three parts, involving a number of rituals that survive to this day. First she would stand before her own family where her father would divorce her from her family gods (today, a father "gives away" his daughter/bride). She would then be brought by the groom to his family home. As the bride could not enter the husband's home and religion of her own volition, the tradition was for the groom to carry his bride over the threshold.

The final part of the ceremony took place at the groom's family altar where she was inducted into the family religion. The bride dressed in white, the color of vestments used in religious worship, and she wore a crown and a veil which also had religious significance. Once inducted into her husband's family and religion, the couple shared a cake to symbolize their union.

THANK THE ROMANS

Today we consider it an inalienable right to own property and to pass it at death to beneficiaries of our choosing. The right of free testation has not always existed. It was the Romans who first allowed widespread testamentary freedom to individual testators.[259] In the words of nineteenth-century historian of ancient jurisprudence Henry Summer Maine (1863): "[T]o the Romans belongs preeminently the credit of inventing the will, the institution, which, next to the contract, has exercised the greatest influence in transforming human society."[260]

The Roman will affected more than the passage of property; beneficiaries also inherited the decedent's standing in the community. Under the concept of *universal succession,* a decedent's heirs continued the decedent's civil life such as his military position and public office.[261] Universal succession preserved continuity of position, authority, and responsibility. The disposition of property through the will was secondary to the assignment of the decedent's status and position.[262] Even the Romans, however, placed limits on testamentary freedom. If a testator wished to disinherit his wife or children he had to expressly state so in his will and state his reasons. There is no evidence that women were given the same rights as men in making wills.

Roman law was heavily influenced by Greek philosophy, grammar, and rhetoric.[263] The Romans borrowed heavily from Greek thinking, especially in the period of the fourth and third centuries B.C. when Greek civilization was in decline and the Roman state was coming into its own. As early as 450 B.C., a Roman commission known as the Twelve Tables was sent to Athens to study Greek culture.[264] As a result, Greek philosophy, in particular the teachings of Aristotle, as interpreted by the Roman Stoics, Cicero (106 – 43 B.C.) and Seneca (4 B.C. - 65 A.D.), was incorporated into Roman law.[265] Although Greek thought inspired Roman laws,[266] the highly structured legal system comprised of lawyers, judges, codes, and procedures was entirely the creation of the Romans.

Heavily influencing the development of Roman secular law was the emergence of Roman Catholic Canon law (the word Canon derives from the Greek word signifying a *rule* or *measuring rod*).[267] Canon law began with the writings of the New Testament and a collection of rules known as the Didache or Doctrine of the Twelve Apostles between 50 and 100 AD. Early Canon law addressed issues of morality, fairness, and equity, on subjects such as divorce, charity, education, slavery, and inheritance. Adherence to these Canons by early Christians came into conflict with the laws of the Roman establishment and led to widespread persecution of Christians. This changed with the conversion of Emperor Constantine to Christianity at the battle of Milvian Bridge in 312 A.D.[268] By 380 A.D., Christianity became the official religion of the Roman Empire, and Christian moral teachings in the form of Canon law were merged with Roman civil law.[269] Since that early union, Western law, and in particular the law of inheritance has been forever imprinted by both Roman and Canon law.

Ironically, while creating a new legal order that would forever inspire Western legal thought, it was the original Roman concept of universal succession that would play a central role in the fall of the Western Roman Empire. Succession was largely left to the discretion of the deceased emperor who could anoint "as his personal heir the man to whom he intended the empire to pass."[270] But this informal system of universal succession (aided by the fact that the Roman will was oral and not written) was open to dispute. In time, the passing of each emperor invariably led to civil war with rival claimants each asserting their right to the throne. Ultimately, competing rivals would not wait for nature to take its course; they would instead kill the emperor and then claim to be his chosen heir. It was these ongoing civil wars in the third century A.D. that accelerated the downfall of the empire and its ultimate destruction by the invading Germanic peoples of the north.[271] Testamentary freedom was largely lost with the fall of the Roman Empire. During the feudal period which followed, property passes to the eldest son under a system known as primogeniture.

Predating the downfall of Rome was the division of the Roman Empire in 300 A.D. into two separate empires: the Western Empire centered in Rome and the Eastern Empire with its capital in Constantinople (known as Byzantium prior to being re-named by the first head of the Eastern Empire, Emperor Constantine, and now modern day Istanbul, Turkey). The division was intended as a governmental reform to restore order to the chaos and ongoing civil wars in Rome. The split did nothing to save the failing Western Empire, but ultimately served as a safe haven for written Roman law, which was completely lost in the West when the Western Roman Empire was plunged into the Dark Ages.

THE ROLE OF RELIGION IN INHERITANCE

BIBLICAL LAW

As one of the central themes of virtually all religions is the preparation of its followers for the afterlife, it is not surprising that organized religion has played a central role in matters of inheritance.

The earliest religious writings are considered to be the word of God communicated to man through prophets. Jews and Christians believed that the Old Testament was communicated directly from God to Moses; the Babylonians believed that the Sun God Shamash had given them the Code of Hammurabi; Egyptian law derived from Thoth; the Persians received their laws from Ahura Mazda by way of Zoroaster, and Muslims from the Prophet Muhammed. The pattern of religious texts passing through prophets persists in the modern era, as for example the Book of Mormon of the Latter Day Saints is believed to be communicated to Joseph Smith from the angel Moroni.[272]

While today most Western cultures mandate their separation, church and state have a long history of competing for what each asserted to be its divine authority. Many fundamental religious sects continue to view religious writings as the principal source of moral guidance and law. Judaism has long regarded law and religion as overlapping if not identical.

Reflecting the times in which they were written, religious texts promote retention of wealth within the family and clan. The Biblical scheme favors sons over daughters, and leaves open the possibility that a widow might inherit her husband's property in the form of a life estate.[273] The Bible, however, permits a form of testamentary freedom through lifetime gifts to virtually any beneficiary, including slaves. Both the Torah and the Quran mandate that property remain within the clan: Orthodox Jews adhere to the view that although the gifting of property to one who is not a Jew is not expressly prohibited, a pious man should not do so. The Quran strictly prohibits bequests to non-Muslims.

Yahweh presented Moses with the following mandatory scheme of intestate succession in the Old Testament:

> And you shall say to the people of Israel, 'If a man dies, and has no son, then you shall cause his inheritance to pass to his daughter. And if he has no daughter, then you shall give his inheritance to his brothers. And if he has no brothers, then you shall give his inheritance to his father's brothers. And if his father has no brothers, then you shall give his inheritance to his kinsman that is next to him of his family, and he shall possess it. And it shall be to the people of Israel a statute and ordinance, as the Lord commanded Moses.[274]

Numbers 36 of the Old Testament assures the balance of power among the original tribes of Israel in the days of Joshua with the following provision pertaining to women inheritors:

> (E)very daughter who possesses an inheritance in any tribe of the people of Israel shall be wife to one of the family of the tribe of her father, so that every one of the people of Israel may possess the inheritance of his fathers.[275]

The Biblical device known as the levirate marriage (Deuteronomy 25:5-10 in the Torah) provides additional protection in the event of the death of a married man. It requires a widow to marry one of her deceased husband's brothers in order to assure retention of ancestral property within the family or clan. Levirate marriages were also widespread among Central Asian nomads, Huns, Mongols, and Tibetans.

In the Biblical scheme, a husband inherits from his wife, but a wife does not inherit from her husband. Numbers 27 and 36 recognize a daughter's right to inherit, but neither mentions any entitlement for wives. Other Biblical references, however, permit "lifetime" gifts to wives. Wives are permitted a life estate in land in order to act as informal trustee for minor sons until they come of age.

Biblical bequests were not in the form of a modern will signed by the testator and intended to become effective upon death. In fact, there is no indication that any Biblical figure ever drafted a will.[276] Instead, the Biblical testator would simply gift property to his chosen beneficiaries during life or make verbal deathbed gifts. Such was the case when Isaac, failing, blind, and confused, mistakenly (with the aid of some trickery) bestowed onto Jacob the birthright intended for his eldest son Esau.

Sirach 33:23 of the Old Testament specifically commends the practice of deathbed distributions: "At the time when you end the days of your life, in the hour of death, distribute your inheritance," but cautions against making gifts too early: "[D]o not give your property to another, lest you change your mind and must ask for it [back]."[277] One of the most well known Biblical examples of lifetime bequests is found in Luke 15:11-32. In the familiar parable of the prodigal son, the father gives his younger son an advance of his inheritance. The story is one of redemption with the father welcoming the return of his son even after he wasted his entire inheritance with "riotous living."

Virtually every kind of property appears to have been subject to the Biblical intestate scheme. Although real property was of particular importance, slaves, silver, gold, and cattle could also be bequeathed and inherited.

ISLAMIC LAW

In the pre-Islamic Arab world (pre-500AD), the tribe was the principal family structure. Under that system, wives were regarded as property and thus had no property or inheritance rights. Even among males, there was a strong tradition that only those who could use a spear and sword could inherit, thus excluding minors and incompetents. In the Quran, the Prophet Muhammed replaced the tribe with the conjugal family as the primary social unit. He adopted a basically patrilineal, male-oriented scheme of inheritance typical of the era, but also established explicit inheritance rights for women that actually predate the inheritance rights accorded women in the Western world.

Islam literally means "surrender," in the sense that its followers should surrender their soul completely to God. According to Hamid Khan, "[f]rom the days of the Prophet, Islam was not just a religion but a complete code for living, combining the spiritual and the temporal, and seeking to regulate not only the individual's relationship with God, but all human social relations."[278]

Islamic inheritance law allows limited testamentary freedom. The right of a decedent to leave to heirs of his choosing is permitted, but is restricted to one-third of his net estate. Islam allots females half the inheritance share available to males who have the same degree of relation to the deceased. For example, where the deceased has both male and female children, a son's share is double that of a daughter's. Additionally, the sister of a childless man inherits half of her deceased brother's property upon his death, while a brother of a childless woman inherits all of her property.

There are parts of the Muslim world that still follow the stringent inheritance prescriptions found in the Quran, just as there are also fundamental Jewish groups that strictly follow the rigid inheritance scheme set forth in the Old Testament/Torah. Fundamentalists of both groups mitigate the discriminatory effect of ancient pronouncements through the use of lifetime gifts and testamentary bequests.

The rules of Islamic inheritance are extremely complex and vary according to various schools of juristic thought, most notably the Sunni and Shia. The Shia scheme of succession is contained in three verses of the Quran (4:11, 4:12, and 4:176) which give specific details of inheritance shares:

- There is no special share for first born sons such as those found in codes of primogeniture in medieval Western cultures;
- There is no birthright to inherit. Therefore, the gift or sale of all of a person's property during life cannot be defeated by heirs apparent;
- There is no right of representation. For example, if a Muslim has two sons and one dies during his lifetime and leaves children, those children do not take their father's share. Instead, the surviving son takes all;
- Stepchildren, illegitimate and adopted children do not inherit (legal adoption as practiced in the West is forbidden in Islam);
- "For the male a share equivalent to that of two females." The rule is based on the Islamic legal presumption that a brother has a legal obligation to provide for his sister's support. The extra share accorded to males is deemed to be fair in light of the fact that men had to provide for their family whereas women did not. Also, men had to pay a dowry in order to marry, while women did not have to pay anything to men;
- If there are no sons, then a daughter inherits one-half of her father's estate. Where there are no sons and two or more daughters, the daughters inherit two-thirds of their father's estate;

- Parents of the decedent inherit between one-sixth and one-third of the estate depending on a number of factors including whether the decedent had children or grandchildren and the gender of such children;
- The sister of a childless man inherits half of his property upon his death, while a brother of a childless woman inherits all of her property;
- Surviving wives inherit one-quarter of their husband's estate if the decedent had no children or male grandchildren.

ROMAN CATHOLIC CANON LAW IN THE MIDDLE AGES

The Middle Ages run from the fall of the Western Roman Empire in about 476 A.D. to the Renaissance period approximatly one thousand years later. The earliest part of the Middle Ages, the period following the fall of the Roman Empire and running until the year 1100 A.D., are sometimes called the Dark Ages, in recognition of the intellectual stagnation that occurred during the period.

It is said that during the Dark Ages, the Western world plunged into "semi-barbarianism and illiteracy."[279] According to historian Rene A. Wormer, the "Roman Empire never actually died… it merely evolved into Christian Europe",[280] and in the process infused Roman legal traditions with church Canon law. Aiding in the church's authority was the fact that only priests and clerics retained their literacy. Even Charlemagne (742 – 814) who was crowned emperor in Rome by the Pope on Christmas Day 800 A.D. never learned to write.[281] The writings of the church provided virtually the only political or legal writings during this period. Literacy and the knowledge of grammar, logic, and rhetoric were barely kept alive in monasteries, but later formed the basis of the expansion of intellectual growth during the High Middle ages.

Roman law was largely lost in the West. It was emperor Justinian (482 – 565 A.D.) of the Eastern Roman Empire who in 533 A.D. compiled and revised the only surviving writings of Roman law into his *Digesta* (which was part of the larger Justinian compilation known as *Corpus Iuris Civilis*).[282] The *Digesta* remained largely unknown to the Western world until it was re-discovered at the University of Bologna by a teacher named Irnerius around

1100, as Byzantine scholars fled from Constantinople to Western Europe to avoid the invading Turks.

HIGH MIDDLE AGES

The High Middle Ages (a period beginning around 1100 and ending about 1350) marked a period of stability as compared to the early Middle Ages. Improved agricultural methods, trade, and a money economy led to steady population growth.[283] The economic growth of the High Middle Ages called for people who could keep records, correspond, and pursue legal studies. The need was met as stronger governments and the church combined to create the great European universities of the day, including those in Bologna, Paris, and Oxford.[284]

Roman law was rediscovered in the 1100s as fleeing scholars from the Eastern Roman Empire returned with Justinian writings.[285] Canon law, which survived weakly through the Dark Ages in monasteries through monasticism saw a similar resurgence during this period. It was also during this fertile period in the High Middle Ages that the teachings of Aristotle were rediscovered in formerly Muslim Spain by traveling Christian churchmen. Lost to the West for nearly a thousand years, Aristotelian teachings survived in the libraries of the great universities of Baghdad, Cairo, Toledo, and Cordoba – the product of the much more advanced Arab civilization that thrived during the Dark Ages along the great southern crescent from Persia to Spain. The rediscovery triggered a debate between faith and reason and the natural and supernatural that forever altered the way we think about nature, society, and even God.[286]

From the late eleventh through thirteenth centuries, the Roman Catholic Church, through Pope Gregory VII (1015 – 1085) and his successors, separated themselves from their civil counterparts and established the Roman Catholic Church as an autonomous entity.[287] Known as the *Gregorian Reform*, the church now spoke the law *(jus dicere)* over church matters as well as over moral and ideological matters such as sex, marriage, family life, education, charity, and inheritance.[288] Key elements of Gregorian Reforms were the imposition of the vows of celibacy and poverty on men of the cloth. Prior to the Gregorian Reforms, priests could marry, and their children could succeed them in their religious positions. These new limitations on the clergy were more than a mere moral prescription; they also served to prevent dilution of the church's wealth through endless division.

The oldest form of Canon law arose from of the Eastern Empire in about 100 A.D. in a collection of rules known as the *Didache*, or *Doctrine of the Twelve Apostles*. The first set of comprehensive Canon laws came to life later, in the twelfth century when the *Decretum* was compiled in Bologna, Italy by a monk named Gratian. The *Decretum* (or *Concordance of Discordant Canons*) soon gained acceptance as the first law book of the church. By the fifteenth century, a whole body of church law had developed to address matters now deemed to be within the jurisdiction of the church.

From the twelfth to fifteenth centuries the Catholic Church claimed a vast new jurisdiction over followers and non-followers on a number of subjects, including inheritance. Church law was flexible, reasonable, and fair, and afforded special care for the disadvantaged – widows, orphans, the poor, the handicapped, abused wives, and neglected children. Canon law became the basis of legal equity, employing remedies such as injunctive relief, specific performance, and reformation discussed in Chapter Ten, *Legal Remedies*. Not surprisingly, the first lawyers and judges were men of the cloth; literate men were educated in Latin, the "language of the law."

Church courts treated both the legality and morality of conflicts before them, which led to their enormously popularity.[289] The division of civil courts and church courts of equity became the genesis of the division of courts of law and equity in the English court system. Early English Chancellors, who were the right hand men of early English kings, were church men trained in Roman Catholic Canon law. Chancellors were engaged by the king to handle special cases of equity that were not served by the rigid system of writs then employed by common law courts. The Court of Chancery, named for chancellors who were their inspiration, was thus born.

The medieval Canon law formulations of rights and liberties contributed to the signing of the Magna Carta in 1215, which limited the rights of the king, guaranteed individual rights, and was the precursor to the development of many constitutions, including the United States Constitution.

LATE MIDDLE AGES

The late Middle Ages (1350 – 1600) are best characterized by the revival of the Greco-Roman tradition in the form of the Renaissance (fueled by the exodus of scholars from Constantinople) and later, the Protestant Reformation. This time was also marked by the Hundred Years' War (1337 – 1453) between royal houses loyal to England and France (the French won), the fall of Constantinople to the Turks (1453), and the bubonic plague or Black Death. Black Death was carried by rats on-board ships reaching southern Europe from the eastern Mediterranean. The first outbreaks were in Sicily and Genoa in 1348, and from there spread throughout Europe. Black Death is estimated to have killed one-third of Europe's population, leaving fields barren and extinguishing industry. These events ended the rapid population growth of the twelfth and thirteenth centuries.[290]

Civil and Canon law were further transformed by the Protestant Reformation. Begun by Martin Luther (1483-1546), Protestant reformers taught that salvation comes from faith in Jesus, not by adherence to the rules of the Pope and Catholic Church. The Reformation was aided by the invention of the Gutenberg printing press, which helped bring the Bible to the common man and removed the clergy's monopoly on literacy. It was the view of reformers that each individual stands directly before God, seeks God's forgiveness, and conducts life in accordance with the Bible and Christian conscience. To the Protestant reformers, the medieval Catholic Canon law obstructed the individual's relationship with God and obscured simple Biblical norms for righteous living. They believed that law was primarily the province of the state, not the church; of the magistrate, not of the minister. The Protestant Reformation triggered a massive shift of power, property, and prerogative from the church to the state. Political rulers now assumed jurisdiction over numerous subjects previously governed principally by the Catholic Church and its law, including inheritance.[291]   Despite their loud condemnations, Protestant jurists nevertheless borrowed heavily from established Roman Catholic Canon law and procedure.[292]

ENGLISH LAW

Like its counterparts in Continental Europe, English law was strongly influenced by Roman and Canon law. The Romans had occupied England from the first century A.D. until the last Roman legions left in 407 A.D.[293] The Catholic Church made its first inroads into England at the end of the Roman occupation, and continued its involvement after the Romans departed. The church brought an interest in learning, writing, and Latin to the new land. According to David Mellinkoff, in *The Language of the Law,* "From that day on, churchmen had an important hand in shaping the common law and its language."[294]

England adopted a system of common law (founded on principles of the obligatory force of previous court decisions, or precedent), rather than the Roman civil law system (where each case is decided anew by application of the civil code and prior decisions have no precedential value).[295] The term common law derives from Henry II (who reigned from 1154 to 1180) who appointed judges, called *missi,* to travel the provinces and consistently apply a uniform legal standard to all subjects.[296]

English courts, particularly ecclesiastical courts, adopted the Roman system of free testation. Freedom of testation was not always the law of England. Testamentary disposition of all property, including land under the Roman model, was permitted during the Anglo-Saxon period that began in the mid-fifth Century and continued until the Norman Conquest in 1066, but thereafter gave way to feudalism.

After the Norman Conquest, jurisdiction over real and personal property was divided between the state and church. In a compromise between the crown and the church, royal courts exercised jurisdiction over real property while succession to personal property (such as clothing, tools, jewelry, and other valuables) was to be the concern of the ecclesiastical courts. Under the feudal system all land was owned by the king, who in turn allocated life estates to nobility in exchange for military service. During the feudal period, land passed undivided to the eldest son under the system of primogeniture. Feudalism is said to derive from the German tribes who invaded Rome from the north and to Charlemagne in particular. The Teutonic origins of feudalism are evidenced in the roots of the word itself: *feud* is the Teutonic word for *fee* or *feh*, which means wages or pay, and *odh* or *od*, means property or possessions. Thus *feud* is wages given for property.[297]

The divided jurisdiction between personal and real property became important in the power struggle between the church and state. In medieval England, the organization of society was based on ownership of land with the eldest son succeeding to his father's military and political office. The church on the other hand concerned itself with divine worship, the care of the sick and poor, and the cultivation of learning and the arts. While the crown levied taxes and military services through the feudal grant of lands, the church extracted a donation of a portion of the decedent's personal property, usually a third, for its deathbed services. According to Ross, "[b]y the time of the Norman Conquest, the recognition of death-bed gifts had come to be associated with the sacrament of penance. It was expected that a dying man would confess his sins to the local priest and make a gift to the church to atone for his sins. To die without making provisions for such gifts would be tantamount to dying without confession and thus to die in sin."[298]

The terms *will* and *testament* are a carryover of the division of authority between the crown and the church. In traditional Anglo-American law, a will was used to dispose of real property, and a testament (Latin, *testamentum*) to direct the disposition of personal property. Today the terms will and testament are used together to describe the modern will; the term testament is mostly ignored.[299] The term *last* (Latin, *novissima verba*)[300] was added to Will and Testament in recognition of the Catholic Church's practice of attending to the last words of a dying parishioner. Another remnant of the division of church and crown is the interchangeable use of the terms *descent* (historically used in reference to passage of real property only) and *distribution* (passage of personal property).

REAL PROPERTY

The feudal period in Western Europe ensued after the fall of the Roman Empire in the mid-400s A.D. Feudalism depended on the grant of land to warriors in exchange for military service. In England, the feudal period began with the Norman Conquest in 1066 and continued for seven hundred years. The period was characterized by ownership of all land by the crown. The king was free to vest use of property to anyone of his choosing. Initially, lords received what amounted to a life estate which the king could re-assign at the death of the lord. Vast interests in land were granted by the king to the great nobles in return for various payments and services including military service. The nobles, in turn, granted smaller portions of land to lesser members of the nobility in exchange for services.

Although the king reserved the right to re-assign feudal lands upon the death of a lord, in what amounted to a life estate, the combination of weak kings and willful nobles led the undivided passage of lands to the eldest son.[301] Primogeniture, which applied only to land, had the advantage of holding lands in larger parcels that were more profitable and avoided endless partitions that would result in parcels too small to support their owner. Coincidentally, the single-heir system was also more compatible with industrialization, as agriculture had become more productive and required less labor. The disinherited constituted a readily available work force which was needed for industrialization.

There were many practical reasons for lands to pass to an eldest son. The extremely short life expectancy of the era created an environment where younger children simply weren't ready to accede to a position of authority at the death of a parent. The eldest son thus became the representative of his family and the lord of his family's lands.

During the period that primogeniture flourished, younger sons and daughters were not wholly unprovided for. There was some expectation that younger family members would function as part of the eldest son's household. Nonetheless, primogeniture was much more favorable to eldest sons than to their younger siblings. The economic future of daughters predominantly depended on whom they married. Younger sons were forced to seek alternate careers in the military or clergy. Interestingly, many of the early Virginia plantation owners were younger sons who left England for a brighter future that included land ownership.

Barons concerned with the devolution of their own estates forced the king to sign the Magna Carta in 1215 which established the orderly succession of estates to heirs subject to the payment of a tax called *relief*. Payment of the tax allowed the king and overlords to pay for military service in gold rather than land and signaled the beginning of the end of the system of primogeniture. By the thirteenth century Europe's economy was transforming from a mostly agrarian system to one that was increasingly money based, also contributing to the end the land-based feudal system.

The Catholic Church, which had accumulated substantial holdings of real estate during the Middle Ages, presented a problem to the new tax system. As a separate legal entity, the church never died, thus depriving the king of the ability to levy his relief. In response, *Statutes of Mortmain* (the term *mortmain* derives from medieval French (*mort main*), and literally means dead hand) were passed by King Edward I in 1279 and 1290 to prevent gifts to the church without royal assent. Later (in the years 1536 to 1541), King Henry VIII would solve the problem once and for all by disbanding the monasteries and confiscating all church land. Modern mortmain statutes survived in England and in the United States through the twentieth century. They addressed the inherent mistrust of the clergy in matters of inheritance by limiting deathbed charitable bequests and the overall percentage of one's estate that could be left to charity. Today, other than a weak remnant of the law that survives in the State of Georgia, mortmain statutes no longer exist in American law.

PERSONAL PROPERTY

During much of the early history of English law, ecclesiastic courts had jurisdiction over personal property. The disposition of personal property was typically a deathbed bequest, orally communicated to the attending pastor or priest at the time of the administration of last rites. The dying declaration was as much about the passage of the decedent's soul as it was about the passage of his things. A portion of the decedent's personal property (usually one-third) was given to the Church to fund the Church's educational and charitable works and to secure the decedent's passage to the afterlife. The balance was divided half to the decedent's spouse and half to his children.

At the urging of King Henry VIII in 1540, the English legislature passed the Statute of Wills to allow men but not women to pass land by will. The Statute of Wills marked the official end of primogeniture by allowing a father the testamentary freedom to leave land to someone other than his eldest son.[302] While testamentary freedom in the disposition of land was certainly an idea whose time had come, the Statute of Wills was seriously flawed. It required no formalities for the proper execution of a will, not even that it be signed or witnessed. After a hundred years of fraud and turmoil, and aided by the growth of literacy, England passed the Statute of Frauds in 1677, which required wills to be in writing and to be witnessed by "three or four credible witnesses." Another reason for passage of the Statute of Frauds in 1677 was the widely held view that the Church had abused its position as spiritual advisor and had become the greasy palmed maître d' to the afterlife. With these two pieces of legislation, the oral deathbed will was replaced by the written will, the priest was replaced by a lawyer, and the passage of real and personal property was merged into a single system governed by secular courts. Europe and, most relevant for the development of American law, England, had again embraced the Roman will and system of testamentary freedom.

While England disposed of primogeniture in favor of broad testamentary freedom, France, following the 1789 French Revolution, and in keeping with its new ideology of equality and fraternity, enacted a system of equal *partition* (sometimes referred to as *partible inheritance*) among the children of the deceased. Where the English system offered no guarantees to children, the French code allotted children a guaranteed share, or *legitime* (from the French words *heritier legitime,* meaning rightful heir), of their parents' estate. Napolean was prescient when at St. Helena he said: "My glory is not to have won forty battles; for Waterloo's defeat will destroy the memory of as many victories. But what nothing will destroy, what will live eternally, is my Civil Code."[302]

The state of Louisiana, at one time a territory of France, follows the French Napoleonic Code. Even after its purchase by the United States in 1803 as part of the Louisiana Purchase, Louisiana continued to follow civil law with its formal adoption of the Napoleonic Code in 1825. To this day, Louisiana is the only state in the United States that grants children a forced share of their parents' estate. The civil code also continues in France, Spain, Germany, Brazil, Mexico, Quebec (Canada), Switzerland, and The Netherlands.

THE AMERICAN MODEL

The colonial break from England coincided with the Enlightenment philosophies that were sweeping Europe and North America. Philosophers such as David Hume (1711-1776) and Thomas Jefferson (1743-1826) espoused "individualism, rationalism, and nationalism" over faith-based adherence to church teachings.[303] Enlightenment philosophy dictated that man was created equal "with inherited rights of life and liberty."[304] Government would receive their moral mandate from a constitution and laws rather than from sacred texts. Secular leaders would represent the will of the people. Church and state were to be separated, and secular laws would govern private property and inheritance.

Despite the break from England and rejection of the concepts of feudalism and primogeniture, the colonies adopted much of the English legal system, including its laws of inheritance. With an abhorrence of aristocracy and family dynasties, American inheritance law focused on individual freedom of disposition.

Freedom of religion, freedom of testation, and the separation of church and state continue to be essential elements of the American fiber. Consistent with those philosophies is the belief that citizens should have the right to own land and to dispose of it at death as they please. Thomas Jefferson, himself a probate lawyer, showed a keen interest in the laws of succession. He had extensively studied the ancient Greek philosophers and Roman inheritance law and was convinced that government ownership of lands and the single-heir principles of primogeniture should be eschewed by the colonies. In 1776 he wrote:

> The opinion that our lands are allodial possessions [the term *allodial* refers to the private ownership of property of its owner without feudal obligation] is one which I have very long held…Was not the separation of the property from the perpetual use of lands a mere fiction? Is not its history well known, and the purposes for which it was introduced, to-wit, the establishment of a military system of defense? Was it not afterwards an engine of immense oppression?… Has it not been the practice of all other nations to hold their lands as their personal estate in absolute dominion? Are we not the better for what we have hitherto abolished of the feudal system?[305]

The preference of male beneficiaries over female children largely disappeared because it was considered incompatible with the colonist's philosophy of equality. Nevertheless, early studies of colonial testamentary patterns show a preference for leaving the family farm or family business to sons regardless of birth order. Although it is widely thought that primogeniture never made it to the American colonies, there is evidence that it existed in some colonies as an informal default scheme for those who failed to execute a will. There is also evidence that some of the colonies followed the Biblical practice of a double share for the eldest son. However, by the time of the American Revolution, the double portion had disappeared and equal distribution became the rule. It was also common for a father to deed the family farm to his sons, granting his widow only a life estate. Sons would run the farm and take care of their mother who would have been physically incapable of running it herself. This early system promoted the multi-generational household that accommodated the needs of all of its occupants: sons owned lands and could thus marry and raise a family; and widows were guaranteed a roof over her head.

MODERN AMERICAN INTESTACY

Intestacy laws provide needed backup in countries like the United States that allow broad testamentary freedom. Laws of intestacy act as a safety net to allocate and distribute assets the decedent failed to allocate by will. Intestacy laws do not govern assets designated in a valid will, owned in trust, assets passing via will substitutes (such as life insurance and retirement accounts which permit beneficiary designations), or jointly owned assets that automatically pass to the surviving co-owner by operation of law. Such designated assets pass entirely outside the jurisdiction of the probate court and the laws of intestacy.

The word intestate derives from the Latin *intestatus* which literally means "having made no will." The intestacy laws of the United States derive from the common law Canons of Descent relating to real property and the English Statute of Distribution enacted in 1670 relating to personal property.

Intestacy statutes allocate property to the decedent's heirs. A living person has no heirs (Latin, *nemo est haeres viventis*) as heirship is determined at the decedent's death.[306] Naturally, there are those who expect to inherit, known as *heirs apparent* who inherit merely by surviving their ancestor.

Intestate laws carry out the decedent's presumed intent but do not attempt to determine the decedent's actual intent. Intestacy laws represent the thinking of the average citizen. Using prevailing distribution patterns culled from valid wills as their guide, lawmakers determine the likely beneficiaries of a rational decedent. Intestacy laws also tend to reflect the interests of government, in that they favor those who were dependent on the decedent during life. Intestacy laws thus prevent the decedent's dependents from becoming dependents of the state. Intestate statutes provide a number of additional important functions:

- They avoid conflict by determining heirs;
- They allow for the fair distribution of the decedent's property;
- They prevent unclaimed property from clogging the wheels of commerce:
- They help define rightful heirs where a will has for any reason been invalidated (including lack of testamentary capacity or undue influence);
- Courts use intestacy laws as the societal standard for what is considered "normal;"
- Courts rely on intestacy statutes in testamentary capacity cases to identify the "natural objects of the decedent's bounty," and in undue influence cases to determine whether the testator's choice of beneficiary was unconscionable.

Intestacy laws also reflect the societal definition of what is considered "family," sending an indirect message as to who "counts" and who doesn't. For example, current statutes of intestacy do not recognize in-laws (including the spouses of predeceased children), unmarried couples (except that roughly one-quarter of the states recognize common law marriages), gay and lesbian unions, and to a great degree, stepchildren. (The first recorded use of the term *in-law* was used in thirteenth century Canon law to determine the degrees of relatedness within which marriage was permitted.)

Although there is always somewhat of a timing lag, for the most part intestacy laws reflect the prevailing view of family and inheritance. The system operates smoothly and fairly once everyone understands the rules. The main purveyors of the rules are estate planning and elder law attorneys who advise their clients on expectation and fairness. Clients often query whether they should leave to in-laws and stepchildren. They quickly decide against such bequests when they are advised that it is not the American custom to do so and that their in-laws will not be leaving to their children.

Modern American intestacy laws reflect our cultural view that a decedent's spouse, children, and grandchildren are the proper takers of our property, with parents, siblings and children of siblings taking in the absence of a spouse and children. Adopted children are treated as natural children.

How is it that our intestate statutes are so insensitive to the needs of stepchildren and in-laws (including the surviving spouses of deceased children)? The answer is that culturally, we expect that the natural parents of stepchildren will provide for them. Testators uniformly leave nothing to in-laws and stepchildren, as they do not consider themselves responsible for their well being. This pattern is consistent with evolutionary principles that suggest that we are inclined to support only those with whom we have a genetic connection. That is not to say that married couples in blended families cannot agree to provide for each other's children. They often do. The question is whether their commitment to stepchildren will continue after the death of the natural parent.

Under the American federalist system, each state has its own intestate rules, making it difficult to summarize the laws of every state. Nonetheless, distinct patterns exist. In non-community or common law states (forty-one of the fifty states), the decedent's estate is divided between the surviving spouse and children, with the natural or adopted children of a predeceased child (i.e., grandchildren) taking a predeceased child's share. Many states grant the surviving spouse a flat dollar figure off the top with the balance divided equally between the surviving spouse and children. This approach effectively gives small estates entirely to the surviving spouse.[307] The surviving spouse's share is determined without regard to his or her resources and regardless of how much was received from the decedent through lifetime and non-probate transfers. If the decedent has no children, most non-community states divide the probate estate between the surviving spouse and the parents of the decedent. If the decedent is a single person with children, state intestacy laws uniformly allocate the entire estate to the decedent's children in equal proportion. If there is no spouse or descendants, the decedent's parents share the estate.

The Uniform Probate Code (UPC) grants surviving spouses an even larger stake than that provided in most non-community property states.[308] The UPC, like other uniform laws, represents advanced national-level thinking which tends to portend future changes in the law. Under the UPC scheme, which has been adopted in whole or in part in about one-third of the states,[309] a surviving spouse is entitled to the *entire* intestate estate if: the decedent had no descendants or parents; or, if all of the decedent's descendants are also descendants of the surviving spouse and there are no descendants of the spouse who are not also descendants of the decedent.

Community property in the U.S. derives from two sources: the Napoleonic civil code as adopted in Louisiana, and Spanish law brought to the U.S. with the annexation of Texas in 1845. In states that employ the community property scheme, spouses generally own rights to half of all marital property, regardless of whose name is on the title. There are currently nine community property states: Arizona, California, Idaho, Louisiana, Nevada, New Mexico, Texas, Washington, and Wisconsin. (Some consider Alaska to be the tenth community property state because it permits spouses to elect out of the state's common law rules if they desire community property treatment.) Community property generally consists of the property acquired during the marriage by the gainful activities of either spouse. Separate property is property acquired prior to the marriage and property acquired during the marriage other than from gainful activities, such as an inheritance.

A surviving spouse in a community property state retains her separate property and is entitled to half of the couple's community property. In intestate estates, the spouse usually takes one quarter of the decedent's separate property and the surviving children take the remaining three quarters. If the decedent had no children, the decedent's community property is divided one-third to one-half to the surviving spouse with the balance to the decedent's parents, or absent parents, then to the decedent's brothers and sisters.

CONCLUSION

Inheritance laws are not static; they continue to evolve to meet the needs of society and the changing family. We have already witnessed the changing entitlement of married women. As domestic unions become more accepted, we may see a corresponding change in the entitlement of unmarried couples under the law. We may even see a greater recognition of stepchildren. Alas, we do not know what the future holds. The only things that are certain are death, taxes, and family inheritance conflict.

The five years spent learning and writing, and my years advising families facing the issues that await us all, have changed and enriched me. Like Marcello Mastroianni on page 56, I wish I could stick around for the next two or three hundred years to watch my family and the world evolve. Unfortunately, it cannot be. Life will certainly go on without me, and the future of inheritance must be left to future commentators. I hope that I have advanced the discussion of inheritance, and that you have been moved in some way by what I have learned and lived. Thank you.

END NOTES

FRONT MATERIAL
[1]The Last Dance: Encountering Death and Dying, Lyne Anne DeSpelder and Albert Lee Strickland

CHAPTER ONE: BEHAVING LIKE ANIMALS
[2]Salmon and Shackelford 337.
[3]Buss 3.
[4]Buss 7.
[5]Buss 6-7.
[6]Buss 142-152.
[7]Buss 109-123.
[8]Buss 124-127.
[9]Buss 19.
[10]Buss page.
[11]Mock 1-7.
[12]Mock 2.
[13]Mock 3.
[14]All figures represent the 2010 estimated Total Fertility Rate as reported by the U.S. Central Intelligence Agency.
[15]Buss 13.
[16]Jones 145.

[17]Jones 147.

[18]Jones 147.

[19]Gilbert 15.

[20]McCullough 87.

[21]McCullough 109.

[22]McCullough 148.

[23]Buss 224.

[24]Buss 224.

[25]Pillemer and Lüscher 25.

[26]Pillemer and Lüscher 313-338.

[27]Sadrin page.

[28]Buss 227.

[29]Buss 202-203.

[30]Buss 215.

[31]Buss 214.

[32]Buss 200-201.

[33]Buss 204.

[34]Buss 204-206.

[35]Buss 207.

[36]Hapworth, Hapworth, and Heilman page.

[37]Mock 121-125.

[38]Buss 233.

[39]Buss 209.

[40]Buss 207.

[41]Brenner 92.

[42]Brenner 92.

[43]Brenner 92.

[44]Brenner 94.

[45]Brenner 97.

CHAPTER TWO: DISINHERITANCE

[46]Rosenfeld, "Legacy" 29.

[47]Rosenfeld, "Disinheritance" 75, 79.

[48]Schwartz 266-267.

[49]Chester 409.

[50]Schwartz 273-274.

[51]Moskowitz 652-653.

[52]Hodel v Irving, 481 U.S. 704, 717 (1987).

[53]See e.g., N.Y. Mut. Life Ins. Co. v. Armstrong, 117 U.S. 591, 600 (1886) for the prospect that one who intentionally kills a decedent cannot collect under the decedent's life insurance policy.

[54]Cahn 139.

[55]Cahn 140.

[56]Rosenfeld, "Legacy" 64.

[57]Rosenfeld, "Legacy" 66-67.

[58]Pennell and Newman 197.

[59]Pennell and Newman 197.

[60]Pennell and Newman 207.

[61]Pennell and Newman 206.

[62]Pennell and Newman 206-207.

[63]Williams, Forgas, and von Hippel, eds. 110.

[64]Martin Luther King, Jr., American Baptist Minister and Civil-Rights Leader, 1929-1968.

[65]Whitman.

[66]Williams, Forgas, and von Hippel, eds. 181.

[67]Leary 479.

CHAPTER THREE: TERROR MANAGEMENT

[68]Hayslip 442.

[69]Moore and Williamson 3.

[70]Moore and Williamson 3.

[71]Mikulincer, Florian, and Hirschberger 20.

[72]Pyszcynski, Greenberg, and Solomon 835.

[73]Pyszcynski, Greenberg, and Solomon 837.

[74]Moore and Williamson 11.

[75]Becker ix.

[76]Freud 304-305.

[77]Lifton introduced the concept of symbolic immortality.

[78]Deshesne et al 732.

[79]Segal 38.

[80]Dechesne et al 724.

[81]Segal 12.

[82]Becker 5.

[83]Pyszczynski et al 436.

[84]Cozzolino et al 278.

[85]Cozzolino et al 278-279.

[86]Mikulincer, Florian, and Hirschberger 22.

[87]Pyszcynski, Greenberg, and Solomon 841.

[88]Milkulincer, Florian, and Hirschberger 20.

[89]Bar-Levav 56.

[90]Milkulincer, Florian, and Hirschberger 25.

[91]Moore and Williamson 11.

[92]Sartre 591.

[93]Sartre 591.

[94]Kreeft 14-15.

[95]Elmer 1.

[96]Bryant and Snizek 929.

[97]Melville 217.

[98]DeSpelder 549.

[99]Elmer 6. Studies have shown that the feeling of control over the death process fostered while preparing a will reduces death anxiety.

CHAPTER FOUR: TOXIC AND ALTRUISTIC INHERITANCE

[100]Vankin 61.

[101]Almost twenty percent of older Americans suffer from mental illness. AARP Public Policy Institute.

[102]Haidt 66.

[103]Dhammapada, verse 252

[104]Matthew 7: 3-5

[105]Haidt 67.

[106]Haidt 69, citing Ross M., & Sicoly, F. "Egocentric Biases in Availability and Attrition." Journal of Personality and Social Psychology. (1979): 37, 322-336. Print.

[107]Haidt 69, citing Epley, N. & Caruso, E. M. "Egocentric ethics." Social Justice Research. (2004): 17, 171-187. Print.

[108]Haidt 73.

[109]Haidt 74.

[110]Principia Mathematica, 1687

[111]Carnegie 54, quoting Knowles, James, ed. The Nineteenth Century: A Monthly Review. London: Kegan Paul, Trench, Trubner, & Co., 1891. Print.

[112]Kirkland.

[113]Schroeder 807-835.

[114]Kirkland.

[115]Sanders.

[116]Kirkland.

[117]Kirkland.

[118]Burrough.

CHAPTER FIVE: THE BROOKE ASTOR STORY

[119]Miller.

[120]Gordon 227-228.

[121]Gordon 3.

[122]Gordon 57.

[123]Gordon 56.

[124]Richardson 346.

[125]Gordon 63.

[126]Gordon 60.

[127]Gordon 58-59.

[128]Gordon 59.

[129]Gordon 9.

[130]Gordon 111.

[131]Richardson 346.

[132]Richardson 349.

[133]Gordon 75.

[134]Gordon 76.

[135]Gordon 47.

[136]Gordon 8.

[137]Gordon 93.

[138]Gordon 91.

[139]Gordon 91.

[140]Gordon 103.

[141]Gordon 23.

[142]Stiegel Vol. 31, No. 2.

[143]Gordon 153.

[144]Richardson 389.

[145]Gordon 277.

[146]Gordon 189.

[147]Barron A31.

[148]Miller.

[149]Miller.

[150]Eligon, "Brook Astor's Son" A1.

[151]Gordon 277.

[152]Ravitz.

CHAPTER SIX: VULNERABILITY IN THE TWILIGHT OF CONFIDENCE

[153]Rowles and Chaudhury, eds. 112.

[154]Attix and Welsh-Bohmer, eds. .5

[155]McNeilly 575.

[156]McNeilly 576-580.

[157]Attix and Welsh-Bohmer, eds. 17.

[158]Attix and Welsh-Bohmer, eds. 18.

[159]Attix and Welsh-Bohmer, eds. 17.

[160]Attix and Welsh-Bohmer, eds. 166.

[161]Sabatino 1.

[162]Attix and Welsh-Bohmer, eds. 57.

[163]Attix and Welsh-Bohmer, eds. 57.

[164]Attix and Welsh-Bohmer, eds. 57.

[165]Attix and Welsh-Bohmer, eds. 159.

[166]Attix and Welsh-Bohmer, eds. 59.

[167]Attix and Welsh-Bohmer, eds. 44.

[168]April 17, 2007 issue of Neurology

[169]Attix and Welsh-Bohmer, eds. 64.

[170]Attix and Welsh-Bohmer, eds. 350.

[171]Gilbert 210.

[172]Chaudhury 232.

[173]Chaudhury 232.

[174]Charles Dickens 78.

[175]Andre Waters, whose picture appears at the beginning of the chapter committed suicide in 2006. Age 44 at the time of his death, his autopsy revealed a brain that resembled that of an eighty-five year old Alzheimer's patient.

CHAPTER SEVEN: TESTAMENTARY CAPACITY

[176]Altman 1691.

[177]Ross and Reed 6-60.

[178]Ross and Reed 3.

[179]Ross and Reed 6-3.

[180]Stindt 42.

[181]Ross and Reed 6-40.

[182]Ross and Reed 6-67.

[183]This requirement was largely due to the fact that Roman wills were predominatly oral. Ross and Reed 2-2.

[184]Bonfield 1911.

[185]Stindt 42.

[186]Stindt 42.

[187]Champine, "Expertise" 29.

[188]Champine , "A Sanist Will?" 554-555.

[189]Ross and Reed 9-20, 9-26.

[190]Ross and Reed 2-9.

[191]Lovelass 179.

[192]Swinburne 34-35, 39-40.

[193]3 Curt. App. 1, 943 (England 1790).

[194]In re Hargrove's Will.

[195]Ross and Reed 6-21.

[196]Black's Law Dictionary 1027.

[197]In re Will of Kaufmann.

[198]Champine, "A Sanist Will?" 553.

[199]Champine, "A Sanist Will?" 554.

[200]Ross and Reed 6-22.

[201]Ross and Reed 6-62.

[202]Marson, Huthwaite, and Hebert 78.

[203]Marson, Huthwaite, and Hebert 78.

[204]In re Stanley Bednarz Trust.

[205]Bradford v Vinton.

[206]Ross and Reed 9-51.

[207]Ross and Reed 9-52.

[208]Marson, Huthwaite, and Hebert 82.

[209]Attix and Welsh-Bohmer, eds. 182.

[210]Attix and Welsh-Bohmer, eds. 182.

[211]Sabatino 10.

[212]Attix and Welsh-Bohmer, eds. 11.

[213]This diagram was inspired from a presentation by Sabatino May 20, 2009.

[214]Attix and Welsh-Bohmer, eds. 64-65.

[215]Marson, Huthwaite, and Hebert 87.

[216]Marson, Huthwaite, and Hebert 84.

[217]100 S.W. 3d 72 (Art. App. 2003).

[218]In re Estate of Garrett v. Garrett

CHAPTER EIGHT: UNDUE INFLUENCE

[219]280 S.E.2d 770, 772 (N.C. Ct. App. 1981)

(*citing* In re Beale's Will, 163 S.E. 684, 686 (N.C. 1932)). Print.

[220]Ross and Reed 7-26.

[221]Ross and Reed 7-26 – 7-39.

[222]Hall, Hall, and Chapman 34.

[223]Hall, Hall, and Chapman 30.

[224]Ross and Reed 7-5.

[225]In re Estate of Alice G. Clark at 14.

[226]Jones and Newton v. Walker at 3.

CHAPTER NINE: LEGAL PROTECTIONS

[227]The latin term *ad litem* literally means for the lawsuit or for the proceeding

CHAPTER TEN: LEGAL REMEDIES

[228]The word "court" is derived from the Latin word curia, which is the rectangular central yard of a Roman home where early adjudications took place.

[229]The merger of law and equity in the U.S. federal court system was officially accomplished with the promulgation of the Federal Rules of Civil Procedure in 1938.

[230]Alabama, Connecticut, Georgia, Massachusetts, Michigan, New Hampshire, Oregon, South Carolina, Texas, and Vermont

[231]Iowa, Kansas, Kentucky, Louisiana, Minnesota, Montana, Nevada, North Dakota, Oklahoma, Utah, and Wyoming

[232]Colorado, Indiana, Maine, Maryland, Nebraska, New Mexico, New York, North Carolina, Rhode Island, and Tennessee

[233]Arkansas, Florida, Hawaii, Illinois, Missouri, South Dakota, Virginia, West Virginia, and Wisconsin

[234]Alaska, Arizona, California, District of Columbia, New Jersey, and Washington

[235]Delaware and Mississippi; two in Courts of Common Pleas in Ohio and Pennsylvania

[236]Blacks Law Dictionary

[237]Anderson 317.

[238]Cohn 2.

[239]Beatty v. Guggenheim Exploration Co. at 380.

[240]If a fiduciary has a duty to bring an action against a co-fiduciary, by law, he would have standing to bring that action.

[241]Johnson 770.

[242]Gordon 269.

CHAPTER ELEVEN: PREVENTION

[243]Dydimus, Arius, Fr 39.2, Dox. Gr. 471.4, quoting Greek philosopher Heraclitus of Ephesus.

[244]National Alliance for Caregiving/AARP.

[245]Rouse v. Branch at 134.

[246]Weigler and Weigler 29.

[247]Weigler and Weigler 29.

APPENDIX: A HISTORY OF INHERITANCE

[248]Witte and Alexander 1.

[249]Cates and Sussman, eds. 1, quoting Friedman, L., "The Law of The Living, The Law of the Dead: Property, Succession, and Society." Wisconsin Law Review (1966): 340-378. Print.

[250]Millet 51.

[251]Genesis: 3-16

[252]Millet 67.

[253]Blackstone 442.

[254]Wormser 29.

[255]Kelly 4.

[256]Kelly 48, 49.

[257]Kelly 5, 6.

[258]Wormser 39.

[259]Maine 166-208.

[260]Maine 188.

[261]Maine 176, 183.

[262]Maine 188-189.

[263]Witte and Alexander 6.

[264]Kelly 46.

[265]Witte and Alexander 6.

[266]Wormser, 93-94. The Roman commission sent to Greece was known as the Ten
Men or Decemviri, and that "the largest source of Roman law was to be found in
the legal customs of the patrician clans" of Rome, and not Greek thought.

[267]Witte and Alexander 71.

[268]Kelly 83.

[269]Witte and Alexander 7.

[270]Kelly 45.

[271]Kelly 45, 80.

[272]Wormser 6.

[273]Hiers 153.

[274]Numbers 27:8-11

[275]Numbers 36:9

[276]Hiers 147.

[277]Sirach 33:19-21

[278]Kahn 1.

[279]Deriving from the Greek word for bearded, the Greeks regarded those who did
not shave as barbarians.

[280]Wormser 179.

[281]Kelly 88, 89.

[282]Witte and Alexander 53.

[283]Kelly 114, 115.

[284]Witte and Alexander 10; Kelly 119-121.

[285]Kelly 80.

[286]Rubenstein ix.

[287]Witte 10.

[288]Witte 10.

[289]Witte 12.

[290]Kelly 161, 162.

[291]Witte 16.

[292]Witte 17.

[293]Mellinkoff 37.

[294]Mellinkoff 49.

[295]Kempin 13-15.

[296]Wormser 242-243.

[297]Wormser 169.

[298]Ross and Reed 2-1.

[299]Mellinkoff 332.

[300]Mellinkoff 78.

[301]Cates and Sussman, eds. 3.

[302]Shammas, Salmon, and Dahlin 26.

[303]Witte 26.

[304]Witte 26.

[305]Witte 26.

[306]Foley 466.

[307]Pennell and Newman 3.

[308]Pennell and Newman 16.

[309]Pennell and Newman 16.

[310]Pennell and Newman 6.

BIBLIOGRAPHY

CHAPTER ONE:
BEHAVING LIKE ANIMALS

Brenner, Gabrielle A. "Why Did Inheritance Laws Change?" *International Review of Law and Economics* 5.1 (1985): 91-106. Print.

Buckley, William F. Jr. "Sonnytime." *National Review Online.* National Review, 8 Aug. 2006. Web. 11 Aug. 2010.

Buss, David M. *Evolutionary Psychology: The New Science of the Mind.* 3rd ed. Boston: Allyn & Bacon, 2008. Print.

Cates, Judith N. and Marvin B. Sussman, eds. *Family Systems and Inheritance Patterns.* Marriage & Family Review. Vol. 5. No. 2. New York: The Haworth Press, Fall 1982. Print.

Daly, Martin and Wilson, Margo. *The Truth about Cinderella: The Darwinian View of Parental Love.* United States: Yale University Press, 1998. Print.

Evans, Dylan, Oscar Zarate, and Richard Appignanesi. *Introducing Evolutionary Psychology.* Cambridge, UK: Icon, 1999. Print.

Gilbert, Daniel. *Stumbling on Happiness.* New York: Vintage Books, 2007. Print.

Hapworth, William E., Mada Hapworth, and Joan Rattner Heilman, *Mom Loved You Best: Sibling Rivalry Lasts a Lifetime.* New York: Viking Adult, 1993. Print.

Jones, Steve. *Darwin's Ghost: The Origin of Species Updated.* New York: Ballantine Books, 1999. Print.

Kluger, Jeffrey. "The New Science of Siblings." *Time.com.* Time Mag., 2 July 2006. Web. 13 Aug. 2010.

Lemke, Julie A. and Seymour Markowitz. "Protecting The Gold In The Golden Years: Practical Guidance For Professionals On Financial Exploitation." *Marquette Elder's Advisor* 7.1 (2005): 27. Print.

Lenzer, Robert, and Devon Pendleton. "Family Feud." *Forbes Mag.* 12 Nov. 2007: 108-115. Print.

McCullough, Michael E. *Beyond Revenge: The Evolution of the Forgiveness Instinct,* San Francisco: Jossey-Bass, 2008. Print.

Mock, Douglas W. *More Than Kin and Less Than Kind: The Evolution of Family Conflict.* Cambride, MA: Belknap Press, 2004. Print.

Pillemer, Karl A. and Rosalie S. Wolf. *Elder Abuse: Conflict in the Family.* Massachusetts: Auburn House Pub. Co.,1986. Print.

Pillemer, Karl A. and Kurt Lüscher. *Contemporary Perspectives in Family Research: Intergenerational Ambivalences: New Perspectives on Parent-Child Relations In Later Life.* Vol 4. Amsterdam: JAI Press (NY), 2004. Print.

Salmon, Catherine A. and Todd K. Shackelford. *Family Relationships: An Evolutionary Perspective.* New York: Oxford University Press, 2007. Print.

Sadrin, Anny. *Parentage and Inheritance in the Novels of Charles Dickens.* Cambridge University Press, 1994. Print.

Shermer, Michael. *Why Darwin Matters: The Case Against Intelligent Design.* New York: Owl Books, 2006. Print.

Williams, Kipling D., Joseph P. Forgas, and William von Hippel, eds. *The Social Outcast: Ostracism, Social Exclusion, Rejection, and Bullying.* New York: Psychology Press, 2005. Print.

Wilson, Edward O., *Sociobiology: The New Synthesis.* Cambridge, MA: Belknap Press, 1975. Print.

CHAPTER TWO: DISINHERITANCE

Brashier, Ralph C. *"Disinheritance And The Modern Family."* Case Western Reserve Law Review. 45 (1994-1995): 85 Print.

Brashier, Ralph C. *Inheritance Law and The Evolving Family.* Philadelphia: Temple University Press, 2004. Print.

Breitman, Rachel and Del Jones. "Should Kids Be Left Fortunes, Or Be Left Out?" *USA Today.com.* USA Today, 26 July 2006. Web. 15 Aug. 2010.

Cahn, Edmond N. "Restraints on Disinheritance." *Univ. of Pennsylvania Law Review* 85.2 (Dec. 1936): 139-153. Print.

Chester, Ronald. "Should American Children Be Protected Against Disinheritance." *Real Property, Probate & Trust Jour.* 32.1 (Fall 1997): 405-453. Print.

Goody, Jack. *Death Property and the Ancestors.* Palo Alto: Stanford Univ. Press, 1962. Print.

Levine, John M. and Norbert L. Kerr. "Inclusion and Exclusion: Implications for Group Processes." *Social Psychology: Handbook of Basic Principles.* 2nd ed. Eds. A. E. Kruglanski & E. TR. Higgins. New York: Guilford Press, 2010. 759-784. Print.

Miller, Robert K., Jr. and Stephen J. McNamee, eds. Inheritance and Wealth in America. New York: Plenum Press, 1998. Print.

Moskowitz, Seymour. "Golden Age In The Golden State: Contemporary Legal Developments In Elder Abuse and Neglect." *Loyola of Los Angeles Law Review Symposium* 36.1 (2003): 589-666. Print.

Pennell, Jeffrey N. and Alan Newman. *Estate and Trust Planning.* Chicago: American Bar Association, 2005. Print.

Rhodes, Anne-Marie. "On Inheritance and Disinheritance." *Real Property, Trust and Estate Law Jour.* 43.1 (Fall 2008): 433-445. Print.

Rosenfeld, Jeffrey P. "Disinheritance and Will Contests." *Family Systems and Inheritance Patterns.* Eds. Cates, Judith N. and Marvin B. Sussman. Marriage & Family Review. 5.2. (Fall 1982): 75-86. New York: The Haworth Press. Print.

Rosenfeld, Jeffrey P. *The Legacy of Aging: Inheritance and Disinheritance in Social Perspective.* New Jersey: Ablex Pub. Corp., 1979. Print.

Schwartz, T. P. "Disinheritance and Will Contests As Reciprocity and Deviance: An Empirical Extension of Gouldner and Rosenfeld Based on Wills of Providence, 1985." *The Sociological Quarterly* 41.2 (2000): 265-282. Print.

Shaffer, Thomas L., Carol Ann Mooney, and Amy Jo Boettcher. *The Planning and Drafting of Wills and Trusts.* 5th ed. United States: Foundation Press, 2007. Print.

Whitman, Walt. "I Sing the Body Electric." *Selected Poems.* New York: Dover, 1991. 12-19. Print.

CHAPTER THREE:
TERROR MANAGEMENT

Bar-Levav, Reuven. *Thinking in the Shadow of Feelings: A New Understanding of the Hidden Forces That Shape Individuals and Societies.* New York: Simon & Schuster, 1989. Print.

Becker, Ernest. *The Denial of Death.* New York: The Free Press, 1973. Print.

Bryant, Clifton D., and William E. Snizek. "The Last Will and Testament: A Neglected Document in Sociological Research," *Handbook of Death & Dying.* Ed. Clifton D. Bryan. Thousand Oaks, CA: Sage Pub., Inc., 2003. 934-940. Print.

Cozzolino, Philip J., et al. "Greed, Death, and Values: From Terror Management to Transcendence Management Theory." *Personality and Social Psychology Bulletin* 30.1 (2004): 278-292. Print.

Dechesne, Mark, et al. "Literal and Symbolic Immortality: The Effect of Evidence of Literal Immortality on Self-Esteem Striving in Response to Mortality Salience." *Journal of Personality and Social Psychology* 84.4 (2003): 722-737. Print.

DeSpelder, Lynne Ann, and Albert Lee Strickland. *The Last Dance: Encountering Death and Dying.* 7th ed. New York: McGraw-Hill Humanities, 2005. Print.

Durkin, Keith F. "Death, Dying, and the Dead in Popular Culture." *Handbook of Death & Dying.* Ed. Clifton D. Bryan. Thousand Oaks, CA: Sage Pub., Inc., 2003. 43-49. Print.

Elmer, Eddy M. "The Psychological Motives of the Last Will and Testament." *www. eddyelmer.com.* Feb. 2001. Web. 19 Aug. 2010.

Freud, Sigmund. "Thought for the Times on War and Death." *The Standard Edition of the Complete Psychological Works of Sigmund Freud*, Vol. 4. London: Hogarth Press, 1953. Print.

Greenberg, Jeff, et al. "Role of Consciousness and Accessibility of Death-Related Thoughts in Mortality Salience Effect." *Journal of Personal and Social Psychology.* 67.4 (1994): 627-637. Print.

Hayslip, Bert, Jr. "Death Denial: Hiding and Camouflaging Death." *Handbook of Death & Dying.* Ed. Clifton D. Bryan. Thousand Oaks, CA: Sage Pub., Inc., 2003. 34-42. Print.

Kamerman, Jack. "The Postself in Social Context." *Handbook of Death & Dying.* Ed. Clifton D. Bryan. Thousand Oaks, CA: Sage Pub., Inc., 2003. 302-306. Print.

Kreeft, Peter. *Before I Go: Letters to Our Children About What Really Matters.* United Kingdom: Sheed & Ward, 2007. Print.

Leary, Mark R. "The Function of Self-Esteem in Terror Management Theory and

Sociometer Theory: Comment on Pyszczynski et al.(2004)." *Psychological Bulletin* 130.3 (2004): 478-482. Print.

Lifton, Robert Jay. *The Broken Connection: On Death and the Continuity of Life.* Washington D.C.: American Psychiatric Press, Inc., 1979. Print.

Melville, Herman. *Moby Dick; or, The White Whale.* Boston: St. Botolph Society, 1892. Print.

Mikulincer, Mario, Victor Florian, and Gilad Hirschberger. "The Existential Function of Close Relationships: Introducing Death Into the Science of Love." *Personality and Social Psychology Review* 7.1 (2003): 20-40. Print.

Moore, Calvin Conzelus, and John B. Williamson. "The Universal Fear of Death and The Cultural Response." *Handbook of Death & Dying.* Ed. Clifton D. Bryan. Thousand Oaks, CA: Sage Pub., Inc., 2003. 3-13. Print.

Pyszczynski, Tom, Jeff Greenberg and Sheldon Solomon. "A Dual-Process Model of Defense Against Conscious and Unconscious Death-Related Thoughts: An Extension of Terror Management Theory." *Psychological Review* 106.4 (1999): 835-845. Print.

Pyszczynski, Tom, et al. "Why Do People Need Self-Esteem? A Theoretical and Empirical Review." *Psychological Bulletin* 130.3 (2004): 435-468. Print.

Rosenblatt, Abram, et al. "Evidence For Terror Management Theory: I. The Effects of Mortality Salience on Reactions to Those Who Violate or Uphold Cultural Values." *Journal of Personality and Social Psychology* 57.4 (1989): 681-690. Print.

Sartre, Jean-Paul. *Being and Nothingness: An Essay in Phenomenological Ontology.* New York: Citadel Press, 1956. Print.

Segal, Alan F. *Life after Death: A History of the Afterlife in Western Religion.* New York: Doubleday, 2004. Print.

Shneidman, Edwin S. *Death: Current Perspectives.* New York: Jason Aronson, 1976. Print.

Shneidman, Edwin S. *Deaths of Man.* New York: Jason Aronson, 1983. Print.

Slemrod, Joel. "Thanatology and Economics: The Behavioral Economics of Death" *The American Economics Review* 93.2 (May 2003): 371-373. Print.

Taylor, Michael R. "Dealing with Death: Western Philosophical Strategies." *Handbook of Death & Dying.* Ed. Clifton D. Bryan. Thousand Oaks, CA: Sage Pub., Inc., 2003. 24-33. Print.

Toynbee, Arnold. "Various Ways in Which Human Beings Have Sought to Reconcile Themselves to the Fact of Death." *Death: Current Perspectives.* Ed. Edwin S. Shneidman. New York: Jason Aronson, 1976. 13-44. Print.

CHAPTER FOUR: TOXIC AND ALTRUISTIC INHERITANCE

Baumeister, Roy F., Evil: *Inside Human Violence and Cruelty*, New York: W.H. Freeman and Company, 1997. Print.

Bryant, Clifton D., and William E. Snizek. "The Last Will and Testament: A Neglected Document in Sociological Research," *Handbook of Death & Dying*. Ed. Clifton D. Bryan. Thousand Oaks, CA: Sage Pub., Inc., 2003. 934-940. Print.

Burrough, Bryan. "Sleeping With the Fishes." *Vanity Fair* Dec. 2006: Print.

Breitman, Rachel and Del Jones. "Should Kids Be Left Fortunes, Or Be Left Out?" *USA Today.com*. USA Today, 26 July 2006. Web. 15 Aug. 2010.

Carnegie, Andrew. *The Gospel of Wealth, and Other Timely Essays*. New York: Century Co., 1901. Print.

Eddy, William. *High Conflict People In Legal Disputes*. Calgary: Janis Publications, Inc., 2006. Print.

Elmer, Eddy M. "The Psychological Motives of the Last Will and Testament." *www. eddyelmer.com*. Feb. 2001. Web. 19 Aug. 2010.

Forward, Susan. *Toxic Parents: Overcoming Their Hurtful Legacy and Reclaiming Your Life*. New York: Bantum, 1989. Print.

Fant, Kenne. *Alfred Nobel: A Biography*. New York: Arcade Publishing, Inc., 1991. Print.

Haidt, Jonathan, *The Happiness Hypothesis: Finding Modern Truth in* Ancient *Wisdom*. New York: Basic Books, 2006. Print.

Kirkland, Richard I. "Should You Leave It All to the Children?" *www.money.cnn.com*. Fortune Magazine 29 Sept. 1986. Web. 12 Jan. 2010.

Lenzer, Robert, and Devon Pendleton. "Family Feud." *Forbes Magazine* 12 Nov. 2007: 108-115. Print.

Miller, Robert K., Jr. and Stephen J. McNamee, eds. *Inheritance and Wealth in America*. New York: Plenum Press, 1998. Print.

Miller, Robert K., Jr., Rosenfeld, Jeffrey P., and Stephen J. McNamee. "The Disposition of Property: Transfers Between the Dead and the Living." *Handbook of Death & Dying*. Ed. Clifton D. Bryan. Thousand Oaks, CA: Sage Pub., Inc., 2003. 917-925. Print.

Noguchi, Yuki. "Buffett To Give His Billions to Charity, With Gates, He Sparks New Era of Mega-Money Philanthropy." *San Francisco Chronicle* 26 June 2006:

A-1. Print.

Redstone, Sumner. *A Passion To Win*. New York: Simon & Schuster, 2001. Print.

Roberts, Sam. "Trustees Begin to Parcel Leona Helmsley's Estate." *New York Times* 22 April 2009: A24. Print.

Sanders, Bethany. "Andrew Lloyd Webber's Kids Won't Inherit His Money." *ParentDish*, 12 Oct 2008. Web. 15 Dec. 2008.

Schoetzau, Barbara. "US Billionaire Buffet to Give Most of His Fortune to Gates Foundation." *VOA News.com*, 26 June 2006. Web. 11 Nov 2009.

Schroeder, Alice. *The Snowball: Warren Buffett and the Business of Life*. New York: Bantam Books, 2008. Print.

Shaffer, Thomas L., Carol Ann Mooney, and Amy Jo Boettcher. *The Planning and Drafting of Wills and Trusts*. 5th ed. United States: Foundation Press, 2007. Print.

Toobin, Jeffrey. "Rich Bitch, The Legal Battle Over Trust Funds for Pets." *The New Yorker* 29 Sept 2008. Web. 20 Aug. 2010.

Vaknin, Sam. *Malignant Self Love:Narcissism Revisited*. 8th ed. New York: Narcissus Publications, 2007. Print.

Vigilant, Lee Garth, Williamson, John B. "Symbolic Immortality and Social Theory: The Relevance of an Underutilized Concept." *Handbook of Death & Dying*. Ed. Clifton D. Bryan. Thousand Oaks, CA: Sage Pub., Inc., 2003. 917-925. Print.

CHAPTER FIVE: BROOKE ASTOR

Astor, Brooke. *Footprints*. New York: Doubleday, 1980. Print.

Barron, James. "Brooke Astor's Son Is Sentenced to Prison." *New York Times* 22 Dec. 2009: A31. Print.

Buckley, William F. Jr. "Sonnytime. *National Review Online*. National Review, 8 Aug. 2006. Web. 11 Aug. 2010.

Dickens, Charles. *American Notes*. New York: Penguin Books, 2000. Print

Dunne, Dominick. "Saving Mrs. Astor." *Vanity Fair*. Oct. 2006: 182-187. Print.

Eligon, John. "Astor Jury's Note Could Help if Defense Needs to Appeal." *New York Times* 7 Oct. 2009: A24. Print.

Eligon, John. "Brooke Astor's Son Guilty in Scheme to Defraud Her." *New York Times* 9 Oct. 2009: A1. Print.

Eligon, John. "Prosecutor Says Astor's Son is 'Depraved'." *New York Times* 17 Sept. 2009: A26. Print.

Gardiner, Sean. "Champion for Elder Justice: Interview with Philip Marshall following the conviction of his father, Anthony Marshall, for the financial elder abuse of Brooke Astor." *AARP Bulletin*. AARP Bulletin, Dec. 2009. Web. 11 Aug. 2010.

Gordon, Meryl. "Inside the Astor Verdict." *Vanityfair.com*. Vanity Fair, Dec. 2009. Web. 19 Nov. 2009.

Gordon, Meryl. *Mrs. Astor's Regrets: The Hidden Betrayals of a Family Beyond Reproach*. New York: Mariner Books, 2008. Print.

McNeilly, Dennis P. and Kathleen H. Wilber, "Elder Abuse and Victimizations." *Handbook of the Psychology of Aging*. 5th ed. Eds. James E. Birren and K. Warner Schaie. San Diego: Academic Press, 2001. Print.

Miller, Russell. "Brooke Astor: The Lady's Fortune Vanishes." *TimesOnline*. The Sunday Times, 11 Jan. 2009. Web. 11 Aug. 2010.

Ravitz, Jessica. "Brooke Astor Would Have Been 'Mortified' By Son's Trial." *CNN. com*. CNN, 20 Feb. 2009. Web. 11 Aug. 2010.

Richardson, John. "The Battle for Mrs. Astor." *Vanity Fair*. Oct. 2008: 345-394. Print.

Stiegel, Lori A. "The Brooke Astor Case: An Appalling Set of Circumstances." A Three Part Interview with Alex Forger. *ABA BIFOCAL*. ABA Commission on Law and Aging, Vol. 31, No. 2 (Nov.-Dec. 2009): 27, Vol. 31, No. 3 (Jan.-Feb. 2010): 60-63, Vol. 31, No. 4 (Mar.-Apr. 2010): 83-91. Print.

Sulzberger, A.G. "Astor Was Often Lucid, Court Is Told." *New York Times* 15 July 2009: A23. Print.

Sulzberger, A.G. "Defense in Astor Case Argues That She Was Simply Absent-Minded." *NYTimes.com*. New York Times, 30 July 2009. Web. 30 July 2009.

Sulzberger, A.G. "Move to Protect Mrs. Astor May Cost an Inheritance." *New York Times* 12 Oct. 2009: A18. Print.

CHAPTER SIX: VULNERABILITY IN THE TWILIGHT OF COMPETENCE

Attix, Deborah K. and Kathleen A. Welsh-Bohmer, eds. *Geriatric Neuropsychology: Assessment and Intervention*. New York: Guilford Press, 2006. Print.

Blazer, Dan G., David C. Steffens, and Ewald W. Busse. *Essentials of Geriatric Psychiatry*. Arlington: American Psychiatric Pub., Inc., 2007. Print.

Chaudhury, Habib. "Self and Reminiscence of Place: A Conceptual Study." *Journal of Aging and Identity* 4.4 (1999): 231-253. Print.

Cheng, Ching-Yu. "Living Alone: The Choice and Health of Older Women." *Journal of Gerontological Nursing* 32.9 (Sept. 2006): 16-23. Print.

Cornell Institute for Translational Research on Aging (CITRA). "Social Isolation, Strategies for Connecting and Engaging Older People, Research Review." *Citra.org*. National Institute on Aging, March 2007. Web. 20 Aug. 2010.

Davidhizar, Ruth, Gregory Bechtel, and Connie Cramer. "Caring for Elderly Patients Who Have Paranoia." *Radiologic Technology* 70.5 (May 1999): 461-464. Print.

Findlay, Robyn A. "Interventions to Reduce Social Isolation Amongst Older People: Where is the Evidence?" *Ageing and Society* 23.5 (Sept. 2003): 647-658. Print.

Gilbert, Daniel. *Stumbling on Happiness.* New York: Vintage Books, 2007. Print.

Grassian, Stuart. *Declaration Submitted to the Court in Madrid v. Gomez,* 889 F. Supp 1146, 1283 (N.D. Cal. 1995).

Gregory, Sean. "The Problem With Football. Our Favorite Sport is Too Dangerous. How to Make the Game Safer." *Time Magazine* 28 Jan. 2010: 36-43. Print.

Herbert, Wray. "Paranoia: Fearful Delusion." *NYTimes.com.* The New York Times Magazine 19 May 1989. Web. 20 Aug. 2010.

Kemp, Bryan J. and Laura A. Mosqueda. "Elder Financial Abuse: An Evaluation Framework and Supporting Evidence." *Journal of American Geriatrics Society* 53.7 (July 2005): 1123-1127. Print.

Lichtenberg, Peter A., Daniel L. Murman, and Alan M. Mellow. *Handbook of Dementia: Psychological, Neurological, and Psychiatric Perspectives.* Hoboken, New Jersey: John Wiley & Sons, 2003. Print.

Rabiner, Donna J., David Brown, and Janet O'Keeffe. "Financial Exploitation of Older Persons Policy Issues and Recommendations for Addressing Them." *Journal of Elder Abuse & Neglect* 16.1 (March 2005): 65-84. Print.

Rabiner, Donna J., Janet O'Keeffe, Janet, and David Brown. "Financial Exploitation of Older Persons: Challenges and Opportunities to Identify, Prevent, and Address It in the United States." *Journal of Aging & Social Policy* 18.2 (2006): 47-68. Print.

Rabiner, Donna J., Janet O'Keeffe, and David A. Brown. "A Conceptual Framework of Financial Exploitation of Older Persons." *Journal of Elder Abuse & Neglect* 16.2 (April 2005): 53-73. Print.

Rowles, Graham D., and Habib Chaudhury, eds. *Home and Identity in Late Life: International Perspectives.* New York: Springer Pub. Co., Inc., 2005. Print.

Schwarz, Alan. "N.F.L. Issues New Guidelines on Concussions." *New York Times* 3

Dec. 2009: A1. Print.

Shenk, Dena, Kazumi Kuwahara, and Diane Zablotsky. "Older Women's Attachments to Their Home and Possessions." *Journal of Aging Studies* 18.2 (2004): 157-169. Print.

Stiegel, Lori A. "Financial Abuse of the Elderly, Risk Factors, Screening Techniques, and Remedies." *ABA BIFOCAL 23.4* (Summer 2002): 1-2, 6-11. Print.

Visser, Pieter Jelle. "Mild Cognitive Impairment." *Principles and Practice of Geriatric Medicine.* 4th Ed. Eds. M.S. John Pathy, Alan J. Sinclair and John E. Morley. England: John Wiley & Sons, Ltd., 2006. 94-101. Print.

CHAPTER SEVEN: TESTAMENTARY CAPACITY

ABA Commission On Law & Aging / American Psychological Assn. *Assessment of Older Adults with Diminished Capacity: A Handbook for Lawyers.* Washington D.C.: American Bar Association and American Psychological Association, 2005. Print.

Altman, William A., Patricia A. Parmelee, and Michael A. Smyer. "Autonomy, Competence, and Informed Consent In Long Term Care: Legal and Psychological Perspectives." *Villanova Law Review.* 37.6 (1992): 1671-1704. Print.

Attix, Deborah K. and Kathleen A. Welsh-Bohmer, eds. *Geriatric Neuropsychology: Assessment and Intervention.* New York: Guilford Press, 2006. Print.

Blazer, Dan G., David C. Steffens, and Ewald W. Busse. *Essentials of Geriatric Psychiatry.* Arlington: American Psychiatric Pub., Inc., 2007. Print.

Bradford v. Vinton, 26 N.W. 401 (Mich. 1886). Print.

Bonfield, Lloyd. "Reforming the Requirements for Due Execution of Wills: Some Guidance from the Past." *Tulane Law Review.* 70. 6.A (1996): 1893-1920. Print.

In re Caterbury's Estate, 165 N.W. 747 (Mich. 1917) (holding that a signature by another at the testator's direction and a mark by the testator is a valid execution). Print.

Champine, Pamela R. "A Sanist Will?" *N.Y. Law School Law Review.* 46. 3&4 (2002-2003): 547-564. Print.

Champine, Pamela R. "Expertise and Instinct In The Assessment of Testamentary Capacity." *Villanova Law Review* 51.1 (2006): 25-94. Print.

In re Estate of Joe Thomas Garret, 100 S.W.3d 72, 72-76 (Ark. App. 2003). Print.

In re Estate of Mann, 184 Cal. App. 3d 593, 603 (1986). Print.

Finkel, Sanford. "Evaluation of Client Competency and Application of the Standards by Experts." *39th Annual Michigan Probate and Estate Planning Seminar.* May 5, 1999, Troy, Michigan. Michigan: Institute of Continuing Legal Education, 1999. Print.

Frolik, Lawrence A. and Mary F. Radford. "'Sufficient' Capacity: The Contrasting Capacity Requirements for Different Documents." *National Academy of Elder Law Attorneys (NAELA) Journal.* 2.2 (2006): 303-324. Print.

In re Hargrove's Will, 262 N.Y.S.2d 571, *aff'd* 42 N.E.2d 608 (1942). Print.

Lovelass, Peter, *A Person's Estate: Who Dies Without Will or Testament.* 11th ed. London: Thomas Davison, Whitefriars, 1823. Print.

Marson, D.C., J.S. Huthwaite, and K. Hebert. "Testamentary Capacity and Undue Influence In The Elderly: The Jurisprudent Therapy Perspective." *Law and Psychology.* 28.1 (2004): 71-96. Print.

Marty-Nelson, Elena, Angela Gilmore, and Eloisa Rodriguez-Dod. "Testamentary Capacity and Validity of Wills." *Tax Management Portfolios.* Vol. 824. 2 ed. Osterville: Tax Management, Inc., 2007. Print.

Reed, Thomas J. "The Stolen Birthright – An Examinatioin of The Psychology Of Testation And An Analysis Of The Law Of Testamentary Capacity – A Modest Proposal." *Western New England Law Review.* 1.3 (1978): 429-533. Print.

Ross, Eunice L. and Thomas J. Reed. *Will Contests.* 2nd ed. United States: Thomson West, 1999. Print.

Sabatino, Charles P. "Diminished Capacity: How to Recognize It and What to Do About It?" *ABA Center for Continuing Education,* Commission on Law and Aging. 20 May 2009. Teleconference and Visual Webcast.

In re Stanley Bednarz Trust, No. 283699 (Mich. Ct. App. June 16, 2009). Print.

Stindt, Thomas E. "Will Power." *The Los Angeles Lawyer.* 23.8 (2000): 37. Print.

Swineburne, Henry. *A Brief Treatise of Testaments and Last Wills.* New York: Garland Pub., 1978. Print.

In re Will of Kaufman, 247 N.Y.S. 2d 664 (1964), *aff'd,* 205 N.E.2d 864 (N.Y. 1965). Print.

CHAPTER EIGHT: UNDUE INFLUENCE

Berkman, Lisa F. "Which Influences Cognitive Function: Living Alone or Being Alone?" *The Lancet.* 15 April 2000: 1315 – 1319. Print.

Birren, James E. and K. Warner Schaie, eds. *Handbook of the Psychology of Aging.* 5th ed. San Diego: Academic Press, 2001. Print.

Champine, Pamela R. "A Sanist Will?" *N.Y. Law School Law Review.* 46. 3&4 (2002-2003): 547-564. Print.

Frolik, Lawrence A. "The Biological Roots of the Undue Influence Doctrine: What's Love Got To Do With It?" *University of Pittsburg Law Review.* 57. 4 (1996): 841-852. Print.

Grassian, Stuart. *Declaration Submitted to the Court in Madrid v. Gomez,* 889 F. Supp 1146, 1283 (N.D. Cal. 1995).

Hall, Ryan C.W., Richard C. W. Hall, and Marcia J. Chapman. "Exploitation of the Elderly: Undue Influence as a Form of Elder Abuse." *Clinical Geriatrics.* 13.2 (Feb. 2005): 28-35. Print.

Kharicha, Kalpa, et al. "Health Risk Appraisal in Older People 1: Are Older People Living Alone an "At-Risk Group?" *British Journal of General Practice.* 57 (April 2007): 271-276. Print.

Madoff, Ray D. "Unmasking Undue Influence." *Minnesota Law Review.* 81 (1997): 571-629. Print.

Marson, D.C., J.S. Huthwaite, and K. Hebert. "Testamentary Capacity and Undue Influence In The Elderly: The Jurisprudent Therapy Perspective." *Law and Psychology.* 28.1 (2004): 71-96. Print.

Ross, Eunice L. and Thomas J. Reed. *Will Contests.* 2nd ed. United States: Thomson West, 1999. Print.

Rowles, Graham D., and Habib Chaudhury, eds. *Home and Identity in Late Life: International Perspectives.* New York: Springer Pub. Co., Inc., 2005. Print.

Stindt, Thomas E. "Will Power." *The Los Angeles Lawyer.* 23.8 (2000): 37. Print.

Trowbridge, Brett. "Psychologists' Role in Cases Involving Disputed Wills, Contracts, Deeds, Accounts, Powers of Attorney and Marriages in Washington." *The Washington Psychologist.* 55 (Aug. 2001): Print.

Turkat, Ira Daniel. "Psychological Aspects of Undue Influence." *Probate & Property, American Bar Association.* 1.2 (Feb. 2005): 36. Print.

CHAPTER NINE:
LEGAL PROTECTIONS

Ball, Jean Galloway. "Financial Abuse Of The Elderly: Civil Remedial Litigation." *National Academy of Elder Law Attorneys, Inc.(NAELA)*. 24 March 2009. Audio Online Seminar.

Blunt, A. Paul. "Estate Disputes and Vulnerable Adults: In re the Estate of Isaac." *Arizona Attorney*. 41 (Dec. 2004): 37-39. Print.

Brank, Eve M. "Elder Research: Filling an Important Gap in Psychology and Law" *Behavioral Sciences and the Law*. 25 (2007): 701-716. Print.

Cohn, I. Mark. "Confidential Relationships – The Unconscious Fiduciary." *NAELA Trusts & Special Needs Trusts Section Newsletter*. (Fall 2008): 1-3, 6, Web. 14 Sept. 2010.

Fishburne v. Furgson's Heirs, 4 S.E. 575, 582 (Va. 1887).

Frolik, Lawrence A. and Richard L. Kaplan. *Elder Law in a Nutshell*. 4th ed. St. Paul, MN: Thomson/West, 2006. Print.

Horwood, Richard M. and Lauren J. Wolven. "Managing Litigation Risks of Fiduciaries." *Tax Management Portfolios*. Vol. 857. 2 ed. Arlington, VA: Tax Management, Inc., 2007. Print.

Kelly, John Maurice. *A Short History of Western Legal Theory*. Oxford: Clarendon Press, 1992. Print.

Larsen, Rikk and Cyrstal Thorpe. "Elder Mediation: Optimizing Major Family Transitions." *Marquette Elder's Advisor*. 7.2 (Spring 2006): 293-312. Print.

Lemke, Julie A. and Seymour Markowitz. "Protecting The Gold In The Golden Years: Practical Guidance For Professionals On Financial Exploitation." *Marquette Elder's Advisor* 7.1 (2005): 27. Print.

Malks, Betty, Jamie Buckmaster, and Laura Cunningham. "Combating Elder Financial Abuse – A Multi-Disciplinary Approach to a Growing Problem." *Journal of Elder Abuse & Neglect*. 15.3 (2003): 55-70. Print.

Pennell, Jeffrey N. and Alan Newman. *Estate and Trust Planning*. Chicago: American Bar Association, 2005. Print.

Pillemer, Karl A. and Rosalie S. Wolf. *Elder Abuse: Conflict in the Family*. Massachusetts: Auburn House Pub. Co.,1986. Print.

Quinn, Mary Joy and Susan K. Tomita. *Elder Abuse and Neglect*. New York: Springer Publishing, 1986. Print.

Roby, Jini L and Richard Sullivan. "Adult Protection Service Laws: A Comparison of

State Statutes from Definition to Case Closure." *Journal of Elder Abuse & Neglect.* 12.3 (2001): 17-51. Print.

Rounds, Jr, Charles E. "Fiduciary Liability of Trustees and Personal Representatives." *Tax Management Portfolios.* Vol. 853. Arlington, VA: Tax Management, Inc., 2003. Print.

Sadrin, Anny. *Parentage and Inheritance in the Novels of Charles Dickens.* Cambridge University Press, 1994. Print.

Wong, Denise W. "Utah's Adult Protective Services Statute: Preventing the Fleecing of Grandma and Grandpa." *Journal of Law & Family Studies.* 6.2 (2004): 429-438. Print.

CHAPTER TEN: LEGAL REMEDIES

Anderson, Roy Ryden. "The Wolf At The Campfire: Understanding Confidential Relationships." S.M.U. Law Review. 53. 1 (2000): 315 - 370. Print.

Ball, Jean Galloway. "Financial Abuse Of The Elderly: Civil Remedial Litigation." *National Academy of Elder Law Attorneys, Inc.(NAELA).* 24 March 2009. Audio Online Seminar

Blunt, A. Paul. "Estate Disputes and Vulnerable Adults: In re the Estate of Isaac." *Arizona Attorney.* 41 (Dec. 2004): 37-39. Print.

Brank, Eve M. "Elder Research: Filling an Important Gap in Psychology and Law" *Behavioral Sciences and the Law.* 25 (2007): 701-716. Print.

Cohn, I. Mark. "Confidential Relationships – The Unconscious Fiduciary." *NAELA Trusts & Special Needs Trusts Section Newsletter.* (Fall 2008): 1-3, 6, Web. 14 Sept. 2010.

DeMott, Deborah A. "Breach of Fiduciary Duty: On Justifiable Expectations of Loyalty and Their Consequences." *Arizona Law Review.* 48.1 Duke Law School Legal Studies Paper No. 113 (2006). Print.

Fishburne v. Furgson's Heirs, 4 S.E. 575, 582 (Va. 1887).

Frolik, Lawrence A. and Richard L. Kaplan. *Elder Law in a Nutshell.* 4th ed. St. Paul, MN: Thomson/West, 2006. Print.

Gordon, Meryl. "Inside the Astor Verdict." *Vanityfair.com.* Vanity Fair, Dec. 2009. Web. 19 Nov. 2009.

Horwood, Richard M. and Lauren J. Wolven. "Managing Litigation Risks of Fiduciaries." *Tax Management Portfolios.* Vol. 857. 2 ed. Arlington, VA: Tax Management, Inc., 2007. Print.

Johnson, Irene D. "Tortious Interference with Expectancy Of Inheritance Or Gift – Suggestions For Resort To The Tort." *Univ. of Toledo Law Review.* 39.1 (2008): 769 -786. Print.

Kelly, J.M. *A Short History of Western Legal Theory.* New York: Oxford University Press, 1992. Print.

Kemp, Bryan J. and Laura A. Mosqueda. "Elder Financial Abuse: An Evaluation Framework and Supporting Evidence." *Journal of American Geriatrics Society* 53.7 (July 2005): 1123-1127. Print.

Klein, Diane J. "Go West, Disappointed Heir": Tortious Interference With Expectation Of Inheritance – A Survey With Analysis Of State Approaches In The Pacific States." *Lewis & Clark Law Review.* 13.1 (2009): 209-231. Print.

Larsen, Rikk and Cyrstal Thorpe. "Elder Mediation: Optimizing Major Family Transitions." *Marquette Elder's Advisor.* 7.2 (Spring 2006): 293-312. Print.

Lemke, Julie A. and Seymour Markowitz. "Protecting The Gold In The Golden Years: Practical Guidance For Professionals On Financial Exploitation." *Marquette Elder's Advisor* 7.1 (2005): 27. Print.

Malks, Betty, Jamie Buckmaster, and Laura Cunningham. "Combating Elder Financial Abuse – A Multi-Disciplinary Approach to a Growing Problem." *Journal of Elder Abuse & Neglect.* 15.3 (2003): 55-70. Print.

Pennell, Jeffrey N. and Alan Newman. *Estate and Trust Planning.* Chicago: American Bar Association, 2005. Print.

Pillemer, Karl A. and Rosalie S. Wolf. *Elder Abuse: Conflict in the Family.* Massachusetts: Auburn House Pub. Co.,1986. Print.

Quinn, Mary Joy and Susan K. Tomita. *Elder Abuse and Neglect.* New York: Springer Publishing, 1986. Print.

Rabiner, Donna J., Janet O'Keeffe, and David Brown. "A Conceptual Framework of Financial Exploitation of Older Persons." *Journal of Elder Abuse & Neglect.* 16.2 (2004): 53-73. Print.

Rabiner, Donna J., Janet O'Keeffe, and David Brown. "Financial Exploitation of Older Persons: Challenges and Opportunities to Identify, Prevent, and Address It in the United States." Journal of Aging & Social Policy. 18.2 (2006): 47-68. Print.

Rabiner, Donna J., David Brown, and Janet O'Keeffe. "Financial Exploitation of Older Persons Policy Issues and Recommendations for Addressing Them." *Journal of Elder Abuse & Neglect.* 16.1 (2004): 65-84. Print.

Roby, Jini L and Richard Sullivan. "Adult Protection Service Laws: A Comparison of State Statutes from Definition to Case Closure." *Journal of Elder Abuse & Neglect.*

12.3 (2001): 17-51. Print.

Rounds, Jr, Charles E. "Fiduciary Liability of Trustees and Personal Representatives." *Tax Management Portfolios.* Vol. 853. Arlington, VA: Tax Management, Inc., 2003. Print.

Sadrin, Anny. *Parentage and Inheritance in the Novels of Charles Dickens.* New York: Cambridge University Press, 1994. Print.

Simes, Lewis M. and Paul E. Basye. "The Organization of the Probate Court In America: I." *Michigan Law Review.* 42.6 (1944): 113-154. Print.

Simes, Lewis M. and Paul E. Basye. "The Organization of the Probate Court In America: II." *Michigan Law Review.* 43.1 (1944): 965-1008. Print.

Wong, Denise W. "Utah's Adult Protective Services Statute: Preventing the Fleecing of Grandma and Grandpa." *Journal of Law & Family Studies.* 6.2 (2004): 429-438. Print.

CHAPTER ELEVEN: PREVENTION

Bashaw, Donna R. "Are In Terrorem Clauses No Longer Terrifying? If So, Can You Avoid Post-Death Litigation With Pre-Death Procedures?" *National Academy of Elder Law Attorneys (NAELA) Journal.* 2.2 (2006): 349-365. Print.

DeSpelder, Lynne Ann, and Albert Lee Strickland. The Last Dance: *Encountering Death and Dying.* 7th ed. New York: McGraw-Hill Humanities, 2005. Print.

Gage, David, John Gromala, and Edward Kopf. "Holistic Estate Planning and Integrating Mediation In The Planning Process." *Real Property, Probate and Trust Journal, American Bar Association* 39.1 (Fall 2004): 509-540. Print.

Girard Trust Co. v. Schmitz, 28 Backes 444, 129 N.J. Eq. 444, 20 A.2d 21 (1941).

Hughes, Scott H. "Facilitative Mediation or Evaluative Mediation: May Your Choice Be A Wise One" *Alabama Lawyer* 59.5 (July 1998): 246-4. Print.

Kharicha, Kalpa, et al. "Health Risk Appraisal in Older People 1: Are Older People Living Alone An "At-Risk Group?" *British Journal of General Practice,* 57(537) (Apr. 2007): 271-276. Print.

Larsen, Rikk and Cyrstal Thorpe. "Elder Mediation: Optimizing Major Family Transitions." *Marquette Elder's Advisor* 7.2 (Spring 2006): 293-312. Print.

Miller, Sharon S. "What Do I Do, and How Do I Do It? A Mediator Speaks to Probate Lawyers." *43rd Annual Probate and Estate Planning Institute.* May 15, 2003, Traverse City, MI. Michigan: Institute of Continuing Legal Education, 2003. Print.

National Alliance for Caregiving/AAPR. *Caregiving in the U.S. 2009.* Untied States: NAC and AARP, Nov. 2009. Print.

Nolan-Haley, Jacqueline M. "The Merger of Law and Mediation: Lessons From Equity Jurisprudence and Roscoe Pound." *Cardozo Journal of Dispute Resolution* 6.1 (2004): 57-71. Print.

Weigler, Carol and Jerard Weigler. "Facilitative Mediation: The Alternative Dispute Resolution Alternative." *Oregon State Bar Bulletin* 63.1 (June 2003): 27. Web. 27 Sept. 2010.

APPENDIX: A HISTORY OF INHERITANCE

Akca, Catherine and Ali Gunes. "Male Myth-Making: The Origins of Feminism." NEBULA: *A Journal of Multidisciplinary Scholarship* 6.3 (Sept 2009): 1-15. Print.

Angel, Jacqueline L. *Inheritance in Contemporary America: The Social Dimensions of Giving across Generations.* Baltimore: John Hopkins Univ. Press, 2008. Print.

Baumeister, Roy F., *Is There Anything Good About Men? How Cultures Flourish By Exploiting Men.* New York: Oxford University Press, 2010.

Blackstone, Sir William. *Commentaries on the Laws of England: Vol. I: Of* the *Rights of Persons.* 3rd rev. ed. Lawbook Exchange, Ltd, 1768. Print.

Brashier, Ralph C. *Inheritance Law and The Evolving Family.* Philadelphia: Temple University Press, 2004. Print.

Brenner, Gabrielle A. "Why Did Inheritance Laws Change?" *International Review of Law and Economics* 5.1 (1985): 91-106. Print.

Cates, Judith N. and Marvin B. Sussman, eds. *Family Systems and Inheritance Patterns.* Marriage & Family Review. Vol. 5. No. 2. New York: The Haworth Press, Fall 1982. Print.

Cecil, Evelyn. *Primogeniture: A Short History of Its Development In Various Countries and Its Practical Effects.* London: John Murray, 1895. Print.

Champine, Pamela R. "Expertise and Instinct In The Assessment of Testamentary Capacity." *Villanova Law Review* 51.1 (2006): 25-94. Print.

"Code of Hammurabi." *Encyclopedia Britannica.* 2009. Encyclopedia Britannica Online. Web. 15 Aug. 2010.

Denman, Donald R. *Origins of Ownership: A Brief History Of Land Ownership and Tenure In England From Earliest Times To The Modern Era.* London: Allen &

Unwin, 1958. Print.

DeRosa, David V. "Intestate Succession and the Laughing Heir: Who Do We Want to Get the Last Laugh?" *Quinnipiac Probate Law Journal* 12.2 (1997): 153-195. Print.

Foley, John P., ed. *The Jeffersonian Cyclopedia: A Comprehensive Collection of the Views of Thomas Jefferson.* New York: Funk, 1900. Print.

Friedman, Lawrence M. Dead Hands: *A Social History of Wills, Trusts, and Inheritance Law.* Stanford: Stanford Law Books, 2009. Print

Green, David, R. and Alastair Owens, eds. *Family Welfare: Gender, Property, and Inheritance since the Seventeenth Century.* Westport, CT: Praeger Pub., 2004. Print.

Griffith, E. David. "Peeling the Onion of History: Ancient Laws of Succession" Parts I-III. *The Colorado Lawyer* 20.1 (Jan. 1991): 49-51. Print.

Hiers, Richard H. "Transfer of Property by Inheritance and Bequest in Biblical Law and Tradition." *Journal of Law and Religion* 10.1 (1993-94): 121-155. Print.

Hirsh, Adam J. "American History of Inheritance Law." Ed. Stanley N. Katz. *Oxford International Encyclopedia of Legal History,* FSU College of Law, Public Law Research Paper No. 258. 3 April 2009. Web. 15 Aug. 2010.

Hoff, Joan. *Law, Gender, and Injustice: A Legal History of U.S. Women.* New York: New York Univ. Press, 1991. Print.

Holob, Marissa J. "Respecting Commitment: A Proposal to Prevent Legal Barriers From Obstructing The Effectuation of Intestate Goals." *Cornell Law Review* 85.5 (July 2000): 1492-1503. Print.

Hooker, Richard, ed. *Hammurabi's Code of Law.* Trans. L.W. King. Washington State Univ. 6 June 1999. Web. 14 Aug. 2010.

"Inheritance and Succession." *Encyclopedia Britannica.* 2009. Encyclopedia Britannica Online. Web. 15 Aug. 2010.

Kelly, John M. *A Short History of Western Legal Theory.* Oxford: Clarendon Press, 1992. Print.

Kempin, Frederick G., Jr. *Historical Introduction to Anglo-American Law in* a *Nutshell.* 3rd ed. St. Paul, MN: West Publishing Co., 1990.

Khan, Hamid. *The Islamic Law of Inheritance.* Pakistan: Oxford University Press, 2007. Print.

Lloyd, Eyre. *The Succession Laws of Christian Countries, With Special* Reference *To The Law of Primogeniture As It Exists In England.* London: Stevens and Haynes, 1877. Print.

Maine, Henry Sumner. Ancient Law: *Its Connection With The Early History Of Society,*

And Its Relation To Modern Ideas. 7th ed. London: John Murray, 1963. Print.

Mellinkoff, David. *The Language of the Law.* Boston: Little, Brown and Co., 1963. Print.

Miller, Robert K., Jr. and Stephen J. McNamee, eds. *Inheritance and Wealth in America.* New York: Plenum Press, 1998. Print.

Millett, Kate. *Sexual Politics.* New York: Doubleday, 1970. Print.

Orth, John V. "After the Revolution: 'Reform' of the Law of Inheritance." *Law and History Review* 10.1 (Spring 1992): 33-44. Print.

Pennell, Jeffrey N. and Alan Newman. *Estate and Trust Planning.* Chicago: American Bar Association, 2005. Print.

Radford, Mary F. "The Inheritance Rights of Women Under Jewish and Islamic Law." *Boston College International & Comparative Law Review* 23.2 (2000): 135-184. Print.

Ross, Eunice L. and Thomas J. Reed. *Will Contests.* 2nd ed. United States: Thomson West, 1999. Print.

Rubenstein, Richard E., *Aristotle's Children: How Christians, Muslims, and Jews Rediscovered Ancient Wisdom and Illuminated the Dark Ages.* United States: Harcourt, Inc., 2003. Print.

Shaffer, Thomas L., Carol Ann Mooney, and Amy Jo Boettcher. *The Planning and Drafting of Wills and Trusts.* 5th ed. United States: Foundation Press, 2007. Print.

Shammas, Carole, Marylynn Salmon, and Michel Dahlin. *Inheritance in America: From Colonial Times to the Present.* Galveston: Frontier Press, 1997. Print.

Witte, John, Jr. and Frank S. Alexander. *Christianity And Law: An Introduction.* New York: Cambridge University Press, 2008. Print.

Wormser, Rene A. *The Story of the Law and the Men Who Made It – From the Earliest Times to the Present.* New York: Touchstone, 1962. Print.

INDEX

Buddha 68
burden of proof 150
Byzantine 238

C

cabinet 176
Canons of Descent 247
Canons of Ethics 214
Cardozo, Benjamin 184
care agreement 199
Carnegie, Andrew 74, 75
Carstone, Richard 23
Castaway 57
CBS 78
Central Asian nomads 234
Chan, Jackie 75
Charlemagne 237
China 90
Christensen III, Henry "Terry" 93, 95-97,
    99, 100
Churchill, Winston 51
Chuzzlewit, Martin 23
Cicero 231
circular logic 136
civil death 38, 224
civil law 39, 232,241, 245
civil rights 133, 170
Civil War 150, 232
clan 222, 223, 227, 230, 233, 234
clean hands 176
clear and convincing evidence 150, 167
Clennam, Arthur 23
Close, Glenn 63, 65
Cluster B Personality Disorder 4, 65, 67,
    81, 108
CNN 76
Code of Hammurabi 39, 221, 228, 229,
    233
cognitive ability 97, 109, 111, 113, 115,
    119, 120, 123, 136, 153, 212
cognitive distortions 51
Columbine 3
common law 38, 42, 147, 174-176, 229,
    239, 241, 247-250
community outreach programs 198
community property 42, 43, 250
compensatory damages 187, 188
Concordance of Discordant Canons 239

concurrent jurisdiction 176, 178
confidential relationship 178
conflict of interest 181
conjugal family 223, 235
conservator 164, 165
consent to mediate 216
consequential damages 188
Constantinople 232, 238, 240
constructive trusts 175, 178
contemporaneous evaluations 131, 142-148,
    164
contemporaneous gift 210
contest 6, 7, 37, 57, 129, 136, 146, 147,
    148, 150, 155, 156, 159, 160, 178,
    186, 188, 203, 204
continuing care retirement communities 198
Copperfield, David 23
court costs 170
Court of Chancery 174-176, 178, 239
court visitors 170
Cove End 94, 95, 99, 105
coverture 224, 225
creationism xix
curtesy 43

D

Dahmer, Jeffrey 130
Dark Ages 232, 237, 238
Darnay, Charles 23
David and Bathsheba 156
deathbed 136, 235, 242, 244, 245
Decretum 239
defectum mentis 132
delivery 138
delusions 113, 116-118, 134
dementia 5, 6, 97, 105, 106, 108, 109, 111-
    117, 119, 122, 123, 128, 139, 140,
    142, 148, 156, 159
Department of Human Services 164
depression 45, 109, 113, 116, 117, 119,
    122, 140, 142, 151, 156
descent 38, 242
determine heirs 177
Deuteronomy 229, 234
developmentally disabled 133
devisees 185
Dhammapada 59
Diagnostic and Statistical Manual of the

G

GAL 168, 192
Gates Foundation 75
Gates, Bill 63, 75, 76
gay and lesbian unions 248
genetic code 12, 17, 18, 24, 30
genetics 12, 17
genome xviii, xix, 12
geology 12
Georgia 42, 43, 244
gerontology xxi, xxii
geropsychology 118
gift 42, 64, 87, 95-97, 99, 103-105, 120,
        132, 138, 139, 145-147, 155, 157,
        159, 160, 163, 165, 166, 186, 187,
        191, 198-200, 202, 207, 210, 228,
        233-236, 242, 244
Girard Trust Co v. Schmitz 203
Goodwill Games 76
Gordon, Meryl xx, 86, 90
grantor 131
Grassian, M.D., Stuart 121
Greco-Roman tradition 240
Greece 39
Greenwood v Greenwood 133
Gregorian Reform 238
Gregorian, Vartan 105
Grimm brothers 32
guardian ad litem 192, 214
guardianship of the estate 166
guardianship of the person 166
Gutenberg printing press 240

H

Haidt, Jonathan 68
hallucinations 57, 113, 116, 117, 121, 134
Hamilton rule 17
Hamilton, William D. 17
handyman 19, 169
Harmon, Hohn 23
Hassam, Childe 98
health care advocate 201
Hearst, Patti 145, 152
Heidegger, Martin 59
heirloom 82, 226
heirs 3, 4, 27, 37, 38, 40, 46, 59, 60, 67, 70,
        136, 177, 181, 185, 188, 205, 213,

        214, 231, 235, 236, 243
heirs apparent 248
Helmsley, Harry B. 77
Helmsley, Leona 63, 70, 76, 102
Henry II 241
Henry VI 33
Herero of Southwest Africa 227
High Court of Justice 176
histrionic 4, 65-67
homestead allowance 43
Homo Habilis 19
Homo Sapiens 19
human behavior xviii, 2, 3, 12, 14, 15, 18,
        31, 52, 223
Hume, David 246
Hundred Years' War 240
Huns 234

I

identity theft 190
idiots 133, 225
illegitimate 150, 228, 236
imbeciles 133
implied fiduciary 179
inclusive fitness 17
independent trustee 213
industrialization 222, 243
informal intervention 164
informal probate 177
informal resolution 164
in-laws xx, 87, 211, 248, 249
In re Estate of Garrett v Garrett 142
insane delusion 128, 134
insomnia 109
instinctive behavior 18, 20, 82, 223
instrumental activities of daily living 111
intelligent design xix
interested parties 130, 167-169, 180, 211,
        214
interference competition 16
interim distributions 212
Internet 78, 107, 118, 149, 208, 218
in terrorem clause 203
intestate 36, 40, 42, 43, 136, 149, 177,
        185, 186, 233, 235, 247, 250
inventory 169, 180, 211
Irnerius 237
irrevocable trust 213

misfeasance 182
missi 241
mistake 184
modern portfolio theory 182
monasticism 238
Mongols 234
Morgenthau, Robert 189
Moroni 233
morons 133
Morrisey, Jr., Francis X. 89, 100, 189
mortality salience 52
mortmain 244
Moses 229, 233, 234
Mozart 19
Mt. Sinai 229

N

naïve realism 69
Napoleonic Code 39, 245, 250
narcissistic 4, 66, 70, 72, 95, 152
Narcissistic Personality Disorder 66
National Center on Elder Abuse 5, 110
National Football League 109, 123
natural objects of bounty 6, 128, 134-136
natural selection 2, 11-14, 18, 21, 24, 29
Nature of Testamentary Act 87, 131
Neanderthal Man 53
neuropsychological autopsy 142
neuropsychology xxi, 123
Newsweek Magazine 92
Newton, Sir Isaac 71
Nickleby, Nicholas 23
Nicomachean Ethics 175
Niger 17
no contest 203, 204
no further inquiry 182
non compos mentis 6, 127
nonfeasance 182
Norman Conquest 241, 242
Numbers 13, 24, 56, 57, 229, 234
nursing xix, 148, 151, 153, 154, 168, 198

O

Old Testament 228, 229, 233-236
Oliver Twist 22
Orman, Suze 208
Orthodox Jews 233

over-medication 153

P

Pandora's box 223
Panzirer, Jay 77
Papua of New Guinea 227
parable of the prodigal son 235
Paramount 78
paranoia 97, 99, 104, 109, 116-118
partible inheritance 245
partition 178, 243, 245
patrilineal 38, 223, 228, 235
pay-on-death xxi, 132
payroll 199
Pelican Bay State Prison 121
Pentateuch 229
personality disorders 4, 5, 64, 65, 66, 67, 71, 72, 116, 154, 196
personal property 41, 81, 156, 176, 185, 201, 215, 241, 242, 244, 245, 247
personal property memorandum 201
personal protection order 171
petitioner 167, 168, 170, 171, 177
Philippe de Montebello 94
physiology 12
Pirrip, Philip 23
plenary guardianship 166
Poe, Edgar Allan 90
policy 91, 159, 203, 204
Pope Gregory VII 238
Pope John Paul, II 52
post-self suicide 60
pre-arrange funeral 203
preliminary injunction 171
prenuptial agreement 202
preponderance of the evidence 150, 169
presumption of sanity 137
pretermittance 39, 40, 43
primitive man 44, 227
primogeniture 25, 32, 226, 230-232, 236, 241, 243-247
Princess Diana 52
probable cause 165, 204
probate court 7, 118, 149, 150, 165, 167, 169, 170, 173, 174, 177, 178, 184, 186, 187, 247
professional home care agencies 198
Professor Nash 121

About the Author

P. Mark Accettura is an Elder law attorney with thirty years of experience in estate planning, Medicaid, Veterans Benefits, trust and estate administration, and inheritance litigation. Mark is a principal with the law firm of Accettura & Hurwitz with offices in Farmington Hills and Royal Oak, Michigan. He is a founding member of the Elder Law Institute of Michigan, PLLC. Mark is the author of numerous books and articles on estate planning and elder law. He received his law degree from the University of Detroit/Mercy School of Law in 1981, and his LLM in taxation from New York University in 1982. Mark was an Adjunct professor at the University of Detroit/Mercy School of Law from 1984 to 1994. Mark is a proud father, son, brother, and husband.